BERLIN

BATTLEFIELD GUIDE

BERLIN
BATTLEFIELD GUIDE

THIRD REICH & COLD WAR

Tony Le Tissier

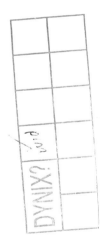

Pen & Sword
MILITARY

First published in Great Britain in 2008 by
Pen & Sword Military
an imprint of
Pen & Sword Books Ltd
47 Church Street
Barnsley
South Yorkshire
S70 2AS

Copyright © Tony Le Tissier 2008
ISBN 978 1 84415 7 662

Printed and bound in Singapore by
Kyodo Printing Co (Singapore) Pte Ltd

Pen & Sword Books Ltd incorporates the Imprints of Pen & Sword Aviation, Pen
& Sword Maritime, Pen & Sword Military, Wharncliffe Local History, Pen and
Sword Select, Pen and Sword Military Classics and Leo Cooper.
For a complete list of Pen & Sword titles please contact

PEN & SWORD BOOKS LIMITED

47 Church Street, Barnsley, South Yorkshire, S70 2AS, England
E-mail: enquiries@pen-and-sword.co.uk
Website: www.pen-and-sword.co.uk

CONTENTS

INTRODUCTION

The purpose of this book is to provide a battlefield guide to the Berlin area and to entice people, whether military history buffs or not, to open a veritable Pandora's Box of interesting aspects of recent history. Some knowledge of German would be useful, but it is not essential.

This is by no means a conventional battlefield guide, for it involves the dramatic change in tactics from large-scale open warfare to fragmented fighting in a built-up area, and is not confined to the specific 1945 battle, but also covers aspects of the Third Reich, the Cold War and subsequent developments encountered along the way.

To put the 1945 battle for the conquest of Berlin into perspective, it entailed fighting on a scale beside which the invasion of Normandy tends to pale into insignificance. Some 150,000 Allied soldiers landed on D-day at a cost of 4,900 casualties of all kinds, about 2,000 of them killed, whereas Marshal Zhukov had over 768,000 troops to attack the German 9th Army defending Berlin on 16 April 1945. Within four days he lost over 37,610 Soviet and about 5,000 Polish soldiers admitted killed, plus 141,800 wounded and 7,804 missing: a total of some 190,000 casualties, although some authorities quote over 300,000 casualties in all. Then Marshal Koniev entered the fray with another 100,000 troops.

Second Lieutenant Karl-Hermann Tams described the opening barrage at Seelow:

At 0300 hours on the morning of 16 April 1945 40,000 guns opened fire simultaneously. It seemed as if the dawn were suddenly upon us and then vanished again. The whole Oder valley bed shook. 40,000 guns, a total known today, amounting to 333 to the kilometre. In the bridgehead it was as light as day. The hurricane of fire reached out to the Seelow Heights. It seemed as if the earth were reaching up into the sky like a dense wall. Everything around us started dancing, rattling about. Whatever was not securely fastened down fell from the shelves and cupboards. Pictures fell off the walls and crashed to the floor. Glass splinters jumped out of window frames. We were soon covered in sand, dirt and glass splinters. None of us had experienced anything like it before, nor would have believed it possible. There was no escape. The greatest concentration of artillery fire in history was directed immediately in front of us. We had the impression that every square yard of earth would be ploughed up.[1]

Suggested preliminary reading for the serious enthusiast consists of my books *Zhukov at the Oder* and *Race for the Reichstag*. For an easier read providing good background knowledge, I strongly recommend my translation and presentation of Helmut Altner's *Berlin Dance of Death* and, for survivors' personal accounts of various episodes, see my books *With Our Backs to Berlin* and *Death Was Our Companion*, while my book *Slaughter at Halbe* covers the fate of the bulk of the 9th Army to the south of Berlin thereafter.

English-language versions of the videos *Durchbruch an der Oder* (*Breakthrough on the Oder River* – Order no. CMG-3021 V) and *Der Todeskampf der Reichshauptstadt* (*The Fate of Hitler's Capital* –– Order no. CMG-1091 V) are both obtainable from Chronos Media GmbH and provide some very interesting viewing.

Chronos Media GmbH

Alt Nowawes 116–118, D–14482 Potsdam-Babelsberg

Tel: 0049-331–704930

Fax: 0049-331–7049315

Email: gass@chronos-media-de

Web: www.chronos-media.de

Layout of Guide

This guidebook is divided into three parts to conform with the three distinct phases of the overall battle: the breakthrough battle for Berlin (the battle for the Seelow Heights); the reduction of Berlin and the battle for the Reichstag.

For the first phase you need transport, a hire car perhaps, with which you can make the basic one-day tour, plus any of the suggested additional explorations in that area, but public transport will suffice for all the city tours except one, and is far more convenient. If you intend including any of the Polish options in your tour, pleasure ensure that your car insurance provides for this.

This book contains three suggested one-day tours in the first section. The first tour covers the essential main elements, and then offers some additional suggestions for visits to the secret Warsaw Pact nuclear warfare headquarters near Seelow, and to the Ostwall fortifications at Miedzyrzecz (Meserich) and the Soviet 33rd Army's cemeteries at Cybinka (Ziebingen) in Poland. **Note: This first phase is dependent upon starting with a visit to Seelow Museum, which is closed on Mondays, so please design your tour accordingly.**

The Berlin excursions are also roughly based on the one-day tour concept, but can be easily adapted to suit the individual concerned.

Good walking shoes are needed throughout and also a strong torch should you consider the Secret Village option. The latter also requires pre-booking (see Chapter 5: Seelow Tour D).

For a more in-depth guide to the city than can be provided in a battlefield context, I recommend *The Rough Guide to Berlin*, published by Rough Guides in the UK at £11.99.

Recommended Maps

For the first phase, I suggest the 1:100,000 map **Landkreis Märkish-Oderland**, issued by Landesvermessung und Geobasisinformation (LGB), available from petrol stations at €6. For Berlin itself, I suggest **Knick Mich!**, a folding map-book at 1:20,000 scale that fits into the pocket, at €7.95.

Terminology

Please note that the word 'Unification' used in the text refers to the 1989 unification of the Federal Republic of Germany with the so-called German Democratic Republic of East Germany, which is usually described as 'Reunification' in Germany. The term 'Allied Occupation' denotes the period of Allied sovereignty within the western sectors of the city, the last vestiges of which were relinquished on 2 October 1990.

Acknowledgements

This book is the result of almost thirty years of accumulating information, for which I am indebted to the many people acknowledged in my previous works. Here I would particularly like to thank Gerd-Ulrich Herrmann and Jürgen Fiehne of Seelow Museum, Dr Reinhard Schmook of the Oderland Museum, and Captain Bill Bellamy and Lothar Loewe for their help with photographs.

My thanks are also due to After the Battle for permission to use photographs taken from *Berlin Then and Now* and to Chronos-Film for some stills taken from German and Soviet newsreels.

Getting There

Berlin has three operating airports, Tegel, Schönefeld and Tempelhof, although the latter is supposed to be closing down, and is serviced by a variety of airlines operating from various airports in the United Kingdom at varying and sometimes very reasonable prices, so it is advisable to shop around. Alternatively, you can travel out in your own car, or use the train or bus services available.

Planning your Trip

Having first read through this book, it is advisable to decide what you would like to do within the time and other factors applicable. I presume that you would like to spend at least one day covering the breakthrough battle features at Seelow and this would fit in best at the beginning of your tour. Flying out from the UK, hiring a car and driving out to Seelow would take the best part of a day. On the other hand, leaving Berlin at 0800 hours, one can drive out to Seelow and complete the first Seelow tour in just one day.

Accommodation

Berlin

There is a tremendous choice of hotel accommodation available in the city. See: www.berlin-info.de/english/hotels.

Seelow Area

The following hotels are recommended in the Seelow area:
Waldhotel Diedersdorf (Grade ** Superior)
Eichendamm 9
Waldsiedlung Diedersdorf
D-15306 Seelow OT Vierlinden
Tel: 0049-3346-88883
Email: waldhotel-Seelow@t-online.de
www.waldhotel-seelow.de
(off the B1 between Diedersdorf and Seelow)

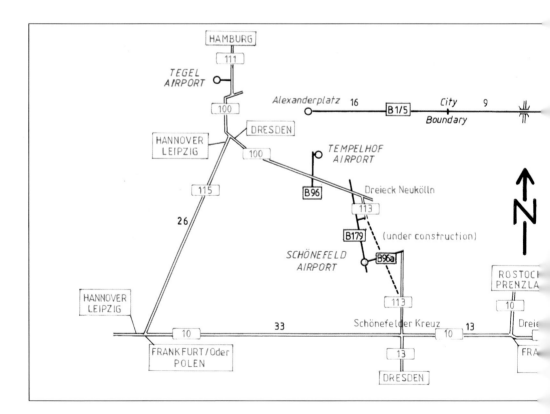

Hotel Brandenburger Hof (Grade ✳✳✳)
Apfelstrasse 1
D-15306 Seelow
Tel: 0049-3346-88940
Email: brandenburgerhof@seelow.de
www.hotel-brandenburgerhof.de
(off the B1 in Seelow)

Seehotel Luisenhof (Grade ✳✳✳✳)
Am Gabelsee
D-15306 Falkenhagen
Tel: 0049-33603-400
Email: seehotel-luisenhof@t-on-line.de
www.seehotel-luisenhof.de
(off the B5 near Falkenhagen – see Seelow Tour D – or off the autobahn route
from Schönefeld Airport)

Getting out to Seelow

From the map below, you can see that there are various routes available to get
you out to Seelow. If you are already in the city, the B1/5 from **Alexanderplatz**
will take you straight out to Seelow, becoming the B1 on the Müncheberg bypass
when the B5 splits off for Frankfurt/Oder.

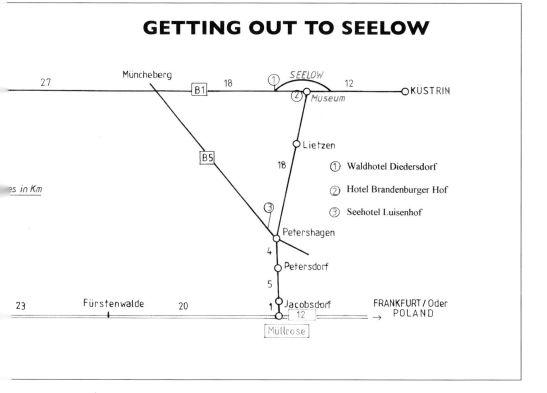

GETTING OUT TO SEELOW

From **Tegel Airport** the road takes you straight out on to autobahn BAB-111 to join the BAB-100, the city ring road or Stadtring, at Junction 4, and at Junction 9, Messedamm, you can, if you wish, turn off on to the BAB-115 signed for Hannover–Leipzig to connect via the BAB-10 for Frankfurt/Oder with the common route onwards from the Schönefelder Kreuz crossroads. Otherwise, you continue along the BAB-100, following the signs for Dresden.

From **Tempelhof Airport** you turn left on to the B96 which takes you to Junction 20 of the BAB-100 and follow the signs for Dresden. At **Junction 25 Dreieck Neukölln**, turn on to the BAB-113, still following the signs for Dresden. The BAB-113 is currently under construction, being designed to bypass Schönefeld Airport and connect directly with the existing southern spur of the BAB-113 leading to the Schönefelder Kreuz crossroads. At present drivers are diverted right to the B179 to Schönefeld Airport, where a right turn on the B96a connects with the BAB-113 spur.

From **Schönefeld Airport** you turn right on to the B96a to connect with the BAB-113 spur.

The BAB-113 then takes you south to the **Schönefelder Kreuz** crossroads, where you turn on to the BAB-10 for 13 kilometres to **Junction 8 Dreieck Spreeau**, following the signs to Frankfurt/Oder. Another 43 kilometres brings you to **Junction 6 Müllrose**, where you turn off left for Jacobsdorf, and then go straight on to Petersdorf and Petershagen. From Petershagen the road continues straight on to Seelow, but if you are planning to stay at the Seehotel Luisenhof, you need to turn left here on the B5; some 1.5 kilometres further on the hotel is signed off on the first road to the right. Driving straight on to Seelow via Lietzen, join the B167 and go on to the main crossroads with the B1. Turn right here for the Museum on the Küstrin road and you will find it halfway down the hill on the right.

For the other hotels, turn left at the B1 Junction. The Hotel Brandenburger Hof is about 400 metres on, just off the main road on the left and clearly signed. For the Waldhotel Diedersdorf continue straight on to the junction with the new bypass, turn left and you will see the hotel signed off to the right.

Comments, Criticisms and Personal Services

The author would welcome any comments, criticisms or requests for personal services for individuals or groups by email to:

Tony@somerset50.freeserve.co.uk

ABBREVIATIONS AND SYMBOLS USED

A	Army	HJ	*Hitler Youth*
Arty	Artillery	Kmk	Kurmark
Aslt	Assault	Lt	Light
Bbg	Brandenburg	Mbg	Müncheberg
BF	Byelorussian Front	Mtn	Mountain
Bty	Battery	Para	Parachute
C	Corps	Pol IR	Polish Infantry Regiment
CP	Command Post	Pz	Panzer
D	Division	PzGr	Panzergrenadier
Fd Arty	Field Artillery	Recce	Reconnaissance
Fd Rep	Field Replacement	SA	Shock Army
Fus	Fusilier	SPG	Self-propelled gun
GA	Guards Army	Sy	Security
Gds	Guards	t	Ton capacity
Gr	Grenadier	Tk	Tank
GRC	Guards Rifle Corps	UF	Ukrainian Front
Grn	Garrison	V	Volks
GTA	Guards Tank Army	VS	*Volkssturm*
GTB	Guards Tank Brigade		

PART ONE

SEELOW
BATTLEFIELD

CHAPTER ONE

THE SEELOW BATTLE SYNOPSIS

In mid-January of the severe winter of 1945, Marshal Koniev's 1st Ukrainian Front and Marshal Zhukov's 1st Byelorussian Front launched a major operation from the Vistula River just south of Warsaw. This operation secured an almost immediate success, smashing the 4th Panzer and 9th Armies of the German Army Group *Vistula*. Marshal Zhukov's troops made such rapid progress that the aim of the operation was altered in the hope of securing a crossing across the River Oder, the last natural obstacle before Berlin, while the ice still held. In this mad rush forwards vehicles had to tow one another to save fuel as they outstripped their logistical support.

On 31 January and 3 February respectively Zhukov's troops crossed the Oder unopposed north and south of Küstrin and established bridgeheads. Surprisingly enough no special effort was made at this juncture to seize Küstrin, where an ancient fortress at the junction of the Warthe and Oder Rivers dominated the only rail and road bridges for miles, and thus was of vital operational importance to either side. Another bridgehead was established south of Frankfurt an der Oder by the Soviet 33rd Army.

Soviet cavalry entering 'Damned Germany'.

Zhukov was prepared there and then to risk an armoured thrust on Berlin, despite his poor logistical state, but Stalin called him off to clear East Pomerania, where German forces were gathering for a counterstroke. This left only limited forces to hold the bridgeheads in the Oderbruch against the troops the Germans hastily assembled to try to drive the Soviets back across the river. Throughout February the Soviets had to rely on artillery support from the east bank, so could

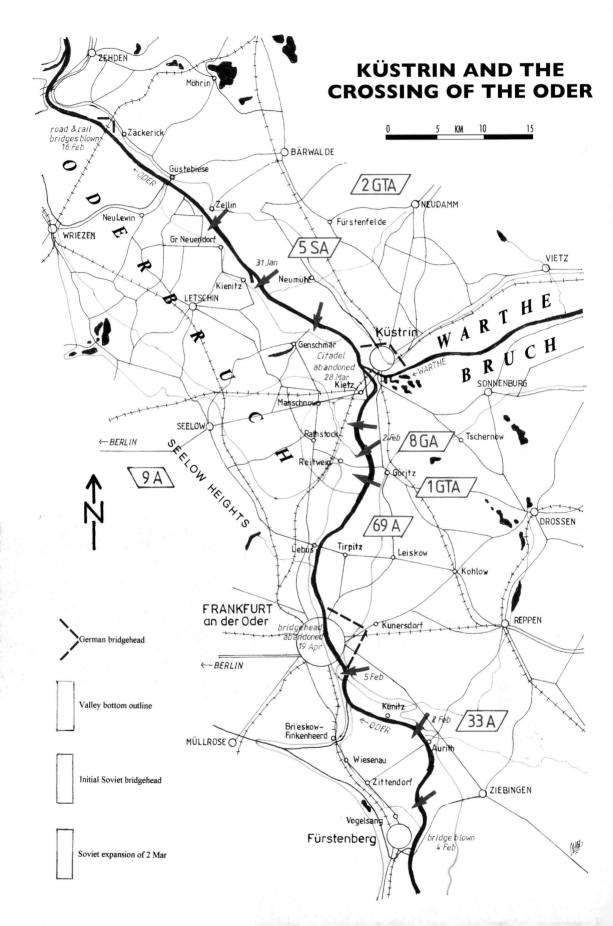

KÜSTRIN AND THE
CROSSING OF THE ODER

0   5   KM   10   15

ZEHDEN
Möhrin
road & rail
bridges blown
16 Feb
Zäckerick
ODER
Güstebiese
BÄRWALDE
2 GTA
Zellin
NeuLewin
NEUDAMM
Fürstenfelde
WRIEZEN
Gr.Neuendorf
5 SA
31 Jan
Kienitz
Neumühl
VIETZ
LETSCHIN
ODERBRUCH
Genschmar
Küstrin
WARTHE
Citadel
abandoned
28 Mar
Kietz
WARTHE
BRUCH
SONNENBURG
Manschnow
SEELOW
Rathstock
2 Feb
8 GA
Tschernow
← BERLIN
Reitwein
Göritz
1 GTA
SEELOW HEIGHTS
9 A
DROSSEN
69 A
N
Lebus
Tirpitz
Leiskow
Kohlow
REPPEN
FRANKFURT
an der Oder
bridgehead
abandoned
19 Apr
Kunersdorf
← BERLIN
5 Feb
Künitz
2 Feb
33 A
Brieskow-
Finkenheerd
ODER
MÜLLROSE
Wiesenau
Aurith
Zittendorf
ZIEBINGEN
Vogelsang
Fürstenberg
bridge blown
4 Feb

⸉ German bridgehead

Valley bottom outline

Initial Soviet bridgehead

Soviet expansion of 2 Mar

do little to expand their positions in the Oderbruch, but the little town of Lebus at the base of the Reitwein Spur was seized on the 12th and this area became the scene of severe fighting that was to last another two months.

Soviet bridge-building on the Oder.

An attempt to expand the southern Oderbruch bridgehead in early March was only partially successful, and then bad weather put an end to further operations until 22 March when a two-day operation succeeded in combining the two bridgeheads and isolating the reinforced Küstrin garrison. The Germans counter-attacked in strength with over four divisions on the 27th, hoping to relieve Küstrin, but their tanks foundered on the minefields laid by the Soviets and the attack had to be abandoned on the second day. The Soviets then directed their efforts on taking Küstrin, which fell on the 29th, although a thousand troops managed to break through to the German lines.

In the meantime the East Pomeranian operation had been successfully completed. Zhukov flew to Moscow to clear his plans for Operation Berlin with Stalin, and a massive logistical operation began to redeploy and restock his armies with personnel, equipment, ammunition and fuel, all within just two weeks. The Germans concentrated on preparing their defences for the inevitable on-slaught to come.

Hitler made an unprecedented visit to the front, consulting with General Busse, the commander of the 9th Army, at CIst Corps Headquarters at Schloss Harnekop on 3 March, and Josef Goebbels, now Reichs Commissar for Defence, addressed some of the garrison at Frankfurt/Oder, Busse's home town.

Zhukov planned to use four combined-arms armies – the 47th, 3rd

Soviet anti-tank riflemen passing a wrecked German Pz IV.

Hitler at Schloss Harnekop.

Goebbels in Frankfurt/Oder.

Shock, 5th Shock and 8th Guards – for the main thrust through the Oderbruch on the Seelow Heights, with the 61st Army and 1st Polish Army covering the northern flank with water crossings, while the 69th and 33rd Armies would destroy the German forces either side of Frankfurt, which could be ignored for the moment, and then thrust for the Berlin autobahn.[1]

Operations commenced on 14 April with a two-day reconnaissance in force, in which the Soviets tried to seek out the German defence preparations; in addition, the ground gained enabled them to prepare ways through the dense minefields for their main offensive.

The opening barrage at 0300 hours (local time) on 16 April was the mightiest

Marshal Zhukov's Operation Berlin planning conference in a school at Landsberg/Warthe.

that had ever been recorded. Zhukov had concentrated 14,600 guns and mortars and over 1,500 rocket-launchers, to which was added the fire of his 3,000 tanks and self-propelled guns, all of which, whether aimed or not, produced the psychological effect he wanted in the thirty-minute concentration. Then 143 searchlights were switched on; this was the signal to advance, but the lights were

A crowded Soviet ferry with rocket-launcher and jeep.

also intended to blind the Germans and extend the daylight hours for his troops to achieve their aims. However, this was largely a flop, for the massive bombardment had created late First World War conditions for the advance and thrown up a cloud of muck and smoke so thick that the searchlights could rarely penetrate it, while at the same time causing night-blindness among the Russian troops. The worst effects of the bombardment on the defence had been countered by the German withdrawal from the first line of defence during the night in anticipation of what would occur.

When daylight came, the rate of advance was further slowed down by the numerous water obstacles and boggy ground encountered in their path. Eventually, goaded by Stalin with rival Marshal Koniev's success to the south, Zhukov ordered in his two tank armies to try to force the pace. The tank armies had not been expected to take part in the breakthrough battle, the aim of which was to open up the start lines for the armoured thrust on Berlin. Consequently they were unprepared for this move, as were the combined-arms armies already fighting the battle, which now found the deployment of their supporting artillery chaotically blocked by the tanks struggling to get through on the limited routes forward.

By the end of the first day the Soviets had gained a foothold on the Seelow

Massed Soviet artillery at the Oder.

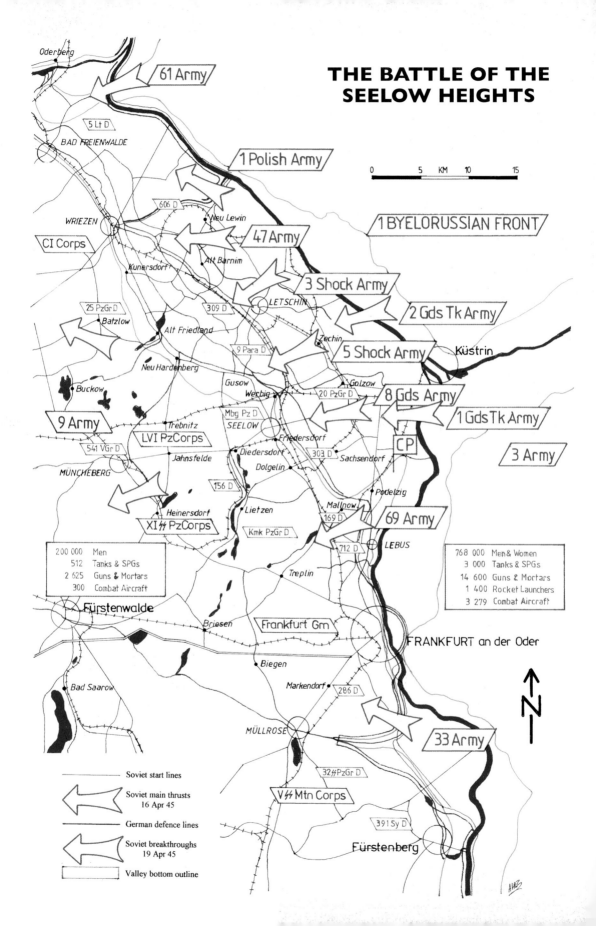

THE BATTLE OF THE SEELOW HEIGHTS

1 BYELORUSSIAN FRONT

Oderberg

61 Army

5 Lt D

BAD FREIENWALDE

1 Polish Army

0   5   KM   10   15

606 D

WRIEZEN

Neu Lewin

CI Corps

47 Army

Kunersdorf

Alt Barnim

3 Shock Army

25 PzGr D

309 D

LETSCHIN

2 Gds Tk Army

Batzlow

Alt Friedland

Zechin

5 Shock Army

Küstrin

9 Para D

Neu Hardenberg

Gusow

Golzow

8 Gds Army

Buckow

Werbig

20 PzGr D

9 Army

Trebnitz

Mbg Pz D

1 Gds Tk Army

LVI PzCorps

SEELOW

Friedersdorf

303 D

CP

3 Army

541 VGr D

Jahnsfelde

Diedersdorf

Sachsendorf

MÜNCHEBERG

Dolgelin

156 D

Podelzig

Heinersdorf

Lietzen

Mallnow

XI ✠ PzCorps

Kmk PzGr D

169 D

69 Army

712 D

LEBUS

200 000	Men
512	Tanks & SPGs
2 625	Guns & Mortars
300	Combat Aircraft

Treplin

768 000	Men & Women
3 000	Tanks & SPGs
14 600	Guns & Mortars
1 400	Rocket Launchers
3 279	Combat Aircraft

Fürstenwalde

Briesen

Frankfurt Gm

FRANKFURT an der Oder

Bad Saarow

Biegen

Markendorf

286 D

N

MÜLLROSE

33 Army

32 ✠ PzGr D

Soviet start lines

Soviet main thrusts
16 Apr 45

German defence lines

Soviet breakthroughs
19 Apr 45

Valley bottom outline

V ✠ Mtn Corps

391 Sy D

Fürstenberg

German victims of the Soviet bombardment.

Heights east of Friedersdorf, had reached the foot of the Heights at Werbig and had made a minor penetration into Seelow itself, but they were being held at these points. The main German defence line along the Seelow Heights, known as the *Hardenberg-Stellung*, was still relatively intact. Elsewhere progress had been disappointing.

On the second day the Soviets broke through at Werbig and Friedersdorf to bypass either side of Seelow, which remained in German hands. The deliberately flooded valley of Lietzen left only the main road from Seelow to Berlin and the area north of it passable to the 1st Guards Tank Army, whose armour was still entangled with the 8th Guards Army. In the north the 1st Polish and 47th Armies closed up to Wriezen, having destroyed the 606th Infantry Division between them, but the 61st Army on the flank had made little progress against the 5th Light Division, nor had the 69th and 33rd Armies on either side of Frankfurt been able to break the German defence. However, the 5th Shock Army in the centre had inflicted severe casualties on the 9th Parachute Division and forced it back across the Alte Oder, where crossing points were found for the 2nd Guards Tank Army. By this point, the Soviet casualties in infantry and armour had reached such staggering dimensions that the Rear Area was scoured for manpower capable of being used as infantry replacements.

Soviet infantry swarming across the Oderbruch.

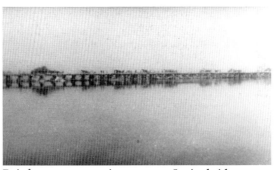

Reinforcements pouring across a Soviet bridge.

Early on the third day the 8th Guards and 1st Guards Tank Armies approached the *Stein-Stellung* at Diedersdorf, where German survivors from the *Hardenberg-Stellung* were now occupying previously prepared positions. With the aid of the Luftwaffe, they inflicted heavy casualties on the Soviet tanks lined up nose to tail on the main road or coming down the open ground of the reverse slope opposite the German positions. That night Zhukov issued orders for the command and traffic control measures now seen to be necessary. He also, most unusually, combined the 1st Guards Tank Army with the 8th Guards Army under Colonel General Chuikov, the latter's commander.

Between them the 47th and 3rd Shock Armies had driven back the remains of the CIst Corps over the Heights, enabling the 2nd Guards Tank Army to reach the higher ground, where they faced the spirited defence put up by the SS *Nordland* Panzergrenadier Division, which had come down from the north during the night and was deployed in some haste behind the shattered 9th Parachute Division by the LVIth Panzer Corps, but was unable to withstand the overwhelming Soviet pressure and was forced to yield ground during the day, while the SS *Nederland* Panzergrenadier Division, of barely regimental strength, went to the support of the XIth SS Panzer Corps.

A wrecked Soviet tank in the Oderbruch terrain.

The German 88mm flak guns exacted a heavy toll of Soviet armour.

General Theodor Busse, Commander of the 9th Army.

Colonel General Vassili Chuikov, 8th Guards Army.

The fourth day saw the inevitable breach of the final German lines north of Buckow and at Müncheberg, but it had been an extremely costly victory. The Soviets admitted the loss of 763 tanks and SPGs, amounting to a quarter of Zhukov's armoured strength, and the Soviet dead are believed in fact to have numbered twice the admitted figure of 33,000 quoted, not counting Polish casualties, against German losses of about 12,000. The Soviet troops were exhausted from the four-day battle and Zhukov's plans for taking Berlin were in urgent need of revision.

The German 9th Army now split into three separate parts, the CIst Corps withdrawing in the north to the screen of the Finow Canal and the LVIth Panzer Corps in the centre being driven back on Berlin as it sought to rejoin the bulk of the 9th Army by the first available bridges over the Spree. The XIst SS Panzer Corps, the Frankfurt Fortress and Vth SS Mountain Corps had held their ground on the southern flank, and General Busse now organised a fighting withdrawal south across the Spree into the complexity of the Spreewald, whose waterways provided scope for a more flexible defence.

8th GUARDS ARMY BATTLEFIELD

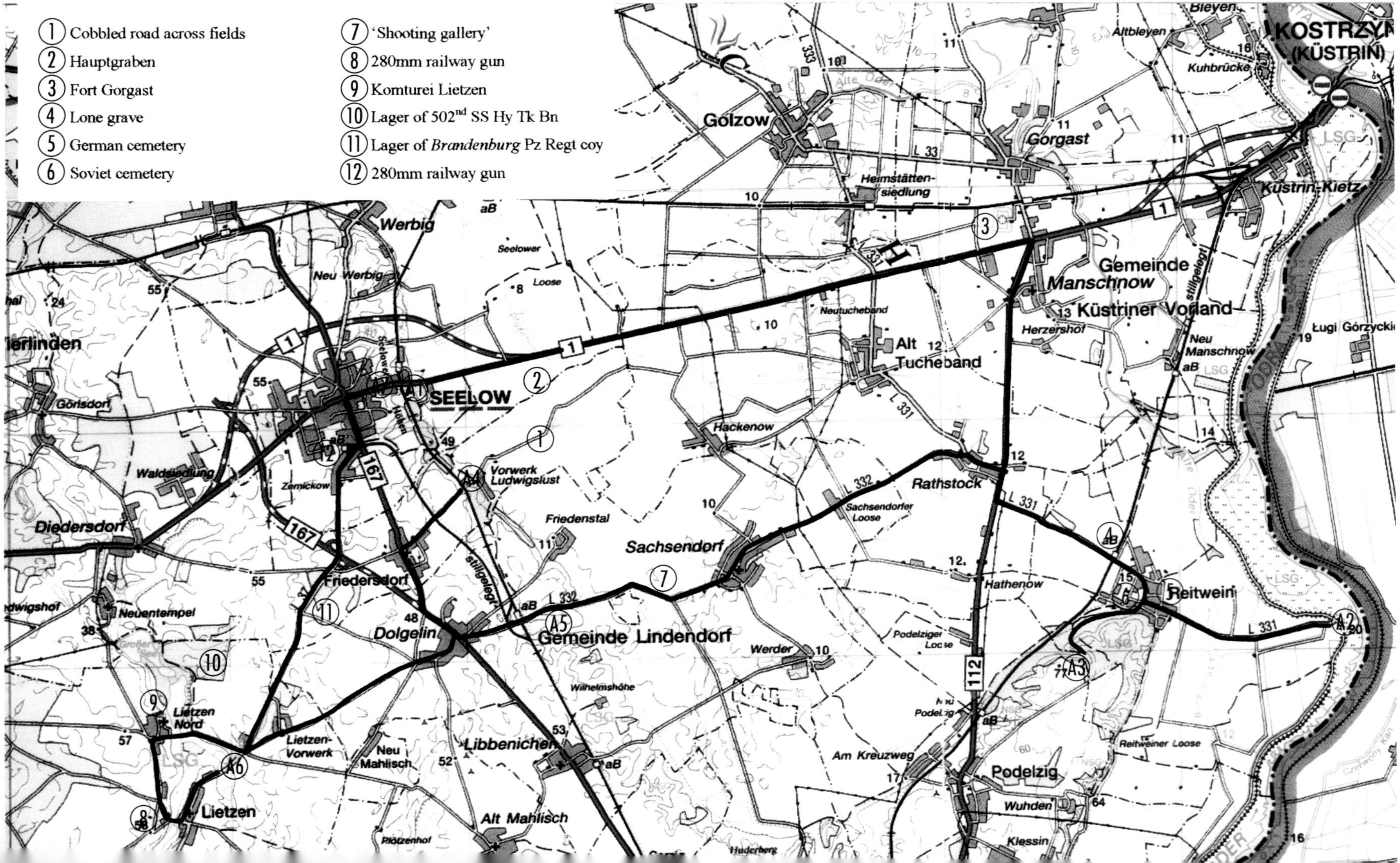

1. Cobbled road across fields
2. Hauptgraben
3. Fort Gorgast
4. Lone grave
5. German cemetery
6. Soviet cemetery
7. 'Shooting gallery'
8. 280mm railway gun
9. Komturei Lietzen
10. Lager of 502nd SS Hy Tk Bn
11. Lager of *Brandenburg* Pz. Regt coy
12. 280mm railway gun

CHAPTER TWO

SEELOW TOUR A: 8TH GUARDS ARMY BATTLEFIELD

OBJECTIVE: This tour covers the Oderbruch battleground of the Soviet 8th Guards Army between February and April 1945.

DURATION/LIABILITY: This day-long tour is dependent upon an introductory visit to the Seelow Heights Museum, which is **closed on Mondays,** and is about a two-hour drive from Berlin.

STAND A1: THE SEELOW HEIGHTS MUSEUM

DIRECTIONS: Leaving **Berlin** on the B-1, the former Reichsstrasse 1 that once linked Prussia from Cleve to Königsberg, you have a drive of about 70 kilometres to reach **Seelow.** When you pass through the village of **Diedersdorf,** you are only a short distance from Seelow. Avoiding the new bypass, turn off right into the town. On the right-hand side of the road there is a boundary stone showing the founding

The Seelow Heights Museum.

date of the town as 1252. Next on the left is an original Prussian milestone, the only survivor of those that once lined the route from Cleve to East Prussia. **Beware,** there is a speed camera just beyond the yellow 'Seelow' sign.

Carry on straight through the town until the road starts dipping downhill and watch out for the museum on your right. The car park is signed off the road to the right beyond the museum office building, which has toilets conveniently situated on the ground floor next to the car park. Steps lead up to the left of the office block to the museum forecourt where there is a display of Soviet weaponry: a T-34/85 tank, a BM-13 'Stalin Organ' rocket-launcher, a 152mm howitzer, a 76mm ZIS-3 divisional artillery piece and a 120mm regimental mortar.

THE SITE: The museum was designed to resemble a log bunker and was built by the East German Government as a tribute to its 'liberators'. Symbolic parades were held here and a lingering emphasis on the Communist-inspired attitude towards the battle remains, while a post-Unification attempt to balance the situation has been made at the entrance with tributes to 'peace'.

Gedenkstätte/Museum Seelower Höhen

Opening hours: 1000–1700 hours daily except Mondays, 1000–1600 hours from November to March. Special arrangements can be made for large parties.

Admission is €3 for adults, which includes a film or slide show.

A pamphlet in English explaining the exhibits on show is available at the desk upon request.

Among the exhibits on the inside wall is a sample of the wooden posts the Soviet engineers used for bridge-building in a manner virtually unchanged since the days of the Romans. Then in the right-hand corner there is a model of a *Mistel* fighter-bomber combination that was used by the Germans against the Soviet bridges. Next comes a display showing the German contribution to the Soviet cause in the form of German Communist volunteers serving in the Red Army and the propaganda work of turn-coat prisoners-of-war, so-called *Seydlitz*-troops of the 'Free Germany' movement, against the Wehrmacht. It does not show anything about the use of these POWs in action against their former comrades, something we shall come across later in our tour.

Around the corner there is a picture of Second Lieutenant Karl-Hermann Tams, who commanded the forward company defending Seelow in the battle, about whom we will learn more later. Another interesting exhibit is a model showing an approach to the Seelow Heights from the Oderbruch in which the boggy state of the latter at the time of the battle is clearly demonstrated.

Far right, next to the entrance, is a model of General Chuikov's 8th Guards Army command post on the Reitwein Spur with the observation posts constructed for Marshal Zhukov and himself on the top. Next to it is a display of photographs showing a plan of the command post and its condition some forty years later. It was deliberately demolished by soldiers of the East German Army when it was at last in danger of collapse. The scorching by flamethrowers of the clay out of which it had been dug had held it virtually intact until then.

Among the items displayed in the centre of this room is a model of a river gunboat as used by sailors of the Red Fleet in this battle, together with a map showing how they were brought forward by rail and water to the Oder River from Pinsk in the Soviet Union.

The museum provides both slide-shows and films in its little cinema. The slide-show is accompanied by an illuminated panoramic model of the battlefield, but the accompanying English commentary is ponderous, and I would recommend asking for the film *Roter märkischer Sand* in English.

Upon leaving the museum bunker, turn sharp left up the steps to the higher level behind. There in the left-hand corner you will see one of the 143 searchlights used by Marshal Zhukov in the battle of 16 April 1945 to provide his troops with a couple of extra hours of light to work in. Taken from the anti-aircraft defences in Moscow and elsewhere in the Soviet Union, these searchlights were tested in great secrecy to evaluate their use in providing light not only to illuminate the battlefield, but also to denote inter-unit boundaries and to blind the enemy. (The British technique of creating artificial moonlight by reflecting off the clouds was not attempted.) However, the test did not allow for the accompanying bombardment that filled the air with smoke and muck, so that in the end the use of searchlights proved a failure, generally adding to the confusion, and causing night-blindness among their own troops and silhouetting them to the waiting Germans.

Next come two rows of red granite gravestones. These are the graves of Soviet soldiers killed in Seelow and originally buried there but later moved here in a

Graves of 'Heroes of the Soviet Union'.

Searchlight and cemetery with the graves of 'Heroes of the Soviet Union' beyond.

The Soviet Memorial.

The Oderbruch.

4th GUARDS CORPS ATTACK ON SEELOW

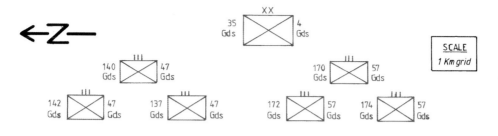

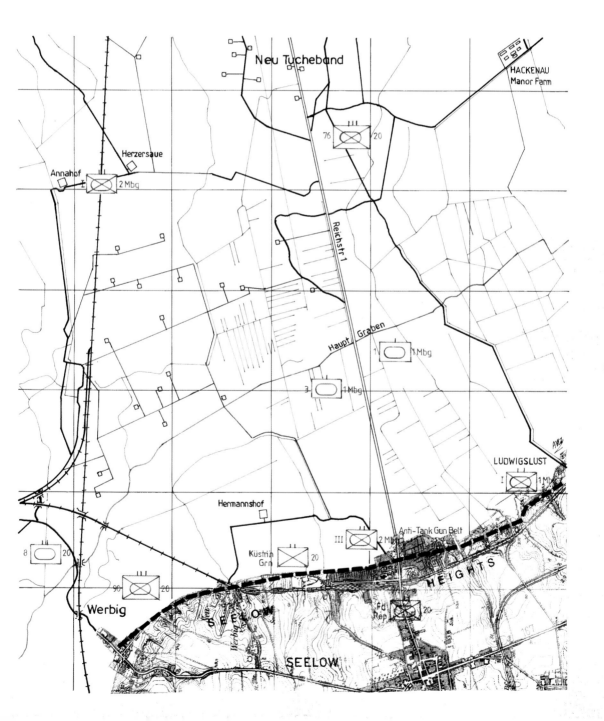

tidying-up operation. The red granite is said to have come from a stock purchased by the Germans from Sweden for the erection of a series of victory columns to mark the expansion to the east. The columns were never built, but the Soviets were able to use this material for the construction of their war memorials and as gravestones. Note that many are shown as 'unknown', for the Soviet soldier had to provide his own form of identity disc, usually a scrap of paper with his details in a tiny tube on a cord necklace. Only the next of kin of those registered as members of the Communist Party had the privilege of receiving notification of a death in action.

The main cemetery here is reserved for sixty-nine holders of the 'Hero of the Soviet Union' medal, the highest Soviet award; all were killed in the battle. Some are buried in double graves, where the initial burial involved using a German wardrobe as a double coffin. One gravestone bears the deceased's photograph; this was stolen soon after Unification and then returned anonymously several years later by post.

The memorial facing this cemetery, which was the focal point for remembrance parades over the years, bears an inscription in Russian and German that translates roughly as: 'Soviet soldiers you will be remembered for ever, chiselled in stone, the names endure, the deeds alive in our memory. You gave your lives to free us from Fascism and war; what burned inside you will remain a torch within us. What you hated, we will hate even more, what you loved, we will love deeply. The cause you died for, will be our reason for living.'

Above is a symbolic statue combining a Russian infantryman with the turret of a T-34/76 tank.

In the far corner of the cemetery is an observation point overlooking the Oderbruch valley below with a small concrete table model of the terrain. From this viewpoint you can look down on to the Oderbruch below. This valley bottom was drained on the orders of Frederick the Great in the eighteenth century and dykes constructed along the banks of the Oder to prevent the flooding that used to occur twice a year. The reclaimed land, an area about 40 kilometres long and 16 wide (25 x 10 miles), was then occupied by thirty groups of settlers from all over his domains. The main characteristic of the terrain is its absolute flatness, broken only by water channels. Little has changed over the centuries except that the fields now tend to be larger as a result of the collective farming of the Communist era.

THE ACTION: In April 1945 a chain of anti-tank and anti-aircraft guns (the famous 88s) extended along the foot of the Heights below. Right across your front, some 2,800 metres away and mainly hidden by the line of trees clipped by the factory chimney below us, is the *Hauptgraben*, the main drainage ditch, which the German engineers had turned into an anti-tank obstacle by cutting away the forward edge. On the left the tree-lined highway leads on to Küstrin and, if visibility allows, you may see the tall chimneystacks in the distance which denote the northern edge of that town. Note the line of trees framing the right-hand side of the field in front of you which marks a 2-metre-wide cobbled track leading to the hamlet of Ludwigslust at the foot of the Heights. This area will be visited later.

On the morning of 16 April Captain Horst Zobel had the remaining two squadrons of his 1st *Müncheberg* Panzer Battalion deployed on this side of the

Hauptgraben on either side of the main road, with ten *Tiger* tanks on the left and ten *Panther* tanks on the right. He had sent four tanks forward to support the 76th Panzergrenadier Regiment on the right-hand side of the road after sending a warning to the anti-tank defences behind him. As soon as the morning mist cleared sufficiently, his tanks began engaging the advancing Soviet armour. Later Zobel saw Soviet tanks advancing along the cobbled track on his right but was under orders not to engage them because of the shortage of ammunition. By nightfall he reckoned to have destroyed some 40 to 50 enemy tanks at no loss to himself, but when the four tanks up ahead were recalled they were knocked out by the German defences as they returned. Zobel then received orders to withdraw up a gully beyond the railway station north of the main road, taking some of the anti-tank guns with him, but the latter proved too heavy and had to be abandoned.

STAND A2: THE ODER RIVER AT REITWEIN

DIRECTIONS: Leaving the museum, turn downhill into the Oderbruch. As you come to the foot of the hill, the flatness of the valley bottom becomes quite evident. The lack of cover from view and fire meant that all movement had to be carried out at night, or during the customary early morning mist. Immediately to your left was deployed the one-day-old IIIrd Battalion of the 2nd *Müncheberg* Panzergrenadier Regiment, including Günther Labes, who described how they had to engage the advancing Soviet infantry, silhouetted like ghosts in the mist by their searchlights, with lacquered steel ammunition that constantly jammed in their rifles and machine guns.[1]

Next you come to the restored *Hauptgraben*, which gives little indication of its value as an anti-tank obstacle today, but German engineers had cut away the leading edge to make it impassable to tanks without bridging material to span it.

Continuing along the highway you can see the isolated farms of Neu Tucheband on your left. Most of these houses were destroyed in the fighting, but their cellars, usually constructed from *Feldsteine*, granite boulders carried down from Scandinavia by the glaciers of the last Ice Age, provided good shelter from direct fire. On your right is the parallel row of trees lining the 2-metre-wide cobbled road leading to Ludwigslust.

As you approach the turn-off for Golzow on your left you pass the point where the Oderbruch narrow-gauge railway used to cross the highway by means of a bridge with embankments on either side, as it did the main Seelow–Küstrin line further on. This narrow-gauge line connected with the main railway lines at Wriezen and Fürstenwalde via Seelow and there are further traces of it to be found later on. The railway embankment here provided a useful shelter for the German defenders in this area when the Soviets united their bridgeheads in late March. The area around Golzow station on the main line and the adjacent First World War veterans' settlement was fiercely contested.[2]

Further on, beyond a factory with a tall chimney and two red-roofed houses to the left of the road, you can see what appears to be a small wood. This is in fact the overgrown Küstrin fortress outwork of Fort Gorgast. Although it must have played a prominent role in the fighting in this area, there is no mention of it in either Soviet or German records, but it appears to have changed hands on 22 March.

Fort Gorgast

Open all year round Monday–Friday, 1000–1600 hours, and the same hours on Saturdays and Sundays from May to October. (This site is included in Seelow Tour B.)

On entering **Manschnow** turn right on the B-112 as for Frankfurt/Oder. This is where two German staff officers were captured at the beginning of February 1945 while travelling to Küstrin, having no idea that the Soviets had already crossed the Oder. The trees in the background on the left behind the village mark the line of the Alte Oder stream that became the Soviet forward boundary in the early days following a counterattack by tanks of the newly arrived 2nd Battalion, *Brandenburg* Panzer Regiment on 5 February.

You will come to a bend in the road and open fields extend to left and right as you approach **Rathstock**. The road here marks the extent of the Soviet advance in the 8th Guards Army's attempt to take the Seelow Heights on 2 March. The German positions on this side of the Alte Oder were overrun, Rathstock was occupied and extensive minefields were laid to protect their positions.

It is relevant here to point out how insignificant the Seelow Heights look from this distance, for they are barely 30 metres (100 feet) higher than the valley bottom, but as you pass through Rathstock the Reitwein Spur begins to loom up to your front left. Turn left on the road leading to **Reitwein** village. As you approach a level crossing, there is a cross marking a grave under a bush on the left. This is unusual, because by the time the Communist authorities ordered the remaining local inhabitants to clear the battlefield of German corpses, they had decomposed to such an extent that most were simply tipped into adjacent trenches and buried unmarked, the vindictive authorities insisting that they be afforded no honour. However, the grave of Werner Müller appears to have been treated differently.

The lone grave of Werner Müller.

Reitwein still bears some scars from the aerial and artillery bombardments it was subjected to between February and April 1945. It was a target for *Stuka* ace Colonel Hans-Ulrich Rudel, famous for his tank-busting feats, who was shot down near here in February and taken to the VIP hospital in the Zoo Flak-tower in Berlin for treatment.

Follow the main road, which turns left at the restored war memorial, and head for the Oder River. A sign indicating German war graves takes you to the little village cemetery on the left, where a mass grave incorporates those who fell nearby.

Now return and continue to the far end of the main road where the dyke rises in front of you. Here there is a restricted vehicular access sign, so park here and continue on foot.

THE SITE: The Oder River flows in a wide curve from the south on your right and it is on this bend that the ice tends to pack in winter, causing the water to overflow its banks. There was a disastrous flood in 1947 as a result of war damage to the dyke and another bad one in 1997, when the *Bundeswehr* was called in to heighten and reinforce the defences.

The area you are now in was a forbidden border area during the Communist rule, and consequently became a nature sanctuary, the area between the embankment and the river itself varying considerably over the year depending on the season and water level. (One former inmate of Colditz, Hugh Bruce, remarked on his visit that he had picked out the sounds of twenty different species of bird in his walk down to the riverbank.)

The Oder River frozen over at Reitwein.

The Oder River at Reitwein in flood.

Until the readjustment of national frontiers in 1945, Germany extended eastwards well beyond the line of the Oder, and the local farmers used their own boats for access to their fields on either side, while the river itself was a major commercial traffic route. Disuse, however, has caused the riverbed to silt up and, although it has been buoyed to indicate the main channel, it is rarely used for barge traffic today. A deserted watchtower on the Polish bank acts as a reminder of how the former socialist brother-countries maintained a strong border interface.

THE ACTION: The pathway takes you down to a stony spit that was reinforced during the *Bundeswehr*'s work on the embankment in 1997; the spit was previously a ferry landing point, as is clear from the spit and track opposite. It is here that elements of the 8th Guards Army crossed over the melting ice on 3 February using bundles of straw soaked in water and frozen, and made a rapid thrust to seize Reitwein and the tip of the Reitwein Spur. The Luftwaffe lost three aircraft here that day.

The only German troops present when the Soviets arrived were some sentries armed only with rifles from the small *Reichsarbeitsdienst* unit stationed in Reitwein to help shepherd refugees through in a system that saw all those fit enough moved on after an overnight stop.

The first Soviet bridge built here was submerged when the Germans released the water from a dam further up the Oder in a deliberate and controlled attempt to

A *Mistel* combination
fighter-bomber conversion.

Trees growing out
of a *Mistel* crater.

The Oder River at Reitwein in spring.

Soviet infantry and Lend-Lease trucks crossing the Oder. Note the crude but robust and easily repairable construction; also the width of the river in full flood.

flood the Oderbruch. This resulted in a heightening of the water table in the valley over the coming weeks, making the ground boggy and difficult for the Soviet armour to manoeuvre across. However, although four tanks were ferried across here at the beginning of the operation, they were almost immediately recalled for the Pomeranian operation. The Soviets marked their submerged bridge with branches sticking out of the water, and so gained a quite unfounded reputation for being able to construct underwater bridges!

Returning to your transport, you pass two vast, water-filled pits on your right surrounded by trees. These are believed to be the craters caused by *Mistel* attacks.

By mid-April 1945 the Soviets had two bridges coming into the embankment at this point, one directly across the river and the other coming in diagonally from the direction of Göritz (today's *Górzyca*).

In all the Soviets constructed some 26 bridges across the Oder and Warthe Rivers, using 13 Pontoon, 27 Field Engineer and 6 Military Construction

Battalions. The Göritz bridge is said to have been destroyed twenty times, and that at Zellin to have cost 387 casualties, including 201 dead, during the seven days it took to construct. However, these Soviet wooden bridges were easily repaired. The 1st Byelorussian Front had fourteen anti-aircraft artillery divisions deployed in defence of its crossing points and installations in the Oderbruch.

STAND A3: ZHUKOV'S COMMAND POST

DIRECTIONS: Driving back into **Reitwein**, you have what was the back of the Reitwein Spur in the coming fighting ahead of you. During this time it was stripped of its trees by shellfire and also by deliberate felling to make bunkers. The whole of the back of the spur was covered in them, and the top today is still covered by a maze of trenches.

Turn left at the village war memorial on Hathenower Weg and then right at the T-junction ahead of you. Up the hillside to your left is the ruined village church, whose verger, an old soldier of the First World War, was captured in his police uniform by the Soviets and was made to dig his own grave before being executed. Such executions were not uncommon as a result of the Soviet soldiers' thirst for revenge

Soviet infantry on the Reitwein Spur.

for the atrocities committed in their own country, whipped on by inflammatory articles written by Ilya Ehrenberg with Soviet sanction. It was not until 14 April that the official line changed with a view to winning over the German population to the Communist cause and sterner discipline was imposed upon the troops.

Opposite on the right is the Soviet cemetery containing the remains of over a thousand soldiers killed in the vicinity. Park a few yards further on and take the narrow track marked *Schukow-Befehlsstand* leading up to the left. At the last

The Soviet cemetery at Reitwein.

Vehicle slots in the woods.

building on the left I was once shown a skull split by an axe; it had just been dug up in the garden, and clearly demonstrated the viciousness of the fighting here. Somewhere among the buildings below on the right was the manor house where Labour Service troops conducted a vain defence of the village under the leadership of the squire, retired Lieutenant Colonel von Wittich, who had volunteered to serve on the staff of the *Raegener* Division assembling on the Reitwein Spur, and arrived with a platoon of infantry to support the *Reichsarbeitsdienst* troops in the village.

You now come to a barrier across the track at the entrance to the woods covering the spur. On the left is a deep cutting into the hillside for the protection of the tanks securing this flank. As you continue along the track you can see traces of a communication trench running roughly parallel to you on the left under the trees. Note that most of the trees are post-war, for the heavy shelling caused the original trees to die of lead poisoning. Those few that survive display shattered limbs.

When you come to a junction turn left, following the sign *Schukow-Befehlsstand*. Traces of sentry posts can be seen on either side of the track. You are now inside the 8th Guards Army's headquarters compound. Note how the railway embankment behind you denoting the front line is desperately close.

Opening up ahead and on your left are three large slots for vehicles dug out of the hillside, and as the track swings right an even deeper slot appears on your right, followed by another slot with two shallow scoops on the far side close to the track. Soviet film footage exists showing officers stepping down into the jeeps that were parked there.

Next you come to the trace of a communication trench coming straight down the hillside on your left and continuing away to the right. The remains of bunkers in the form of shallow pits begin to appear on either side of the track.

The path to the *Schukow-Befehlsstand* leads off to the right. Just above the track you have been following are the remains of General Chuikov's command post bunker, a model and photograph of which feature in the Seelow Museum. The near entrance has been restored with wooden logs shoring up the sandy soil covering the clay into which it was dug but, as mentioned before, the tunnels have been collapsed.

Follow the steep pathway up to the top of the hill, passing a sample of bunker construction techniques and other restoration work on original bunkers and trenches; you also pass the top end of the communication trench you passed earlier on the track. You finally emerge at Marshal Zhukov's observation post, where a sign warns that you enter at your own risk. That on the right was General Chuikov's. You need to be careful here, for the cliff edge in front of you is mere sand held together by tree roots. Trees now obscure the view Zhukov would have had across the valley, although it should be remembered that the weight of the

The restored entrance to the 8th Guards Army command post.

Zhukov's command post site in 2005.

Marshal Zhukov and his staff conducting the battle.

artillery bombardments would have seriously obscured the view anyway. However, the height of this position would have been helpful for radio communication with his subordinate formations.

Soviet photographs show Zhukov in this pit, which had a flat wooden coaming fitted to the sides and a camouflage net overhead; he is surrounded by his staff, including his lady doctor. Of particular significance is a photograph showing the worry on his face at one point, presumably when he realised that he would have to report that he would not be able to meet his timetable for taking the Seelow Heights, to Stalin's intense disapproval. It should be remembered that Zhukov had effectively been demoted before this battle to the command of a single army group or front, and lived in constant anticipation of arrest through Stalin's displeasure. Indeed, he kept with him a small suitcase ready packed for prison.

Note the trenches to the left of this position. These were a necessary part of the defences as the Germans tried to force the Soviets back down the spur.

Returning to your transport, drive back out of the village. If you are running late in your schedule at this stage, you could take a quick lunch-break at the village pub, *Zum Hochzeitsmarkt*, which is, however, **closed on Mondays and Tuesdays**.

STAND A4: LUDWIGSLUST

DIRECTIONS: Back at the main road, turn right for **Rathstock** and then left into the village. Note the ruined church and some damaged buildings on the way through. At the fork in the road at the end of the village turn left for **Sachsendorf**.

The Saumberg (right) from the 'shooting gallery'.

You pass the village cemetery and some post-war houses, but the road junction was the limit of the Soviet advance until the reconnaissance in force on 14 April, when it became important to lift some of the mines blocking the route forward for the main attack on the 16th. You pass the remains of a collective farm of the post-war Communist era as you move on to Sachsendorf, a long, narrow village, whose name indicates that it was founded by people coming from Saxony at the invitation of Frederick the Great.

In April 1945 this village was defended by soldiers of the 302nd Grenadier Regiment of the 303rd *Döberitz* Infantry Division, supported by the 920th Self-Propelled Artillery Training Brigade, which was in fact a battalion-sized unit of self-propelled guns. Towards the far end of the village there is a small Soviet cemetery on the right and then the village churchyard, which is believed to contain a mass grave of the German dead lost here.

On exiting Sachsendorf you come to what I have dubbed the 'shooting gallery' for reasons that will soon become clear. If you can imagine yourself as a Soviet tankman, you would now have your first view of the Seelow Heights confronting you. The Oderbruch narrow-gauge railway traversed the field diagonally on your right to cross the road at the point ahead just before it turns right and passes through a gap in the trees. The railway then continued along a now ruined causeway to climb the Heights up ahead. Your road now runs alongside a deep drainage ditch to link up with the *Hauptgraben* at the next bend, keeping you virtually parallel to the line of anti-tank guns along the foot of the Heights at a deadly range of about 1,000 yards – hence the 'shooting gallery'! The tanks were sideways on with their weaker armour facing the devastating 88s. Then when they reached the *Hauptgraben*, they had to wait for their engineers to bridge the obstacle in open terrain, the boggy ground severely restricting their manoeuvrability.

As you get closer you can see the lines of bushes that have since grown in the trenches along the forward slopes. What appear to be re-entries have precipitous sides and offer no exit for tanks. The only way up is by the road.

On the left where the slopes close in on the road, you can still see the pit for an anti-tank gun, and there is another one behind it in line with the next hedgerow. A *Bundeswehr* artillery officer once commented that no tank would have got past him if he held that point, but the Soviets kept coming and eventually a wall of wrecked tanks provided cover for others to go past and climb the hill to the right, the road ahead being barricaded at the crest where the Frankfurt/Oder–Seelow railway crosses.

Here at Dolgelin railway station was the command post of the 303rd *Döberitz* Infantry Division, whose commander, Colonel Scheunemann, was seriously wounded while climbing into an armoured personnel carrier in a belated attempt to escape. The Soviet tanks that had broken through then turned right in an attempt to roll up the German defences.

You now move on to see what happened next. Drive across the level crossings to meet the main road (B-167) in **Dolgelin** and turn right as for **Seelow** as far as the next village of **Friedersdorf**. Passing the large barn used as an artillery observation

The railway bridge at Ludwigslust.

Dolgelin railway station.

The cobbled road leading into Ludwigslust.

point during the battle on the left and the church on the right, turn right at the village pond and drive on. Note the massive *Feldsteine* used in the construction of the barn just beyond the pond on your left. Follow this road, passing over the point where the narrow-gauge track led to Seelow and start dipping down towards the Oderbruch. The field on the right is where the Soviet tanks coming from Dolgelin railway station appear to have engaged the German defences from the rear, enabling a breach from below.

THE SITE: You now come to the railway bridge that crossed over the narrow re-entry you are in. This was barricaded at the time of the battle. You can see evidence of bunkers on the steep banks on either side and there are the remains of defences on the ground above either side of the bridge. Go through the bridge and emerge in the hamlet of Ludwigslust, where the previously mentioned 2-metre-wide cobbled track across the fields comes in.

THE ACTION: This was the site of the only breach in the Seelow Heights defences effected by the 8th Guards and 1st Guards Tank Armies on 16 April 1945. Further Soviet progress was checked at 1500 hours that day by a company of the *Brandenburg* Panzer Regiment coming from the woods west of Friedersdorf, which managed to hold its ground until noon next day.

Now return to **Friedersdorf**, turning right at the village pond to take a lunch-break at *Zum alten Speicher* (**closed Mondays**).

STAND A5: THE SAUMBERG

DIRECTIONS: Returning to **Dolgelin** railway station by the B-167, park next to it. Then cross the road and turn left along a track that runs past a barn and a new farmhouse. On the top of the hill in front of you is a little wooden shelter which marks your aiming point, the crest of the **Saumberg**. To reach it follow the tree-lined track uphill to the right until you meet another track going off to the left, which leads to the top of the hill.

THE SITE: From here there is a panoramic view of the Oderbruch. On a clear day you should be able to see the whole length of the valley to the north.

Opposite across the Oder you can see the high ground on either side of the Warthebruch that joins the Oderbruch at Küstrin, with its chimneystacks to the north of the town. On your right the Seelow Heights curve round into the Reitwein Spur. In the middle ground Sachsendorf in the centre is flanked by the village of Hackenow on the left and the hamlet of Werder on the right, and across the big field in front of you, you can see the line of the 'shooting gallery'.

THE ACTION: The German defence here consisted basically of the 303rd *Döberitz* Infantry Division, with its three two-battalion grenadier regiments deployed with the 300th near Hackenow, the 301st in Sachsendorf and the 302nd near Werder. They were supported by the battalion-sized 920th Self-Propelled Artillery Training Brigade in Sachsendorf as previously mentioned. The 4th Battery of the 1st Battalion, 26th Flak Regiment, was also deployed in this area with its 3rd Platoon somewhere below to the left of the road, this side of the *Hauptgraben*. The latter was obliged to abandon its guns in the face of the overwhelming Soviet advance and the gunners went on to fight as infantry in defence of the railway line near the station. All around the clumps of bushes usually denote where trenches and bunkers existed.

The Reitwein Spur from the Saumberg.

During the night preceding the battle General Heinrici, the Army Group Commander, ordered the evacuation of the forward line of trenches, so that the devastating opening barrage mainly fell on empty positions. The opening barrage

The 'shooting gallery' from the Saumberg.

The view north-eastwards from the Saumberg.

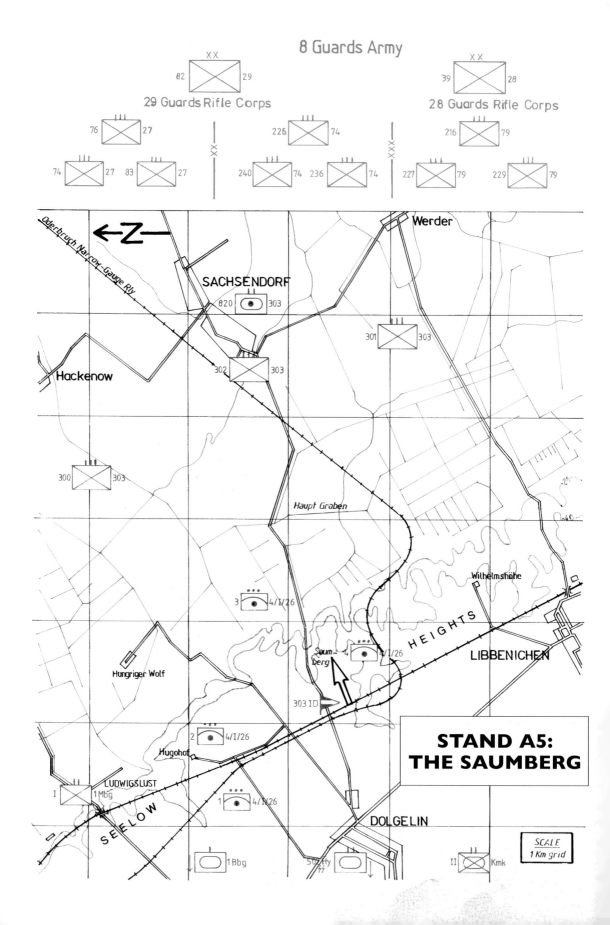

8 Guards Army

29 Guards Rifle Corps

28 Guards Rifle Corps

**STAND A5:
THE SAUMBERG**

SCALE
1 Km grid

Colonel General Gotthardt Heinrici.

(at 0300 hours) on 16 April 1945 was the mightiest that had ever been recorded. Zhukov had concentrated 14,600 guns and mortars and over 1,500 rocket-launchers, to which was added the fire of his 3,000 tanks and self-propelled guns, all of which, whether aimed or not, produced the psychological effect he wanted in the 30-minute bombardment.

Then the 143 searchlights were switched on as the signal to advance; they were also intended to blind the Germans and extend the daylight hours for Zhukov's troops to achieve their aims. However, as previously mentioned, this was largely a flop, for the massive bombardment had thrown up such a cloud of muck and smoke that the searchlights could rarely penetrate it, while at the same time the intensely bright lights caused night-blindness among the Soviet troops.

Friedhelm Schöneck, serving with the 309th *Berlin* Infantry Division further north in the Oderbruch near Sietzing, wrote:

It is 3 o'clock but still night. The night has gone mad. An ear-deafening din fills the air. In contrast to what we have experienced previously, this is no bombardment but a hurricane tearing apart everything in front of us, over us and behind us. The sky is glowing red as if it will crack open at any moment. The ground rocks, heaves and sways like a ship in a Force 10 gale. We crouch down in our defensive positions, our hands grasping our weapons in deadly fear, and our bodies shrunken into tiny crouching heaps at the bottom of the trench.

The bursting and howling of the shells, the whistling and hissing of shrapnel fills the air or what remains of it for us to breathe. Screams and orders are choked by steel, earth and the acrid smoke of the volcano that has suddenly opened up on top of us with incredible force.

One would like to be a mole and dig oneself in a flash into the protective earth, would like to find a solution in nothingness, but we lie as naked as earthworms on a flat surface, exposed to a pitiless trampling, defenceless and without hope.

The infernal drumming continues. Into the middle of it dash hurtling furies, aircraft rushing in to attack right over our positions to complete the mad stirring of the whirling, bubbling witches' cauldron we find ourselves in.

Our trench system has disappeared,

Two members of the 9th Parachute Division killed in action.

collapsed or flattened by thousands of shells and bombs. The dug-out we are sitting in has become even narrower, the walls driven inward, packing us together like sardines in a tin can. We tremble and pray, the beads of rosaries slipping through soldiers' dirty hands. We have lost all shame. Dear God, hear us calling to you from this hell! Kyrie eleison![3]

General Chuikov attacked here with his 29th Guards Rifle Corps, while his reduced 28th Guards Rifle Corps advanced on the line Werder–Libbenichen on the right. His main emphasis, of course, was on Seelow with his 4th Guards Rifle Corps. However, it was here at Dolgelin railway station and at Ludwigslust that he scored the most success on the first day before the tanks of the 1st Guards Tank Army were ordered forward by Marshal Zhukov, adding to the confusion that already existed on the ground. Chuikov later described his attack as follows:

For the first two kilometres our rifle units and tanks advanced under cover of the moving barrage successfully, though slowly. But then the machines, which had to get past the streams and canals, began to be left behind. Coordinated action between artillery, infantry and tanks was thus lost. The moving barrage, which had been carefully calculated for a certain length of time, had to be stopped, and the artillery switched over to support of the infantry and tanks by means of consecutive concentration of fire on different points. The enemy conducted a particularly stiff resistance at the *Hauptgraben*, which skirts the foot of the Seelow Heights. The spring floods had turned it into an impassable barrier for our tanks and self-propelled guns. The few bridges in the area were kept under enemy artillery and mortar fire from beyond the Seelow Heights and from dug-in tanks and self-propelled guns, all well camouflaged.

Our advance slowed down even more. The troops were unable to move until the engineers had set up crossings. Any kind of manoeuvre by motor vehicles or tanks was impossible for the roads were jammed, and to try to move across country, in this marshy valley with its well-mined fields, would have been impossible.

It was our Air Force that saved the day. Controlling the sky over the battlefield, our bombers, fighters and attack aircraft silenced the enemy batteries at the back of the German defence area. Finally the *Hauptgraben* was crossed, and our troops began storming the Seelow Heights.

By noon the 8th Guards Army had broken through the first two lines of enemy defences and reached the third, but failed to take it off the march.

The slopes of the Seelow Heights were too steep for our tanks and self-propelled guns, so they had to search for more gentle ways up. They found them along the roads that led to Seelow, Friedersdorf and Dolgelin, but there the Germans had

Colonel General Vassili I. Chuikov directing the 8th Guards Army.

formidable strongpoints which could be suppressed only by accurate and very powerful artillery fire. This meant that our artillery had to deploy closer to the Seelow Heights.[4]

Wrecked Soviet tanks in the Oderbruch.

You also get some idea of what it was like out on the ground for the German troops from Lieutenant Colonel Helmut Weber, who commanded the 300th Grenadier Regiment down below on the left. He evacuated his forward positions during the night as instructed, but several hundred unarmed reinforcements, who had arrived around midnight and had been swiftly divided up and sent forward to the various companies, were still on the move when the Soviet bombardment started. Weber's command post in the *Hungriger Wolf* Farm had been hit by shellfire the day before, so he had moved back 200 metres or so into some trenches, where it again came under fire and all communications were lost. Eventually his right-hand battalion reported that it was in new positions abreast of his old command post position, but nothing was heard of the left-hand battalion, so he sent his bicycle platoon to man some trenches behind it. It was not until the next day that contact was re-established with the remains of this battalion, whose commander had had to clear Soviet troops from on top of his bunker while still under artillery fire. When Weber went to seek artillery support for his right-hand battalion from his accredited artillery battalion he discovered that the latter had run out of ammunition two days previously!

Once the Soviet tanks started crossing the *Hauptgraben*, the 2nd Battalion of the *Kurmark* Panzergrenadier Regiment, the 2nd Battalion of the *Brandenburg* Panzer Regiment and the 1st Company of the 502nd SS Heavy Tank Battalion were deployed from Corps Reserve. The *Brandenburg* countered the Soviet thrust on Friedersdorf, as already described, while the *Kurmark* bolstered the defences of Dolgelin.

The six *Tiger* IIs of the 502nd arrived at Dolgelin railway station at about 1030 hours and found themselves confronted by twenty Soviet tanks behind the anti-tank barrier blocking the Sachsendorf road, but they could not immediately engage as their gun barrels could not be depressed far enough. Taking up a more favourable position, the *Tigers* then began engaging the Soviet tanks and soon destroyed eleven of them. Two of their own tanks were hit by Soviet tanks that they had failed to notice in a dip, but these two *Tigers*, despite track and hull damage, were able to remain in action. The *Tigers* then began firing at targets down in the Oderbruch, including the columns of Soviet armour approaching the Heights carrying infantry, whom they blew off with high explosive. However, not being equipped with night-sights, which were then a rarity, the *Tigers* withdrew to the west of Dolgelin at nightfall for replenishment and safety as they had no infantry cover. Later that evening Lieutenant Colonel Weber found his 14th Company guarding them and warned the tank commander that without the support of the tanks the position could not be held.

With the focus of the Soviet attack now on Seelow itself and the Ludwigslust–Friedersdorf breach, Dolgelin became the northern flank of the German XIth SS Panzer and Vth SS Mountain Corps. These elements of the German 9th Army on either side of Frankfurt/Oder would hold out until the final lines of defence were breached at Müncheberg on 19 April, when General Busse ordered a withdrawal into the Spreewald to the south-west.

Traces of German positions can be found all over the Saumberg as you make your way back to Dolgelin railway station.

STAND A6: LIETZEN

DIRECTIONS: Drive back into the village and across the main road into Alte Poststrasse, passing the ruined church with its stork's nest. At the far end of the village drive straight on for **Lietzen**. You are now on the Lebuser Plateau, where the German artillery and main armoured forces were deployed. The village of Lietzen was where Helmut Altner saw action as a new recruit in the 1314th Grenadier (Field Training) Regiment of the 156th Field Training Division, as described in his book *Berlin Dance of Death* (or *Berlin Soldier*).

THE SITE: Pass through the hamlet of **Lietzen Vorwerk** and approach a crossroads. Half-left is a rounded hill topped with bushes. This is where the so-called *Hindenburg-Stellung* Line branched off the line of the flooded valley behind, the latter serving as an effective anti-tank obstacle. The bushes on the hill conceal trenches, behind which is the German field cemetery. It was from here that Helmut Altner and his comrades had to engage turn-coat German *Seydlitz*-troops mixed with Soviets when the latter attacked on the 18th.

Turn left at the crossroads and around the first bend you come to the German

The German field cemetery at Lietzen.

Dolgelin church and the stork's nest.

field cemetery on the left. This has been considerably extended since Unification, as newly found remains are constantly added to the original wartime graves. The hill to the right of the road with its farmhouse is where the windmill stood that was attacked by unmarked *Stuka* aircraft on the 17th, flown by either Soviet or turn-coat German airmen. Drive on over the hill into the village. On your right is the dam of the village pond. In April 1945 the valley was flooded right across to this height, and Altner and his comrades were able to use the dam as a footpath to the village.

The site of Lietzen windmill

Pass the village inn and you will come to a T-junction. The house facing you formerly contained Altner's battalion command post. Turn right to pass between the lake above and the village pond. Up the hill on your right stood the village station on the narrow-gauge track between Fürstenwalde and Seelow. A 280mm gun of the 8th Battery, 100th Railway Artillery Battalion, was stationed here, only to be destroyed by air attack on the first day of the Soviet offensive. Further on the road runs parallel to the disused narrow-gauge

The pond at Lietzen

railway until you come to **Lietzen-Nord**, or **Komturei Lietzen** as it used to be called.

When you come to a T-junction turn right. The road to the left leads to Diedersdorf on the B-1 via Neuentempel. This road was literally smashed to pieces by the Soviet artillery during the battle and is still closed to traffic as a through route.

Ahead of you on the left is a gateway in the estate wall with an iron water pump,

The entrance to Komturei Lietzen.

Komturei Lietzen from across the valley.

The oldest barn in Germany, complete with stork's nest.

where Altner washed himself on one occasion. Turn through the gate and drive on. You are now on the Komturei Lietzen estate. This was occupied by Altner's battalion during the battle and the divisional commander lived in the manor house.

By a curious coincidence the Komturei was used by the *Reichswehr* for its field headquarters in the 1933 army manoeuvres conducted by General Kurt Freiherr von Hammerstein-Equord, in which the defence of the Seelow Heights against an enemy attacking across the Oder was practised.

Under the East German government the whole area became a monstrous communal pig farm conglomeration. Fortunately the original owner was able to reclaim his land after Unification and it has since been cleared out.

On your right is what is said to be the oldest barn in Germany, complete with stork's nest. Beside it is a table giving the dates of arrival and departure of the birds each year, and the number of chicks produced, showing a remarkable consistency in timings. Apparently the storks nesting east of the Elbe fly via the Bosphorus to and from Africa, the chicks assembling somewhere on the Oder and flying together ahead of their parents, whereas those nesting west of the river go via the Straits of

Komturei Lietzen

Prior requests to visit should be made by telephone 033470–4960, or fax 033470–49660, or Email info@komturei-lietzen.de. English can be used for the last two.

The flying angel.

The combined altar and pulpit with a
child's grave set in the floor.

Gibraltar. Sadly one of the adult storks died in 2002 and at the time of writing the
nest still remains unused.

The manor house is all that remains of what was once a caravanserai of the
Knights Templar built in 1232. The church next to it dates from the same period
and contains three items of particular interest: an angel suspended from the ceiling
on a chain, whose outstretched palm serves as a christening font, a child's grave set
in the floor from a time when these would have been most uncommon and an
eighteenth-century collapsible wooden altar-cum-pulpit which survived the war
bundled up in a cellar.

STAND A7: SEELOW

DIRECTIONS: Leaving the Komturei, turn left and go back up to the crossroads
where you began the Lietzen circuit. Here you turn left for **Seelow**. The woods set
back on the left are where the 502nd SS Heavy Tank Battalion was laagered. On
the right you pass a small lake. Drive on until you come to woods on either side of
the road. These contain the remains of several dug-outs. As you emerge on the far
side, you cross a lane linking Friedersdorf on the right with Diedersdorf on the
B-1 to your left. This was the route taken by part of the 1st Guards Tank Army
from Ludwigslust on the afternoon of 17 April 1945, during the encirclement of
Seelow, as the defending company of the 2nd Battalion, *Brandenburg* Panzer
Regiment, was beaten back and other Soviet tanks poured over the Heights on the
far side of Seelow.

Carry on through the former hamlet of Zernickow, which has recently been
incorporated into Seelow, crossing the remains of the old narrow-gauge railway

with the station on the left. Another 280mm gun of the 8th Battery, 100th Railway Artillery Battalion, was positioned here and was also destroyed by air attack on the first day of the Soviet offensive.

Turn left on the main road (B-176) and continue to the second set of traffic lights, where you turn right on the B-1 as for **Küstrin** and the museum once more.

THE SITE: Pass the town hall on the left, then the road turns a corner to the left and there is a straight stretch with a pedestrian-crossing up ahead. This is where the main barricade blocking entry to Seelow from the Oderbruch stood, flanked by rows of cottages. Second Lieutenant Karl-Hermann Tams had two light anti-tank guns as part of his defence here, and his company of assorted soldiers and sailors, who had been assigned to the infantry after the loss of their ships, fought to clear the Soviet infantry from the cottages on the night of 16 April.[5] Continue as far as the museum, turning right opposite it for the railway station, where fierce fighting took place on that first day between survivors of the Küstrin garrison and elements of the 8th Guards Army.

Turn around. There was an 88mm gun in the grounds of the cheese factory on your left, but this must have been knocked out early on, for just short of the B-1 you cross over the bridge where the tanks broke through, bypassing the main road bridge over the railway, which Tams had blown as the battle commenced. The railway cutting here served as shelter for the improvised *Berlin* armoured train, consisting of a locomotive pulling five flatcars carrying tanks that could not be used otherwise for lack of fuel, and was an effective part of the defence between here and Werbig.

Turn right back on the B-1 for **Seelow** and pass on your right the spot where the

tanks emerged from the gully on to the road and were blocked by the barricade at the pedestrian-crossing ahead. Carry on over the crossroads signed for **Berlin**. Set back on your left is the town church, the tower of which was demolished before the battle by German engineers, as were others, so as to prevent Soviet artillery observers from using them as aiming marks. Opposite the Hotel *Brandenburger Hof* on the right is the town cemetery containing many of the German soldiers who died in the fighting or from wounds in the field hospital located in the town. On the corner of the road outside the cemetery is a newly erected memorial to

Second Lieutenant
Karl-Hermann Tams.

SEELOW VILLAGE

1 Present Museum
2 Armoured Train (Tanks on flatcars)
3 Blown Bridge
4 Tank Penetration
5 Barricade with two Anti-tank Guns
6 Tams's Company Command Post
7 Field Replacement Battalion Command Post
8 280mm Railway Gun
9 Cemetery

all victims of war, and just inside the cemetery is a memorial erected by veterans of the 76th Panzergrenadier Regiment of the 20th Panzergrenadier Division to their comrades. Both these memorials were unveiled on the 50th anniversary of the battle.

This is where you break off if you are staying on in the Seelow area for further excursions, otherwise you can continue on this route as outlined separately in Seelow Tour G for the return to Berlin.

The 76th Panzergrenadier Regiment's memorial.

The military section of Seelow town cemetery.

CHAPTER THREE

SEELOW TOUR B: THE SOUTHERN ODERBRUCH

OBJECTIVE: This tour expands the territory covered on your first day to provide a more in-depth picture of the most important part of the battlefield in the southern Oderbruch valley, in particular the railway triangle at Werbig, the battle for Küstrin, the siege of Klessin and the fighting around Lebus.

STAND B1: THE KRUGBERG

DIRECTIONS: Leaving **Seelow** north on the B-167, take the road off to the right for **Werbig**. The first road on the right, now a cul-de-sac, is the re-entry up which Captain Horst Zobel's tanks tried to drag some of the 88mm guns of the anti-tank defences on the evening of 16 April 1945. Then cross over the new bypass and follow the line of the ridge until the road ahead drops down to the left. At this point a rough track leads off the road to the right marked *Friedenswald*. Follow this across the field to the piece of statuary visible on the skyline, where you park.

THE SITE: Around you are some odd items of statuary left over from an exhibition held here shortly after Unification and the establishment of a plantation in the interest of 'World Peace'. Then walk round to the left where a copse crowns the crest of the **Krugberg**, as this part of the Seelow Heights is called. Some traces of dug-outs and trenches can still be found in this area.

The view east from the Krugberg.

THE SOUTHERN ODERBRUCH

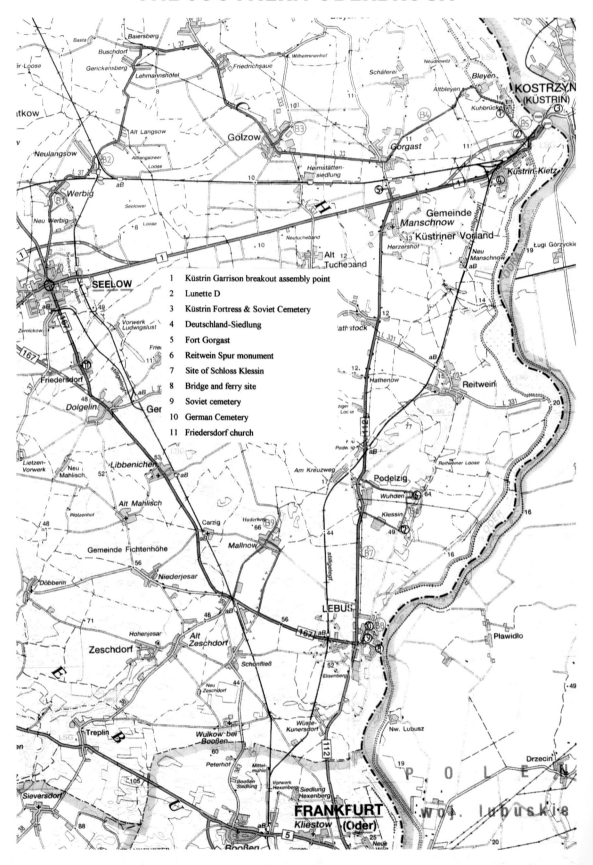

1   Küstrin Garrison breakout assembly point
2   Lunette D
3   Küstrin Fortress & Soviet Cemetery
4   Deutschland-Siedlung
5   Fort Gorgast
6   Reitwein Spur monument
7   Site of Schloss Klessin
8   Bridge and ferry site
9   Soviet cemetery
10 German Cemetery
11 Friedersdorf church

THE SITE: This is where the 90th Grenadier Regiment of the 20th Panzergrenadier Division withstood the assaults of the 4th Guards Rifle Corps of General Chuikov's 8th Guards Army on the evening of 16 April. Dr Fritz-Rudolf Averdieck, then a signals sergeant with the 90th Grenadiers, was in a shallow bunker here on the open hilltop and later described the events of that day:

> On Monday, the 16th April, we were awakened at 0400 hours by the Russian bombardment. Every time we tried to get out and run to the armoured personnel carrier, there were flashes of lightning in the still-reigning darkness and dirt and shrapnel whistled around our ears. An enemy battery had taken our command post as its aiming mark. Eventually it fortunately moved its fire back some 70 metres across the fields. This inferno continued until 0600 hours and then the aircraft appeared. A squadron of twin-engined bombers dropped a carpet of bombs over a wood behind us in which there was all sorts of artillery. However, our batteries fired only very seldom. The nakedly exposed Heights and roads were meanwhile being controlled from the air, our own air effort being exceptionally weak.

Regimental Signals Sergeant Fritz-Rudolf Averdieck.

The view across Werbig and the hidden railway triangle.

By midday, from the sounds of battle and rumours, the enemy were already past us on the left and right. The remains of the detachments deployed in front of us were caught in our positions. Our troops were running from their trenches towards us as the Russian infantry appeared and, before we knew it, the Ivans were already on our Heights. With hastily assembled forces . . . they were driven back halfway down again and our new positions held for the night. Air activity and continual mortaring robbed us of any sleep this night and caused some deaths in the supply column.[1]

Looking out over the Oderbruch, the area in front of you is framed by the Berlin–Küstrin railway line on your left and the B-1 on your far right. Between them, some 4 to 7 kilometres out, is the line of a post-war drainage ditch, the only new feature in this area. Below on your left is part of the village of Werbig with the railway triangle in which the north–south and east–west lines merge. This is where the forward elements of the 9th Rifle Corps of the 5th Shock Army and the 4th Guards Rifle Corps of the 8th Guards Army converged in the attack on this corner of the Seelow Heights.

The triangle was within the 20th Panzergrenadier Division's boundary and was originally the responsibility of the 90th Panzergrenadier Regiment, but the latter took such a pounding during the Soviet reconnaissance in force on 14 and 15 April that the 1st Battalion, 2nd *Müncheberg* Panzergrenadier Regiment, was called out of reserve to fill the forward position around the *Annahof* farm. The 8th Panzer Battalion was deployed in this area, as was the battalion-sized 245th Self-Propelled Artillery Brigade, supporting the 26th Parachute Regiment of the 9th Parachute Division deployed on the left.

STAND B2: THE TRIANGLE

DIRECTIONS: Leave the Krugberg and return to the road, turning right to pass through Werbig. Go on to enter **Neulangsow** and the triangle for a look around.

THE SITE: This triangle of railway tracks surrounded by watercourses formed a strong defensive position, for here the north–south line has to rise in order to cross the main east–west track, so that two sides of the triangle consist of high embankments penetrated only by narrow tunnels for the roads to pass through. The cobbled road leading to the *Annahof* position soon becomes too badly damaged to drive on.

THE ACTION: Kurt Keller of the 1st Battalion, 2nd *Müncheberg* Panzergrenadier Regiment, wrote:

The *Annahof* position was vacated when the news arrived that Russian tank units had thrust past us and were moving on the Werbig railway junction, threatening to encircle us.

We then set off with our battalion commander to the regimental command post near a stream in Langsow not far from the goods station. On the way I was slightly wounded for the second time that day and was bandaged in the cellar of the regimental command post.

The two-level station at Werbig.

As the Russians were trying to surround us, the troops gathered at the regimental command post. Some of the soldiers decided to withdraw toward the Eberswalde–Seelow [north–south] railway line. I myself with a larger group tried to get past the goods station in Werbig, where there were some Russian T-34 tanks, and to break through toward Seelow or Reichsstrasse 1.[2]

Lieutenant General F.E. Bokov with the 5th Shock Army wrote that Corps and divisional artillery was directed on this area and the railway line east of it, but it took two bombardments before the Soviet infantry could progress. The 220th Tank Brigade advanced under cover of the bombardments and participated in the attack at point-blank range. Bokov added that Werbig railway station changed hands three times.

Sergeant Waldmüller of the 8th Panzer Battalion described his experience here:

A farm near us is on fire. It is still dark and a bit foggy. Our infantry are streaming back toward us in the dawning light. It is difficult to distinguish between our own and the enemy soldiers in the mist. The Russians have hardly any tanks in our sector, but are attacking with masses of infantry and anti-tank guns. We pull back westward along the village street. I get the task of securing the village's north-westerly exit. Russian infantry are bypassing the village to the north. The sun comes through and the fog lifts a little. Russian anti-tank guns and infantry push forward to the eastern end of the village street. Our platoon leader, Second Lieutenant Scheuermann, gives the order for me to withdraw by the village's south-western exit. We are the last vehicle!

In turning round our driver, an old Afrika Korps hand, drives into a heap of cobblestones, which causes our right track to come off. I radio for help. The vehicle in front of us, Sergeant Walter Bauer's SPG, comes back. Under fire from the Russian anti-tank guns and infantry, we attach his tow wire to our tank and our tow wire to our torn-off track. In this way, at the last second, he

One of the bridges in the Triangle.

pulls us out of the village for 4 kilometres to where we can fix our track again.[3]

Kurt Keller described the road tunnels through the railway embankments as being choked with wrecked tanks and dead bodies, the slaughter of 'thousands' of Russian infantrymen being assisted by the *Berlin* armoured train, which when not in action sheltered in the cutting alongside where the Seelow Heights Museum now stands. He claims this armoured train was responsible for the destruction of about 56 Soviet tanks. He continued his account:

After some of the fleeing troops had come under fire from about nine T-34s in breaking out via the goods station, the Russians shelled us with their artillery and other tanks for a further one and a half hours, so that we had to crouch down in shell holes between the goods station and the regimental command post as best as we could. We tried jumping from one shell hole to another back to the regimental command post to find better cover and then to break through via the farmsteads to Werbig. However, this did not work out, as we were taking heavy casualties from the Russian sub-machine-gun and mortar fire, as well as machine-gun fire. Sometime between 1100 and 1130 hours our last regimental commander, a major from Bruchköbel, surrendered with the remains of the regiment.

After the surrender the Russians shot all the wounded that were unable to march any more, as well as some soldiers that were not wounded, standing them up against the wall. I myself was stood up against a wall three times until an older Russian took me away, saying to me 'You are not SS' and placing me in a group of prisoners being led away.[4]

STAND B3: GOLZOW

DIRECTIONS: You now go back to the road and drive on to **Buschdorf**, passing one of the wide irrigation ditches that severely hampered and channelled movement in this area. Reaching the T-junction, turn right for **Golzow**. At the crossroads in the centre of Golzow turn left on the road for **Genschmar**. The village church used to stand on a diamond in the centre of the crossroads here with the road running round it, but its ruins were removed after the war. Drive on until you come to the bridge over the Alte Oder, where you turn round and stop.

THE SITE: It was in this corner that Captain Horst Zobel of the 1st *Müncheberg* Panzer Battalion was dug in with his 3rd Squadron of *Tiger* tanks on 22 March when the Soviets launched their attack to combine their bridgeheads, cutting off Küstrin. The site of the farm he used is now covered in trees.

THE ACTION: Zobel described the action on the 23rd:

We were about 100–150 metres from the stream and bridge, with completely flat and open country in front of us. We had four tanks in the orchard of about 75 square metres. There was a massive single-storey building on the north side of the orchard with several outhouses. We were supposed to, and had to, hold this farm, for once the Russians crossed the bridge, the divisional front could easily be rolled up from that flank. The fruit trees were very young and had no leaves at this time of year, so we had no cover from view at all.

This little plot of land became the Russians' goal for their artillery, mortars, anti-tank and tank fire. At first we pressed our tanks close to the buildings, but these were soon shot to pieces. The hits were so accurate and so dense that we were constantly having to change position. In the end we moved from one corner to another, hour after

Colonel (Retd) Horst Zobel addressing British troops on a battlefield tour in 1996.

hour. Between the loud explosions of the heavy and extra-heavy calibre artillery came the lighter sounds of mortars and the sharper crack of tank and anti-tank shells. And all the time, as the shells were landing so densely that we kept thinking the next one must be a hit, we kept changing location again and again, back and forth, here and there. So it went on the whole day long, and a day can be dreadfully long.[5]

You now go back into the village, where the large house on the right still bears the scars of the fighting here. Its cellar served as a command post for Colonel Helmut von Loisecke of the 90th Panzergrenadier Regiment during the abortive German counterattack on 27/28 March. He reported:

The countryside was completely open and flat, dropping a little away to the north toward the brook, along which there were a few trees and bushes. The farmstead immediately south of the bridge 500 metres north of Golzow was still in our hands, while the other farmstead east of Golzow was occupied by the enemy, although north of the brook. In the distance one could see the colourful roofs of Gorgast, the greenhouses on the western edge and the tall clump of trees in the manor park.

On the 27th March the 2nd Battalion moved into the assembly area east of Golzow station while the 1st Battalion remained on the western edge of the

The 90th Panzergrenadier Regiment's command post.

village ready to follow. The *Tiger* Battalion rolled forward at 0300 hours and the attack began. I had my command post in the building immediately east of Golzow station. It was the most practical from a communications point of view, as from here I could best reach all parts of the regiment, as well as the artillery, the tanks and Division, while combat was in progress.

Our artillery bombarded Gorgast. Infantry weapons opened up. Soon came a message from the 2nd Battalion that they had broken through the first enemy lines. Further reports said that the right-hand company of the 2nd Battalion was engaged with the enemy in a strongly defended farmstead 1,000 metres east of the railway station, and the left-hand company was under heavy enfilade fire from the sector north of the brook, where Panzergrenadier Regiment 76 was

Colonel Helmut von Loisecke commanding the 90th Panzergrenadier Regiment.

attacking. One could hear heavy fire coming from there too. Finally the right-hand company of the 2nd Battalion took the farmstead, where the tanks remained in position. The left-hand company also was unable to advance as the enemy north of the brook were firmly ensconced in their buildings and were maintaining a constant enfilading fire on the regiment's whole attack front. Our own tanks could not progress further because of enemy mines. The fighting came to a halt. I could not withdraw my troops without the tanks as the tanks could not stay there without infantry protection.

The day began to dawn and what I feared occurred. As soon as the morning mist lifted the enemy began to shoot at the stationary tanks, which presented an easy target on the plain. At 1100 hours a bombardment by all calibres began, including *Stalin-organs*. The soldiers, receiving no support from either their own artillery or the Luftwaffe, began to leave their positions, at first individually and then in groups. It was a panic. I stopped them near the command post and led them forward once more and in a short while the old front line was regained. The enemy had not followed up. In the evening we shortened the line so as to start making a line of defence. The tanks were towed away during the night of 28/29 March and the enemy artillery fire died down.[6]

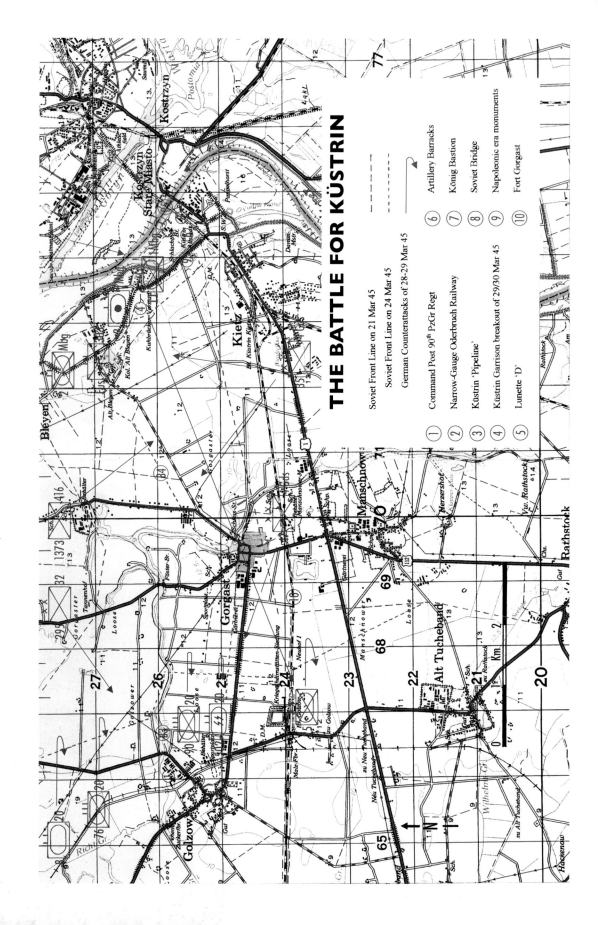

THE BATTLE FOR KÜSTRIN

Soviet Front Line on 21 Mar 45

Soviet Front Line on 24 Mar 45

German Counterattacks of 28-29 Mar 45

① Command Post 90th PzGr Regt

② Narrow-Gauge Oderbruch Railway

③ Küstrin 'Pipeline'

④ Küstrin Garrison breakout of 29/30 Mar 45

⑤ Lunette 'D'

⑥ Artillery Barracks

⑦ König Bastion

⑧ Soviet Bridge

⑨ Napoleonic era monuments

⑩ Fort Gorgast

STAND B4: THE KÜSTRIN PIPELINE

DIRECTIONS: Go back into **Golzow** and turn left for **Gorgast**, passing the battle scene just described. Where the main road turns right in Gorgast, go straight on, following the signs for **Altbleyen**.

THE SITE: While Captain Zobel was defending the bridge in Golzow, his 2nd Squadron of self-propelled guns and tanks had been located at Gorgast. When the Soviets launched their attack on 22 March, the fortress commandant of Küstrin commandeered this company to augment his garrison. Up to this point the road from Gorgast to Bleyen had served as the lifeline to Küstrin. Apart from serving as a supply route, this vital corridor, or 'pipeline' as they called it, had enabled the evacuation of the entire civilian population of the town, although it was only usable at night and by tracked vehicles. Holding this route open had proved no easy task.

THE ACTION: As you come to **Altbleyen** you can see the dykes surrounding the Neu Bleyen and Kuhbrücken-Vorstadt enclosures beyond. When the Soviets closed in, there were four battalions defending this area, the two-battalion 2nd *Müncheberg* Panzergrenadier Regiment, the 2nd Battalion, 1st *Müncheberg* Panzergrenadier Regiment, and the 303rd Fusilier Battalion.

It was from here that the Küstrin garrison made its breakout attempt at 2300 hours on 29 March in defiance of Hitler's explicit instructions. Some 1,318 men, including the commandant and 118 *Volkssturm*, are said to have got through to the German lines.

STAND B5: KÜSTRIN FORTRESS

DIRECTIONS: Pass the hamlet of **Kuhbrücken-Vorstadt**. To your left now is the Vorflut Canal, which cuts off a bend in the Oder, forming an island opposite the Küstrin fortress, one of whose outer fortifications, Lunette D, is on your right immediately before you come to the railway line. Next is the road bridge and you must decide whether to take advantage of the convenient parking area here and walk across, or take the car.

Crossing the island on foot, you pass through the former artillery barracks, augmented by newer Soviet barrack blocks, and cross the bridge into **Poland**. Before you are the remains of the walls of the **Küstrin** fortress, now bearing the Polish name **Kostrzyn**.

THE SITE: The near bastion, with an anti-tank gun on the point, contains a Soviet cemetery. The garrison town that existed within the walls was levelled by the Poles after the war so the stonework could be used in the restoration of Warsaw. After years of neglect the site has been cleaned up and now resembles another Pompeii, but it is largely overgrown. The fortress walls bear many scars from the siege of 1945.

Since 1423 Küstrin had developed from a fortified town with its castle standing at the junction of the

The Soviet memorial on
Bastion König.

Warthe and Oder Rivers into a massive fortress, and defensive outworks or lunettes had also been established on the approaches to the bridges leading to the fortress, although by 1945 the original fortifications were truly obsolete. One of the fortress's claims to fame was that the future King Frederick the Great was imprisoned here by his father for attempted desertion and had been obliged to watch the decapitation of his companion as part of his punishment.

On the last day of January 1945, when Soviet tanks made a surprise penetration of the Neustadt suburb across the Warthe, Küstrin was totally unprepared for its fortress role. Not only were there inadequate troops to defend it, but also there was a basic lack of arms and ammunition, all of which would subsequently have to be brought through the gap between the two Soviet

An aerial view of Küstrin fortress. At top right the Warthe River has flooded over the peninsula on which the fortress stands, with the Oder River curving through the centre from bottom right. Below centre is the artillery barracks island with its two lunettes. Across the canal on the left is Lunette D. The Soviets built an additional bridge across from the Schloss bastion, at bottom centre of the fortress.

bridgeheads at night. Three Lend-Lease *Sherman* tanks and a *Valentine* of the 2nd Guards Tank Army were knocked out before the Soviets withdrew.

Himmler's nominee as fortress commandant, SS-Lieutenant General Heinz-Friedrich Reinefarth, did not arrive until 2 February, by which time the town was all but completely surrounded. As an army sergeant Reinefarth had been awarded the Knights' Cross, and then had transferred to the Waffen-SS, where he gained rapid promotion and the addition of the Oak Leaves to his Knights' Cross. Undoubtedly a brave soldier, he was also known as 'the Butcher of Warsaw' for his work in the ruthless suppression of the Polish Home Army uprising the previous year.

An aerial view of Küstrin Altstadt showing the Schloss and the tower in which the future King Frederick the Great was imprisoned.

One of the knocked-out *Sherman* tanks incorporated into a barricade.

SS-Lieutenant General Heinz-Friedrich Reinefarth.

Having failed to take Küstrin off the march, the Soviets were obliged to lay siege to the citadel, using elements of the 5th Shock Army from the north and the 8th Guards Army from the south. The citadel finally fell on 29 March and those of the German garrison who could broke out that same night, some 1,318 of them getting through to the German lines, including Reinefarth himself. It is estimated that the defence and attempted relief of the Küstrin fortress cost the Germans about 5,000 killed, a further 9,000 wounded and evacuated to their own lines, and another 6,000, mainly wounded, taken prisoner, while the Soviets lost about 5,000 killed and 15,000 wounded.

The bridges across the Warthe and Oder Rivers here remained prime targets for the Luftwaffe and the vital railway bridge bringing Soviet and Lease-lend supplies from right across the Soviet Union was destroyed yet again on 16 April and took a week to repair. The Soviets constructed a supplementary bridge from a central point in the fortress to the island, linking with Kietz on the mainland. They also improvised footways over the wrecked bridges with planks of wood.

You now cross back over the bridges into Germany. On the right at the end of the artillery barracks island are two memorials dating back to the Napoleonic era. The inscription on one reads: 'To the Prussian soldiers who were shot by the French on the 22nd February and 20th April 1807 as guerrillas on the Göhrin.' The other reads: 'Leutnant Wilhelm von Falkenhayn and a number of soldiers fell here on the Torschreiber Bridge in the battle for Cüstrin on 31 October 1806. Erected on 20 March 1914 by the Club for Cüstrin's History 100 years after the liberation of the town by General von Hinriss.'

Blown bridges under fire at Küstrin with a Soviet gunboat in the foreground.

The Soviet cemetery on Bastion König.

STAND B6: THE REITWEIN SPUR

DIRECTIONS: Returning to where you left your transport, follow the B1 through the former suburb of **Kietz**, which was taken by the 8th Guards Army on 4 February 1945, driving through the village along a straight road parallel to the railway. At the far end, where a railway line crosses the road, there is a separate, modern Deutschland-Siedlung on the left that was originally intended for the especially large families urged by the Nazi regime. On the right is the railway station from where one can take a shuttle train to Kostryzn.

Drive on to **Manschnow**, where there is an opportunity to visit **Fort Gorgast**, signed off to the right.

Fort Gorgast

Open all year round Monday–Friday, 1000–1600 hours, and the same hours on Saturdays and Sundays from May to October.

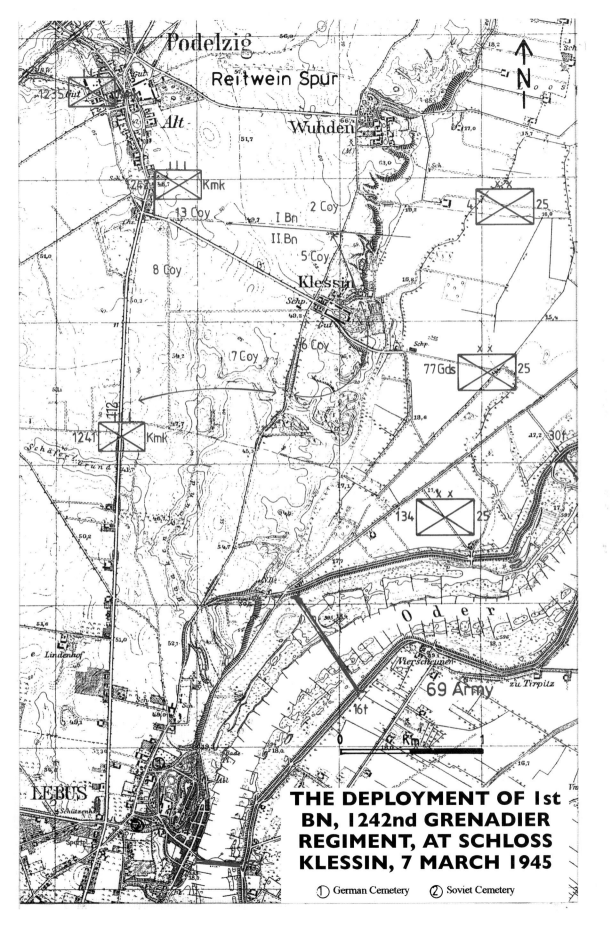

THE DEPLOYMENT OF 1st BN, 1242nd GRENADIER REGIMENT, AT SCHLOSS KLESSIN, 7 MARCH 1945

① German Cemetery ② Soviet Cemetery

The entrance to Fort Gorgast.

From Manschnow crossroads take the B-112 as for **Frankfurt/Oder** through Rathstock and up the Reitwein Spur to the village of **Podelzig**. This is where the first countermeasures to the 8th Guards Army's crossing at Reitwein were organised by Major General Adolf Raegener, the previous commandant of Küstrin, with an improvised staff and an ad hoc collection of hastily assembled units that came to be known as the *Raegener* Division.

THE SITE: From here you take the cobbled road leading left, Wuhdener Weg, to the hamlet of **Wuhden** situated on the far edge of the Reitwein Spur escarpment. Throughout February and March 1945 the ridge on your left witnessed a desperate struggle by the Germans to try to force the Soviets off the spur. An attack to clear the spur was launched by Raegener's troops on 4 March, while the newly arrived 1st Battalion of the *Kurmark* Panzergrenadier Regiment headed for the Reitwein crossing point along the valley bottom to the right, but both were beaten back.

You now come to Wuhden and work your way into the little village square to see the memorial erected in 1995 in honour of the soldiers killed in this area. The inscription reads:

> Those who live in the memory of their comrades are not dead
> Only those who are forgotten are dead
> We remember our fallen comrades and all those who died in the war 1945
> Reitwein Spur with the villages Podelzig, Wuhden and Klessin, 1995

THE ACTION: On 2 March a thrust along the Reitwein Spur by the 8th Guards Army drove the Germans back to Podelzig, leaving a battalion of the 1st *Potsdam* Officer-Cadet Grenadier Regiment isolated in Wuhden. Hitler promptly declared Wuhden a 'fortress' to be defended to the last man, but it was totally unprepared for this role, its only resources being a potato store and a single well. Air supply was decided upon and a transport aircraft allocated for making night drops, but the Soviets promptly brought up their anti-aircraft artillery and soon rendered this means of supply impracticable. An armoured thrust to relieve the garrison met such a hail of anti-tank gunfire that the tanks hardly got across their start line. A subsequent dash at night by three *Panther* tanks of the 2nd Battalion, *Brandenburg* Panzer Regiment resulted in one getting through to provide radio communication for the beleaguered garrison, now reduced to a combatant strength of only 150–160 men.

Corps turned down all requests for permission for a break-out as being contrary to Hitler's orders. Eventually the divisional commander decided on his own responsibility to order a break-out on 12 March, by which time the potato store and the well had been destroyed and only 80 of the original 400 men were still on their feet. The wounded had to be abandoned. Nevertheless, the *Kurmark* continued to report Wuhden held for a further four days until formal permission finally came through. The survivors were then rewarded with their commissions as second lieutenants and fourteen days' leave.

You leave Wuhden and take the road left to **Klessin** until you reach a T-junction. Turn left and up ahead of you on the left is a barren space between the trees on the first bend in the road. This is the site of the manor house (Schloss) and outbuildings of Klessin, which stood in a long rectangle with the manor house at the far end overlooking the valley. Most of the houses that stood to the north of the rectangle have been replaced by the new ones alongside the road you have just come along.

The view from the Schloss is now completely obscured by trees, but this was a

The memorial to the fallen on the Reitwein Spur.

Schloss Klessin before the battle.

All that remained
of Schloss Klessin
after the battle.

valuable outpost for the defenders overlooking the Soviet bridging points below.

On 7 March the 1242nd Grenadier Regiment, mainly officer cadets from the Wetzlar academy, assumed responsibility for this sector, Klessin having also been declared a 'fortress', and by the 11th the Soviets had surrounded the position. All attempts to get through with counterattacks failed, except for two tanks, while the cadets conducted a heroic defence. On the 19th the Luftwaffe succeeded in dropping 13 containers at a cost of two aircraft shot down, but these containers could only be recovered at night because of the heavy machine-gun and anti-tank gunfire.

On the morning of 23 March the Soviets broke into the manor house, forcing the defenders back, and that evening permission was received to break out. Under cover of a well-directed artillery concentration and a diversion by a subsidiary group, the main body managed to reach the gully to the south of Klessin, only to encounter a platoon of Soviet troops entering from the other end. Fortunately, the Germans came across some Panzerfausts that the Soviets had captured and turned them against the Soviets, killing all of them. Under the continuing barrage this

The Schloss Klessin site today.

group of just twenty-six men reached the German lines near the main road, being joined shortly afterwards by about thirty-five men of the diversionary group, some severely wounded.

Little remained of the Schloss. The rusting hulks of the destroyed tanks of both sides and tens of thousands of mines had to be removed. The hamlet was later reconstructed as a line of houses along the Wuhden road with only two cottages on the original site.[7]

STAND B7: THE *SCHÄFERGRUND*

DIRECTIONS: Cut straight back along Altklessiner Weg to the B-112 and turn left for **Lebus**. About 2 kilometres along you come to a depression known as the *Schäfergrund*, extending to the right of the road.

THE ACTION: Rudi Lindner of the 1241st *Wetzlar* Officer-Cadet Grenadier Regiment wrote of the fighting in this area in February 1945:

On the 18th February the regiment was given the task of conducting a counterattack with the support of the 2nd Battalion of the Panzer Regiment 'Kurmark' with the aim of constricting the Lebus bridgehead. The orders for the attack read: 'Thrust down both sides of the Podelzig–Lebus road as far as the crossroads in Lebus and split the enemy bridgehead.'

The main point of attack was set east of the road, which is also where the tanks were committed. The order of advance was as follows: in the first echelon, west of the road the 1st Battalion, east of the road the 2nd Battalion, with the 2nd Battalion, Panzer Regiment 'Kurmark'; in reserve, one company of the 1st Battalion behind the 2nd Battalion; the direction of advance was south toward Lebus.

Preparation for and support during the attack was implemented by the mass of the Panzergrenadier Division 'Kurmark's artillery and mortars, as well as a squadron of Me-109s.

On the 18th February, following thirty minutes' artillery preparation, our regiment, together with the 2nd Battalion, Panzer-Regiment 'Kurmark', went into the attack and immediately ran into a massive barrage from the Soviet artillery that forced our infantry to dig in after having gained only a little ground. East of the road, the tanks managed to push through to within 1500 metres of the northern edge of Lebus. Support for the attack from our own low-flying aircraft had only lasted thirty minutes.

The infantry had become separated from the tanks as a result of the artillery barrage, and the tanks ran into a strong enemy anti-tank artillery belt. Under these circumstances, the divisional commander, Colonel Langkeit, called off the hopeless attack and had the tanks return to the start line.

That evening elements of the Russian 69th Army in regimental strength conducted a night attack from the northern edge of Lebus on our regiment, which had gone over to the defence. The

Rudi Lindner, seen here in the rank of colonel in the East German Army; he eventually retired as a major-general.

attacking Russian troops were able to make a breach in our defences, occupy the *Lindenhof* and effect a breach along the road running north.

Early on the 19th February, the divisional reserve counterattacked and forced the enemy back to the track fork 2 kilometres south of the *Schäfergrund*. However, the counterattack came to a halt here when the enemy committed new forces.

This was the first baptism of fire for our regiment, involving high casualties. These were needless victims to no tactical advantage, on the contrary, involving loss of ground.[8]

Artillery support for the *Kurmark* troops was substantially increased over the second half of February and the beginning of March so that the division could call on fire from up to 250 guns at a time. The ammunition supply was temporarily generous and these resources could lay up to 8,000 shells on an area of 11,000 square metres to support or quell an attack. Bombardment conditions on the Reitwein Spur were described by First World War veterans as comparable to those experienced at Verdun in 1916.

STAND B8: LEBUS

DIRECTIONS: Continue to the Lebus roundabout, where you turn left into the town and drive straight down the hill towards the river as far as a car park on the left opposite a little restaurant, and walk down to the old ferry crossing point on the Oder.

THE SITE: Lebus dates from the year 966 and was the seat of a bishop from 1133 until the end of the fourteenth century, when the bishopric was moved to Fürstenwalde, having been for a while on the frontier between Christianity and the pagan east.

THE ACTION: It was here that the 69th Army launched a surprise attack across the still-frozen river on 12 February with two divisions and 30 to 50 tanks and took the town, which had been only partially evacuated of its civilian population. The remaining civilians were rounded up and those unsuited for hard work were sent east across the Oder while the rest were put to work building fortifications and burying the dead. The Soviets then found some 50 or 60 fishing boats stored in the town from which they were able to construct a floating bridge.

Go back up the hill and take a turning to your right marked *Kriegsgräberstätte*. First on your right on the crest of the hill is the Soviet cemetery, and some distance further along is the German cemetery, also on your right.

The ferry and Soviet bridge site at Lebus.

The Oder River at Lebus.

The German cemetery at Lebus.

The Soviet cemetery at Lebus.

STAND B9: MALLNOW

DIRECTIONS: From the German cemetery turn back for the roundabout and take the B-167 as for **Seelow**, coming to the railway level crossing. Here, a *Tiger* tank was used as an emergency stop-gap; it was driven straight from the workshops, armed with only five shells but plenty of machine-gun ammunition, and was used to block the expansion of the Soviet bridgehead.

Then take the road off to the right signed for **Mallnow**.

THE SITE: Upon arriving in the village, turn left at the T-junction, then right and left on to Podelziger Weg, which takes you out to a car park for a nature reserve. From here walk out parallel to the road to the edge of the ridge, the Huderberg, where the trenches of the important artillery observation post that was located here are still clearly visible.

Back in the village, the cemetery at the ruined church contains the war graves of those killed in the vicinity.

THE ACTION: On the night of 2 March 1945 some 36 Soviet tanks broke through to Mallnow from the Lebus bridgehead, many being destroyed by artillery fire. The

The remains of the German artillery observers' trenches on the Huderberg looking north-eastwards across the Oderbruch.

next day tank-busting Colonel Rudel's elite *Stuka* squadron joined in to destroy or chase off the rest. As previously mentioned, he was later shot down in this area and hospitalised at the Zoo Flak-tower.

Drive back to the B-167 and turn right to return to **Seelow**.

Your tour is over for the day but, if there is some time to spare, you might consider visiting the church in **Friedersdorf** on the way back to Seelow. Built in 1702, the present church on the site was seriously damaged in 1945, but it has been beautifully restored and provides a most interesting representation of traditional Prussian village life. The village was, and is once more, the seat of the von der Marwitz family, the remains of whose manor farm buildings, including a vast barn, stand on the opposite side of the main road. Entry to the church may be obtained by contacting the von der Marwitz family at their home behind the church until 1700 hours on weekdays; later than that and at weekends contact Herr Thomas Dresel at the first house facing the village pond around to the left.

Lieutenant General (Retd) Hans-Joachim von Hoppfgarten, former Chief of Staff of the *Kurmark* Panzergrenadier Division, seen here on a 1992 staff ride to the Huderberg.

Well-kept graves in Mallnow churchyard.

The little graveyard contains the family graveyard with its memorial stones and a powerful post-First World War sculpture of a grieving man by Arno Breker, who later became one of Hitler's favourite sculptors and provided statues for the Olympic Stadium in Berlin.

Inside the church there's a special side balcony for the Graf's family, and an interesting memorial to the Graf von der Marwitz, a Gendarmerie general in Frederick the Great's army, who refused the latter's orders to sack an enemy village because 'it wasn't done'. This caused him to be dismissed and shunned for several years before the king relented and restored him to favour.

The village church at Friedersdorf.

CHAPTER FOUR

SEELOW TOUR C: THE NORTHERN ODERBRUCH

OBJECTIVE: This tour expands the territory hitherto covered to the northern part of the Oderbruch valley. Among other things, it encompasses the first crossing of the Oder River by the Soviets at Kienitz and the battlefield of the 1st Polish Army.

STAND C1: LETSCHIN

DIRECTIONS: Leave **Seelow** on the B-167 as for **Wriezen** and pass through the village of **Gusow**. Signed off to the right as you pass through is the *Kriegsgräberstätte*, the local cemetery containing the graves of 83 named and 15 unknown soldiers; there is also a new war memorial.

Continue along the B-167 and take the next right for **Letschin**. Near the railway

The new war memorial at Gusow.

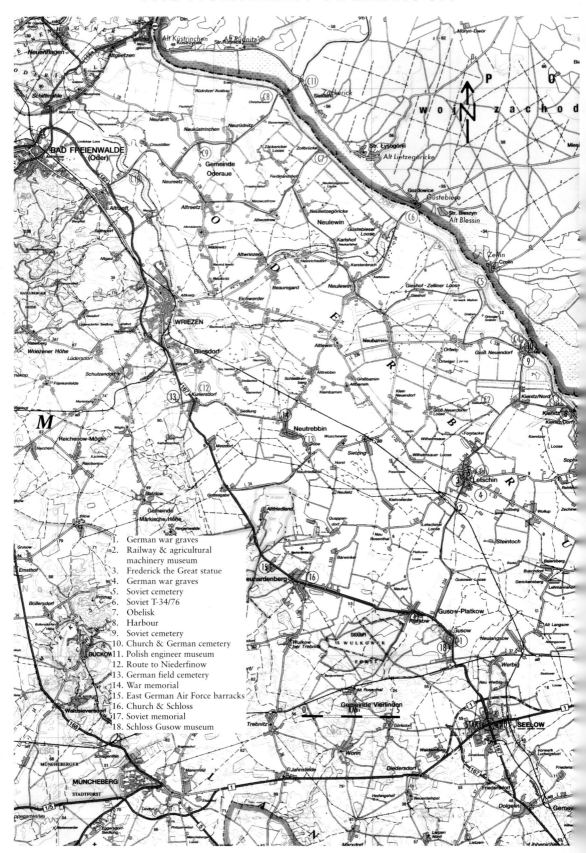

1. German war graves
2. Railway & agricultural machinery museum
3. Frederick the Great statue
4. German war graves
5. Soviet cemetery
6. Soviet T-34/76
7. Obelisk
8. Harbour
9. Soviet cemetery
10. Church & German cemetery
11. Polish engineer museum
12. Route to Niederfinow
13. German field cemetery
14. War memorial
15. East German Air Force barracks
16. Church & Schloss
17. Soviet memorial
18. Schloss Gusow museum

Frederick the Great, who developed the Oderbruch.

The German war dead buried in the town cemetery.

The Soviet cemetery on Letschin town square.

crossing you come to a railway and agricultural machinery museum on your right that contains a large collection of material on these subjects, operated by a local society of enthusiasts who restore their artefacts beautifully.

THE SITE: Coming to the main square of Letschin, the first thing you see is an excellent statue of Frederick the Great on the left. This statue was hidden in a barn towards the end of war and did not emerge again until after Unification.

The Soviet cemetery here is located behind bushes in the square on the right, while 117 German soldiers are buried in the town cemetery 500 metres down the road to the right opposite the statue.

STAND C2: SOLIKANTE

DIRECTIONS: Continue through the village and turn right at the roundabout for **Kienitz**. About 1 kilometre along take the turn-off to the left for **Solikante**, and drive down the minor road leading to it for about 200 metres.

THE ACTION: This is where Gerhard Tillery, whom we will encounter again on this tour, experienced the attack on 16 April 1945:

> I got up at 0330 hours, still half asleep, and took post, but did not have to be as alert as in the front line. It was very misty. I made the rounds of our quarters, and at ten to four woke up my relief and was happy that I could now sleep into the morning.
>
> As I was going back down into the cellar, I heard the well-known 'Flup, flup' sound coming from Ivan. He was firing his mortars. I took this to be his morning concert and carried on down. The first Russians salvos fell on the front line, but the hits started coming closer until they started landing in our vicinity. But there was more to it than that, more than the usual morning concert. Our building received several direct hits. Ivan was laying a violent bombardment down on us. Hit after hit followed the discharges and the din that came from their anti-aircraft and anti-tank guns and heavy artillery too could be heard. Then the runner came from the company command post: 'Alert! Take post immediately!'
>
> I reached the trenches jumping from shell hole to shell hole under the heaviest fire. The earth was being ploughed up systematically, one crater overlapping the next. The trenches were already suffering and beginning to cave in. One of the comrades from my section was wounded with a splinter in his backside.
>
> On the 14th, two days previously, I had thought that that was the real bombardment, but what the Russians were giving us now was far, far worse. I did not think that anyone could survive. Every bit of earth was being churned over. I jumped in the holes where there had already been an explosion, as every soldier knows that no two shells land on the same spot. The minutes stretched into hours. At last after three hours the firing eased up and moved on behind us, but we knew that the second part was on its way. Now we could shoot back again, being no longer exposed to the shelling.
>
> Men were running back from the front line, in a state of shock and without

The Solikante-Amt Kienitz battlefield looking north-east from the approach road.

their weapons. Panting and trembling, they called out to us: 'Ivan is coming!'

Only a few had survived the shelling in the front line and been able to flee from the Russians, who were following close on their heels. One could not see them as it was so misty that one could hardly see ten metres, but one could hear them. The 'Urrahs!' were getting louder. I had handed in my machine gun for repair the day before because of the constant jamming, so Staff Sergeant Buchel sent me back to the company command post to get it. I found it, although the place was deserted, but when I came out again I could hear Russian voices in the immediate vicinity, and could not go back. The Russians had already reached our trenches. There was only one way out and that was to the rear.

I ran westwards as fast as I could, but I had my heavy machine gun to carry. Apart from this, I had a box of ammunition, the Russian sub-machine gun, my pistol, hand-grenades and all my equipment on me. Clearly I could not run very fast. The Russian voices were getting closer and soon they would be catching me up. I had to discard something. First went the Russian sub-machine gun, then the hand-grenades went into the dirt, then the ammunition box, and finally I wanted to throw the machine gun away.

Suddenly I heard called from behind: 'Stoi! Ruchi verch!' The machine gun flew in a high curve into the dirt. I tugged at my ammunition pouches, but could not get them off. As I turned around I could see the outline of my pursuer, who already had his rifle up to his cheek. Then he lowered it again. 'Damn it, Tillery!' he said. 'Bring the machine gun with you!' It was no Russian, but a comrade from my platoon, Hans Kaldekowitz, who had a head wound. When the Russians arrived they had not been able to get away in time and were overrun. Then they had mixed in with the advancing Russians and gradually got ahead. Later a large part of the company was to meet up again.[1]

STAND C3: KIENITZ

DIRECTIONS: Return to the main road and turn left for **Kienitz-Nord** (formerly Amt Kienitz), and then turn right for the main village of **Kienitz**, where a Soviet T-34/76 tank on a plinth dominates the main square.

The plaque here reads: '31 January 1945 – Kienitz, the first place to be freed from Fascism on our state territory. Fame and honour to the combatants of the 5th Shock Army and 2nd Guards Tank Army.' Another point to notice is that every street bears the same name, Strasse der Befreiung ('Liberation Street'), which was an imposition by the former East German government. (Nearly all the streets in the Oderbruch area bear Communist-inspired names to this day.)

Drive out of the far end of the village, going straight on where the main road turns right at a telegraph pole topped by a stork's nest, and you will come to a metal obelisk commemorating the Soviets' arrival in the early hours of 31 January and the establishment of their first bridgehead. One can drive as far as the river down the cobbled road ahead, but the dyke roads are forbidden to traffic.

Note the old harbour on the left where the farmers used to unload produce from their fields on the far side of the river prior to 1945.

The Soviet T-34/76 monument in Kienitz.

The Soviet cemetery at Gross Neuendorf.

The obelisk
commemorating the
Soviet crossing of the
Oder River.

THE ACTION: Marshal Zhukov described the arrival of his troops here in his memoirs:

> At the moment the detachment burst into the town of Kienitz, German soldiers were blissfully walking the streets, and officers were sitting in a restaurant. Trains on the Kienitz–Berlin line were running on schedule, and communications were operating normally.[2]

This has been quoted faithfully by others, but it could not be more inaccurate. The crossing had taken place in the dead of night over a frozen river. The only people awake in the village at the time were the baker and his assistant. Asleep on a train carrying six anti-aircraft guns at the narrow-gauge railway station were 13 officers and 63 youngsters of the Labour Corps (Reichsarbeitsdienst), who were captured. Only a few lightly clad individuals fled across the fields to get away to warn the incredulous officials in the nearest town of Wriezen.

STAND C4: GROSS NEUENDORF

DIRECTIONS: Turn back on your route to **Lietzen-Nord**, where you turn right on the road leading to **Gross Neuendorf**, where the first thing you come across is a neat Soviet cemetery.

THE SITE: Move on into the village, turning left on Alte Dorfstrasse, and you will come to Parkweg and the village church. The church was so fought over and damaged that the northern part has not been rebuilt and the bells have been set up in a wooden frame outside. Two of these bells commemorate the von Sydow family, Hans Christian, a colonel, Georg Sigismund, a director, and Georg Wilhelm, a naval captain.

Walking straight on from the church through the cemetery, you come to the military section, marked **Kriegestote 1945**.

The German cemetery at Gross Neuendorf.

The sheared-off village church and belfry.

The Zellin bridge site.

STAND C5: THE ZELLIN BRIDGE

DIRECTIONS: From Gross Neuendorf drive on to **Ortwig**, where a road to the right leads out to the Oder dyke. The road bends to the left before the dyke, runs parallel to it and then turns left again. At this point a track runs back to the dyke, where there is a place to park. From here you can walk down to the river on a broad, surfaced roadway.

THE SITE: This is the site of the Zellin bridge, which cost 387 Soviet casualties, including 201 fatalities, in the seven days it took to build. Zellin, across the river, is now *Czelin*. A bit further downstream to the left are the four foundation piers for a pylon that once carried power cables across the Oder.

STAND C6: GÜSTEBIESE LOOSE

DIRECTIONS: Continue via **Gieshof** to **Neubarnim**, where you turn immediately right for **Neulewin**. In Neulewin turn right again and follow the road out of the village for **Güstebiese Loose**, going right to the end, over the dyke and down to the water's edge opposite *Gozdowice*, the former Güstebiese.

THE SITE: Return to the dyke. In the line-up for Operation Berlin this was part of the Soviet 47th Army's territory, but their Polish neighbours' 1st Infantry Division to the north had experienced considerable difficulty in attempting to make river crossings near the blown combined road and railway bridge at Zäckerick (*Siekierki*) during the reconnaissance in force on 14 and 15 April, suffering considerable casualties in the process. At the last minute the Poles were allowed to bring in troops to force the Alte Oder from this point.

1st Polish Army

The Soviet-sponsored 1st Polish Army, together with the 2nd Polish Army serving under Marshal Koniev further south, had been raised from conscripts of military age found within the old Polish borders and from among those prisoners taken by the Soviets in 1940 (when the Soviet Union joined in the German invasion of Poland) who had not been fit enough to join the exodus to form the British-sponsored Polish forces in 1942. The 1st Polish Army was so weak in officers and NCOs that Russians had to be used in many capacities, and most units were still at only 70 per cent of establishment. General Stanislaw Poplawski, the army commander, was himself a Soviet Army officer, although Polish born. The army structure was unusual in that there was no interim corps level of command, the army headquarters directly controlling the five infantry divisions.

THE ACTION: There were no Soviet bridges within the newly allocated Polish sector, so Polish engineers had to ferry across the 3rd Infantry Division and two regiments of the 2nd Infantry Division, the former having the task of securing the near corner as it wheeled left north of the Alte Oder channel, while the latter secured the Oder embankment northwards to allow other troops to cross the flooded river. This operation proved successful and some heavy tanks were brought across in support, but the day's objectives were not achieved in full.

Assault river crossings were made against fierce opposition near the tiny hamlet of Zollbrücke, using the Soviet 234th Amphibious Vehicle Battalion with its female drivers, and the 1st Infantry Division eventually succeeded in establishing a bridgehead near the destroyed road and

General Stanislaw
Poplawski, Commander
of the 1st Polish Army.

The ferry crossing site at Güstebeise.

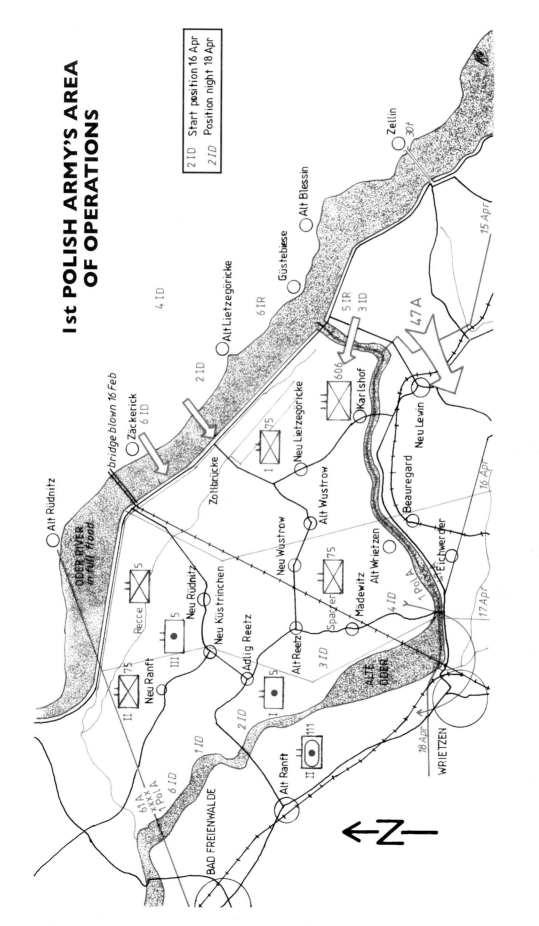

1st POLISH ARMY'S AREA OF OPERATIONS

2 ID   Start position 16 Apr
2 ID   Position night 18 Apr

Zellin
30t
Alt Blessin
Güstebiese
Alt Lietzegöricke
6 IR
4 ID
Zäckerick
6 ID
2 ID
bridge blown 16 Feb
Alt Rüdnitz
ODER RIVER
in full flood
5 IR
3 ID
47 A
606
Karlshof
Neu Lewin
Zollbrücke
I   75
Neu Lietzegöricke
Beauregard
Neu Wustrow
Alt Wustrow
Eichwerder
Recce
5
Neu Rüdnitz
5
Neu Küstrinchen
Adlig Reetz
Alt Wrietzen
1 Pol A
75
Madewitz
4 ID
Sparren
III   5
75
II
Neu Ranft
I   5
Alt Reetz
3 ID
ALTE ODER
II   111
Alt Ranft
21 D
1 ID
17 Apr
16 Apr
15 Apr
61 A
xxxx
1 Pol A
6 ID
18 Apr
WRIETZEN
BAD FREIENWALDE

←N—

rail bridges opposite Zäckerick, but at a cost of 1,365 men, including 112 officers.

The experiences of Lieutenant Erich Hachtel give some idea of the confusion that reigned behind the German lines that morning. As commander of the heavy weapons company (150mm howitzers and 120mm mortars) of the 75th Light Infantry Regiment, 5th Light Infantry Division, he had his command post close to the regimental command post in Königlich Reetz (now Altreetz). He wrote:

Oberleutnant Erich Hachtel.

At 0930 hours I was summoned to the regimental command post. Lieutenant Colonel Liebmann turned to me: 'Herr Hachtel, have you contact with the front?' I replied in the negative, adding that I had had no contact since 0900 hours. I discovered that the regiment also no longer had contact with the 1st Battalion and so no one knew exactly what was happening. Lieutenant Colonel Liebmann looked at me and said: 'Take your tracked motorcycle combination forward, make contact with the 1st Battalion and report back to me what it looks like up front.' With this task I raced first south to a dike and then along this to the *Oder-Stellung* near Neulietzegöricke. Soldiers lying in their holes on the left side of the dike looked at us in amazement. We had driven along the front line and the area around us with its shell holes reminded one of a moon landscape. They must have been soldiers of the 3rd Battalion under its commander, Major Sparrer, who with his unit was known as 'Combat Group *Sparrer*'.

We reached the shattered village of Neulietzegöricke and found the command post of the 1st Battalion of the 75th Light Infantry Regiment on a big square in the middle of the village. The battalion commander reported that everything in his sector was in order and firmly in our hands. A breach in his 1st Company's sector had been cleared and the assailants driven back into the Oder with cold steel. As I then learned, they had been members of a Polish division, as one could tell from the dead left behind. With this message on as yet positive progress in the fighting, I returned to the regimental staff.

I then made my way to the left flank of our regiment to look at my platoon's firing positions. I drove alone on a motorcycle via Neuranft and then eastward along an arrow-straight road leading to Neuküstrinchen. Suddenly Russian aircraft appeared in the sky and attacked the convoy I was overtaking on the road. I saw how the machines wheeled to come over our road one after another, raking the road with their armament. People jumped madly aside seeking cover, horses broke loose, rearing up to collapse or gallop off the road with their wagons. I saw this distressing sight and accelerated away, seeing no other possibility of getting out of this mess. Once more I was lucky and so came to our firing positions safe and sound. Second Lieutenant Vogel came up to me straight away and reported that everything was in excellent order, being very pleased with our results. My visit to the observation post confirmed this. When I was about to leave, I noticed that my motorcycle had received two hits but, thank God, was still mobile!

So all attacks were repelled in our sector of the Oder and our front line remained firmly in our hands, although the situation to the south with our right-hand neighbour, the 606th Infantry Division, was threatening. Strong Russian tank units had broken through there, increasing the pressure already coming from the Küstrin area. Our 3rd Battalion under Major Sparrer's command was facing south and had to secure our right flank. This battalion was really meant as a reserve, but through the dangerous, obscure situation with our right-hand neighbour, the 606th Infantry Division, the battalion came to experience the enemy's full pressure and thus, with its attached elements, had to bear the main burden as 'Combat Team Sparrer'.[3]

Lieutenant General Friedrich Sixt, Commander of the 5th Light Infantry Division.

STAND C7: ZOLLBRÜCKE

DIRECTIONS: Returning to **Neulewin** turn right for **Kerstenbruch**, where you turn right again for **Karlshof**, crossing over the Alte Oder, the original course of the Oder, which makes the northern part of the Oderbruch an 'island'. From Karlshof drive on through **Neulietzegöricke** to turn right at the next T-junction for **Zollbrücke**.

THE SITE: This was the site of another of the many ferries that used to ply across the Oder prior to the end of the Second World War.

THE ACTION: As previously mentioned, this position was taken against fierce opposition by assault units of the 1st Polish Infantry Division on 16 April 1945, crossing in the vehicles of the Soviet 234th Amphibious Vehicle Battalion with its female drivers.

The river at Zollbrücke.

An amphibious unit in action on the Oder.

STAND C8: THE ZÄCKERICK BRIDGES

DIRECTIONS: As you are not allowed to drive along the dykes or their service roads, turn back inland here for **Altwustrow** and **Altreetz**, where you turn right for **Neureetz** and there right again to drive through **Neuküstrinchen** and **Neurüdnitz**, then follow the sign to **Bienenwerder** to reach the banks of the Oder next to the remains of the Zäckerick road and rail bridges.

THE SITE: These bridges formed a critical point in the German defence of the northern Oderbruch.

THE ACTION: As early as 29 January the newly formed HQ Army Group *Vistula*, then commanded by Reichsführer-SS Heinrich Himmler, had ordered a special unit

to secure this crossing point and destroy it only when the enemy was immediately before it. Despite several Soviet attacks, the Zäckerick bridgehead was able to hold out until 16 February. The price for this dubious success was very high, for only about 45 of the original 200 soldiers

A Polish pontoon bridge at Zäckerick. (Note the dependence upon horses.)

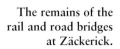

The remains of the rail and road bridges at Zäckerick.

reached the safety of the west bank, having held a crossing open for over two weeks that neither German military personnel nor refugees could use.

STAND C9: NEUKÜSTRINCHEN

DIRECTIONS: Return the way you came via **Neurüdnitz** to reach **Neuküstrinchen**, where you turn left down the main street to reach the church known as the Oderbruch Cathedral.

THE SITE: Frederick the Great had this large church built here to cater for a wide area. Opposite the church is the voluntary fire brigade station, which contains an interesting little museum about the fighting in this area.

The Neuküstrinchen Museum

Access can be obtained by contacting either Herr or Frau Köhler at 53 Dorfstrasse (the village high street).

Inside the church there are rolls of those killed in the neighbouring villages during the fighting and a memorial outside to those with no known grave in the church grounds. The inscription reads in German, Russian, Polish and Hungarian: 'To the fallen soldiers with no known grave. While we know about these horrible things, we ask you, Lord, to look upon history as our fallen comrades saw it. Give all the peoples of the earth freedom, peace and justice.'

The Neuküstrinchen memorials.

STAND C10: THE ALTE ODER

DIRECTIONS: Return to **Neureetz,** where you turn right as for **Altranft,** and come to the **Alte Oder** channel at **Neugaul.**

THE ACTION: The Alte Oder channel presented a considerable obstacle for the 1st Polish Army on 19 April 1945. A German soldier recalled:

Fog covered the foreground; it was completely foggy. I saw suspicious shadows in the fog. A Second Lieutenant going by identified tanks with his binoculars. Several tanks, five or seven, came up to the dyke and fired with their guns. Infantry attacked from Croustillier. We could not hold off the tanks with just carbines and a few sub-machine guns. We had no artillery support or *Panzerfausts*. The inexperienced Luftwaffe soldiers and our small

A JS-2 heavy tank of the 1st Polish Army crossing the Alte Oder.

group pulled back over the log footbridge. We dug in as best as we could in the old Oder dyke north of the sugar factory and lay under constant fire.

Next day the Polish engineers constructed two 30-ton and three 16-ton bridges for their supporting armour across the Alte Oder south of Neugaul. Meanwhile the 4th Polish Infantry Division wheeled north through Wriezen, following its fall to the 47th Army, to roll up the German resistance from the southern flank.

STAND CII: SIEKIERKI

OBJECTIVE: The 1st Polish Army's cemetery at Siekierki, Poland.

LIMITATIONS: Please ensure that your car insurance is valid for travel in Poland.

DIRECTIONS: Drive on to join the B-167 at the traffic lights and turn right to drive on to the next crossroads, where you turn right again on the B-158a for **Hohenwutzen** and Poland (**Polen**).

Having crossed into Poland, take the first turning right out of the checkpoint area, which takes you through woodland down to the Oder riverbank, and drive on through Kostrznek (Alt Küstrinchen) and Stari Rudnica (Alt Rudnitz) until you come to a disused railway station on your left. Just beyond the railway station is the 1st Polish Army's magnificent cemetery set back off the main road on the left. There is also a small museum to the left of the cemetery entrance.

Going on into the village of **Siekierki** (Zäckerick), you come to a monument and another small museum devoted to the Polish army engineers who operated in this area, and there is an external display of river-crossing equipment.

1st Polish Army's cemetery at Siekierki.

These villages along the east bank of the Oder River are much depleted from their pre-war status as a result of being pillaged for building materials for the reconstruction of Warsaw, so that large areas are now derelict.

The 600th SS Parachute Battalion is said to have defended the approaches to the river above Alt Küstrinchen to the last man. The dead were then buried in their trenches and the site bulldozed over and planted with potatoes. The site today is overgrown wasteland.

You then return to the B-167 by the way you came.

OPTION

If you are interested in technical marvels, it may well be worth your while to carry on the few extra kilometres to Niederfinow to see the extraordinary lift that conveys barges and other canal traffic 36 metres in five minutes from one canal level to another. The *Schiffshebewerke Niederfinow* was opened in 1934 and is one of the very few operational in the world.

Turn right at the traffic lights and drive past Bad Freienwalde on the B-167 to Falkenberg, where you turn off right for Niederfinow, then drive through the village, over the Finow Canal as for Liepe, and you will come to it.

STAND C12: KUNERSDORF

DIRECTIONS: Upon reaching the B-167, turn left as for **Wriezen**, which the new road now bypasses, and drive on through the hamlet of **Vevais** towards the village of **Kunersdorf**. Where the main road bends to the left halfway between these villages, there is a track off into the woods on the right that leads to the German field cemetery, which is up the hillside to the right of the track and signed *Deutsche Soldatenfriedhof*.

THE ACTION: This is where units of the 25th Panzergrenadier Division and the 2nd Battalion, 118th Panzergrenadier Regiment, of the 18th Panzergrenadier Division, which had been brought forward from Army Group Reserve during the

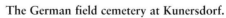

The German field cemetery at Kunersdorf.

Kunersdorf's distinctive church.

previous night, manned the line on 17 April following the virtual collapse of the 606th Infantry Division the previous day.

On that day the Soviet 47th Army launched a strong attack from the line Thöringswerder–Altlewin with infantry, armour and cavalry forces. Soviet aircraft then prevented effective German counterattacks, but the 47th Army still claimed to have repelled two counterattacks of up to battalion strength supported by fifteen tanks and self-propelled guns!

Lieutenant Gerhard Hahn, who was with the 2nd Battalion, 119th Panzergrenadier Regiment, reported:

> At 0600 hours the battalion attacked in the flat valley bottom of the Oder near the Kunersdorf manor farm, 5 kilometres south of Wriezen, driving the Russians back over the Friedland Strom Canal. The battalion took up defensive positions in the drainage ditches south of the Kunersdorf farm towards Metzdorf under a heavy enemy artillery barrage.
>
> Renewed enemy attacks with strong artillery and armoured support were repulsed. The Russians and Germans are lying opposite each other in the parallel ditches. During the afternoon the enemy launched an attack against the battalion's front. Hardly any artillery fire, but losses from Russian snipers. Heavy casualties for the battalion today, especially in the 5th and 7th Companies. Company commander, 7th Company, severely wounded.
>
> The Russians have broken through to the Seelow Heights left and right of the battalion, enemy tanks pushing through to the west. By evening farms can be seen burning about 5 kilometres off.
>
> There is a danger that the battalion will be cut off. During the night of 17/18 April 1945 the companies could still be supplied with food and ammunition, and the dead and wounded taken back.[4]

STAND C13: NEUTREBBIN

DIRECTIONS: Cut across the main road at **Kunersdorf** to take the road to **Neutrebbin**. Arriving at the village high street, you come across a well-maintained memorial to the village's war dead dating back to the nineteenth century. Turn right here and you will come to another particularly fine statue of Frederick the Great in the village centre. Plaques on either side of the plinth bear the inscriptions: 'Here I have conquered a province in peacetime that cost me no soldiers' and 'It is not important that I live, but it is important that I work as long as I live to make my people happy.'

Turn left, away from the statue, then follow the village street to the eastern end of the village and turn right for **Gottesgabe**.

THE ACTION: Gerhard Tillery, who was involved in the German withdrawal in this area, recorded:

> The following morning, the 18th, we occupied positions on the north-eastern edge of Neutrebbin, where our regiment gathered. Only 34 assembled, all the rest being either dead, wounded, captured or missing. Our company was still comparatively strong with about ten men remaining.

Neutrebbin's memorial to the dead of many wars.

We deployed ourselves in front of the village. The Russians soon arrived and made an attack, coming to within a few metres of our positions and we even captured one. Suddenly the four self-propelled guns that had been supporting us vanished and now the Russians started coming at us with tanks. As we could hardly defend Neutrebbin with less than forty men, we withdrew. We already had two men killed and several wounded in the village.

Drive out of Neutrebbin to a crossroads, where you turn right for Gottesgabe.

Tillery continues his description:

We withdrew about 3 kilometres over open fields until we came to a canal about 10 metres across that ran between Neutrebbin and Gottesgabe, and here we deployed once more. The self-propelled guns from Neutrebbin reappeared in our support but, when the Russians attacked with tanks in big numbers, they had to be blown up as they were unable to cross the canal.

We pulled back to another ditch, where we were stomach deep in cold water, as otherwise the Russians would have seen us. My camouflage suit was soaked through and was running with water, and I still had to carry my machine gun and a box of ammunition, so I took off my padded trousers and threw them away; after all, it was spring. I could hardly get out of there. With every step my feet sank deep in the mud.

The Russians soon spotted us and brought the ditch under mortar fire. One bomb landed in the ditch and killed three men. Then we had to cross an open field. The Russians were firing even when individuals crossed, using mortars and accurately. At the end of the ditch lay a man wounded in the leg, who asked me to help him across. Although mortar bombs landed close, we managed to get across unscathed.

Then we came up against the military police and everyone who had a weapon had to go back into the line, but staff clerks and supply personnel were allowed to go – a factor that did little to raise our fighting morale.

I had become separated from my unit again. Although I knew

The ditch between Neutrebbin and Gottesgabe.

Neuhardenberg village green with its Schinkel-designed church.

that it was close by, the military police refused to let me find it. I was given a confused, thrown-together section to deploy along a line of trees in front of Gottesgabe. We had communication to the rear by means of a runner. When I sent the runner back with a message, he failed to reappear. I sent another runner back with the same result, so I went back myself to find out what was happening. I did not find a soul. They had all gone back without telling us.

A unit of 15- and 16-year-olds of the *Hitler Youth* had made an attack from Gottesgabe and been driven back with heavy casualties. I was deployed with my section along the eastern edge of the village. During the night the Russians thrust their way into the village with tanks and we had to withdraw.

We deployed again about 200 metres west of Gottesgabe. Suddenly about forty men came toward us. We opened fire, thinking they must be Russians, and by the time we discovered they were Germans, two of them were already dead.[5]

Continue along the B-167, passing **Altfriedland** and its fish farms, then, as you approach **Neuhardenberg**, you pass between two former military installations, the one on the right housing the German Democratic Republic's state air force squadron and the one on the left the airfield.

The village church at Neuhardenberg, designed by the famous German architect Karl Friedrich Schinkel, dominates the centre of the village green. The village was named after Karl August Fürst von Hardenberg, who was given the estate in 1814 by King Friedrich Wilhelm III in reward for his services in the administrative reform of the Prussian State. His successor in 1944 was Carl-Hans Graf von Hardenberg, who was one of those involved in the 20 July plot against Hitler. He attempted to commit suicide when the Gestapo came to arrest him, but only wounded himself and was subsequently lucky enough to survive incarceration in Sachsenhausen concentration camp.

The estate was confiscated by the Nazi government and remained expropriated throughout the period of the German Democratic Republic, which renamed the village Marxwalde in 1949. Following Unification, the family was able to reclaim this property as well as the Komturei Lietzen estate (encountered in Seelow Tour A), and the village was renamed accordingly, although as one word, in common with post-war practice.

Schloss Neuhardenberg

Open for exhibitions Monday–Sunday 1100–1900 hours.

Drive on to **Platkow**, where a Soviet war memorial is located on the village green commemorating their losses against the German 9th Parachute Division in this area.

The next village is **Gusow**, where the Schloss has an interesting but somewhat disjointed exhibition of tin soldiers in historical settings, and you finish in **Seelow**.

Schloss Gusow

Closed Mondays; open April–September 1000–1800 hours, October–March 1000–1700 hours.

The Soviet war memorial at Platkow, marred by a blackened face. The names of the individual dead were added to the structure on plaques at a later date.

FALKENHAGEN SECRET VILLAGE

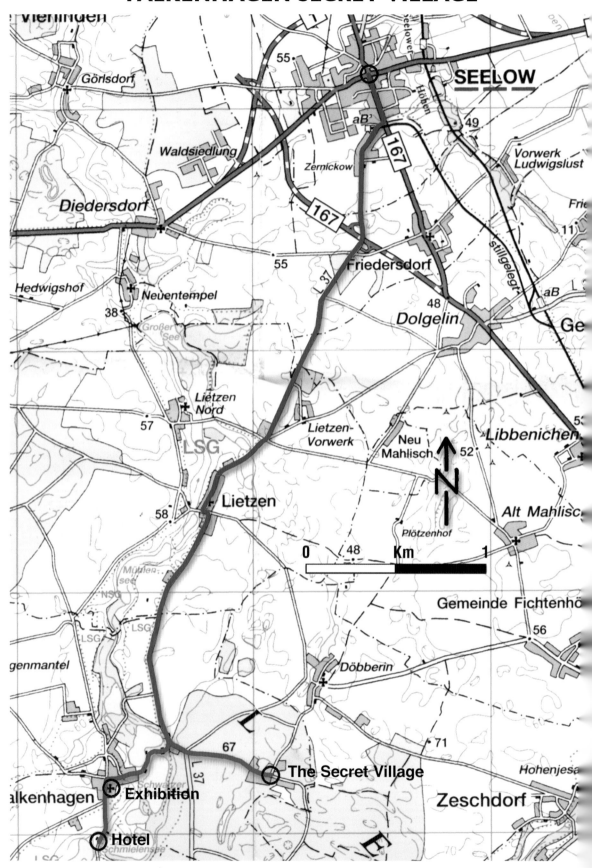

SEELOW TOUR D: FALKENHAGEN SECRET VILLAGE

OBJECTIVE: A conducted tour of a top secret Soviet command post located underground in a former German poison gas factory.

LIMITATIONS: Prior arrangements for a conducted tour of the village, which is private property, need to be made with Herr Hajo Schumacher, the proprietor of the Seehotel Luisenhof, Am Gabelsee, D-15306 Falkenhagen (Tel 033603-400, Fax 033603-40-400). He charges €100 for a tour, irrespective of the numbers involved. **A powerful torch is needed!**

DIRECTIONS: Drive south out of Seelow on the road you took back from **Lietzen** on your first day. Continue through Lietzen, turning left where you previously turned right at Altner's battalion command post, and carry on for about 2 kilometres until the road is joined by one coming in from **Falkenhagen** on the right.

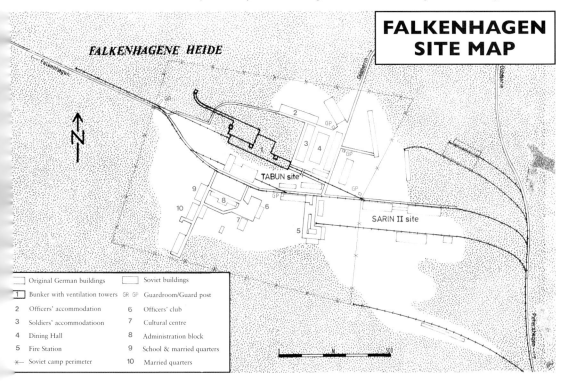

FALKENHAGEN SITE MAP

FALKENHAGENE HEIDE

TABUN site

SARIN II site

☐ Original German buildings		☐ Soviet buildings
☐ Bunker with ventilation towers	GR GP	Guardroom/Guard post
2 Officers' accommodation	6	Officers' club
3 Soldiers' accommodatioon	7	Cultural centre
4 Dining Hall	8	Administration block
5 Fire Station	9	School & married quarters
✕— Soviet camp perimeter	10	Married quarters

To reach the **Seehotel Luisenhof**, turn into the village and follow the signs for the hotel.

If you would like a preview, there is a small exhibition (in German) in the church on your way. The church is kept open and the exhibition is inside beneath the clock tower. It includes a model of the original factory, which is worth seeing.

Alternatively, the factory itself can be reached by turning left at the road junction mentioned above and proceeding 200 metres to where another road forks off left to **Döbberin**. At this point you leave the metalled road and go straight ahead on to an unmarked concrete track into the woods. Follow this until you come to a manned guard-post, which is the usual rendezvous point for conducted tours.

THE SECRET NERVE-GAS FACTORY

The original site was that of a factory for the manufacture of poison gas, built as the result of a decision made by the Wehrmacht's *Heereswaffenamt* (Army Weapons Administration) in 1938 to manufacture Chlortrifluoride for the recently discovered nerve-gas *Tabun*. Chlortrifluoride, or *N-Stuff* as it was called, is an aggressive, highly inflammable substance that needs very special handling. Production was to take place underground, and in order for it to remain perfectly dry, the factory needed a concrete shell some 5 metres thick to prevent any intrusion from the water-table. As it would take time to complete the construction of the bunker, in which only German-born nationals could be employed, some above-ground laboratories and plants were erected to enable the preliminary development of the manufacturing process from laboratory to factory-scale production. In fact the bunker took a full five years to complete, not being ready until 1943.

When Albert Speer became the Minister for Armaments and Munitions in 1943, he decided to implement the production of *Sarin II*, a later generation of nerve-gas, at the same site. The two products and those concerned with them were kept completely separate. A small satellite camp of the Sachsenhausen concentration camp was set up that year in the woods north of the site, but whether the inmates were employed in the construction of the *Sarin II* installations, or used in the assembly of V-weapons in part of the above-ground installations remains uncertain.

Considerable effort was made by the Germans to camouflage the site from aerial observation. Transportation was by a special narrow-gauge track connecting with the main lines at Briesen. These tracks followed the contour of a new concrete road through the forest that was built to carry local traffic away from the site and were countersunk in the road surface to conceal their profile. Production also required heavy consumption of electrical power, and immediate post-war maps show a line of overhead pylons stopping abruptly a considerable distance from the site. This clue to something unusual in the vicinity that would merit such a supply was later removed. During the war the Germans continued to rely on camouflage for the protection of the site and no anti-aircraft guns were deployed that might have attracted attention to it.

The upper level of the five-storey factory is concealed under a natural hill in such a way that a railway line ran right through it in a tunnel. Three ventilation towers projected above the hill, but below the height of the tops of the trees that covered it.

Part of the *Sarin II* production site.

During the brief period the factory was operational, between October 1944 and February 1945, some 22–30 tons of Chlortrifluoride were produced. By this time the site was under SS control and it seems that V-weapons were also assembled here. When the Red Army established bridgeheads across the Oder River at the beginning of February 1945, production was hastily abandoned and the satellite concentration camp disbanded.

THE SITE: In April 1945 the command post of the 1314th Field Training Grenadier Regiment was located here, as described in Helmut Altner's *Berlin Dance of Death*:

> We march past massive workshops that rise out of the dark like threatening giants and stop in front of one of them, the command post of our regimental commander. . . .
> Then we fade into the background and tour the deserted workshops and factory streets. Camouflaged entrances lead to the underground workshops, whose open doors are an invitation to share their secrets. V-weapons are no longer being assembled here, for the workers have become soldiers, and boxes of ammunition and *Panzerfausts* lie next to the gleaming bodies of the flying bombs, while cobwebs and dust lie finger thick on the workbenches.[1]

After the war the factory and its site were stripped by the Soviets of everything that could be moved as part of their reparations scheme. Having no further interest in the site at that time, the Soviets handed it back to the local authorities and it was not until the 1950s that the Soviet Army returned to set up a signals establishment here. This is believed to have been the principal communications facility for the headquarters of the Group of Soviet Forces in Germany at Zossen-Wünsdorf following the discovery of the Anglo-American spy tunnel intercept from the southeast corner of the American sector of Berlin in April 1956.

The conversion of the factory into a Warsaw Pact nuclear command bunker began in the 1970s. The Soviets left the original production structures alone, apart from the original accommodation block and two halls that they used for basketball. To the original accommodation block they added officers' quarters, another large

The camp kindergarten.

accommodation block and a hotel with a separate, communal mess hall, all within the outline of the original structures. They also built a cultural centre, an officers' club, family accommodation, including a kindergarten and a school, and even some new family accommodation blocks shortly before their departure in 1992.

On your way through to the factory you pass the kindergarten and married quarters aside on the right, then the original offices and accommodation block with the original site workshops opposite. Next on the right is a sort of parade ground with the Soviet cultural centre in the background and the officers' club to its left. Then you come to a sort of warehouse on the right with a loading platform for the railway on which the Soviets built a guardhouse. Opposite is a wooden barrack block and then one of the laboratories. Turn left at the end here and left again, the area now

The railway and loading bay with a Soviet guardpost on the platform.

The officers' club and camp cinema.

The camouflaged entrance to the installation.

behind you being the never-completed area for the production of *Sarin II*. Ahead of you is the camouflaged entrance to the tunnel with one of the ventilation towers just visible in the trees. The first part of the tunnel is as it was originally, but then you see a structure on the left over the railway line that was built by the Soviets, who blocked off the tunnel at either end and installed airproof personnel entrances incorporating a series of three massive steel doors about 1 metre wide, 2 metres high and half a metre thick.

Between these doors they built

The entrance to the command bunker.

Inside one of the decontamination chambers.

decontamination facilities overlooked by control cubicles, with a hospital close behind. One of the ventilation towers was filled with filters for use in the event of a biological attack, when the other two could be cut off.

Down below the various production chambers were converted into the control bunker role with raised floors under the communications rooms allowing easy access for the technicians; there was a special wallpapered and self-contained suite for the commander, and other facilities for the senior officers. The soldiers appear to have been allocated collapsible bunks hinged to the corridor walls and denoted by painted numbers. The main operations room had a false ceiling reducing its original height. It appears that the bunker was manned on a monthly rotation basis with the commander and staff being flown in from the Soviet Union.

When you emerge into daylight again, turn left to pass the remains of the special accommodation built for those taking part in the Warsaw Pact exercises, including a hotel and separate mess-hall.

On their departure the Soviets stripped the premises once more, before handing it over to the German State Property Office in 1992 as 'Falkenhagen Garrison – Military Settlement No. 1', an item that had not even been listed previously.

Warsaw Pact staff accommodation.

CHAPTER SIX

SEELOW TOUR E: THE OSTWALL FORTIFICATIONS AT MIEDZYRZECZ (MESERITZ)

OBJECTIVE: The German fortifications of the Tischtiegel (*Trcziel*) defensive belt at Miedzyrzecz on the pre-war boundary with Poland.

LIMITATIONS: It is important to check that your car insurance is valid for travel within Poland.

DIRECTIONS: Crossing at **Kostrzyn** (*Küstrin*), go round the fortress to the right and take Route 133 left for 63 kilometres to **Skwierzyna** (*Schwerin an der Warthe*), where you turn right for 18 kilometres on Route 3 (E-65) to **Miedzyrzecz**

Soviet troops examining the Meseritz fortifications.

THE OSTWALL FORTIFICATIONS

(*Meseritz*), then look out for the tourist information centre (Biuro Uslug Turystycznych) at 7 Reymonta Street for final directions.

THE SITE: After the First World War the Polish border encroached to within 150 kilometres due east of Berlin, leaving the German government under threat of invasion. Consequently a defensive construction plan was drawn up entitled *Oder-Warthe-Bogen* (the bend between the two rivers); it had an estimated budget of 500 million Reichsmarks and work commenced in 1935. Only 60 of the 160 planned installations were completed along the 110-kilometre front, but these included armoured turrets for machine guns, 10cm howitzers with a range of 6 kilometres, and flamethrowers, and armoured emplacements for anti-tank guns and 15cm howitzers. Flooded areas and other obstacles were also included in the plan.

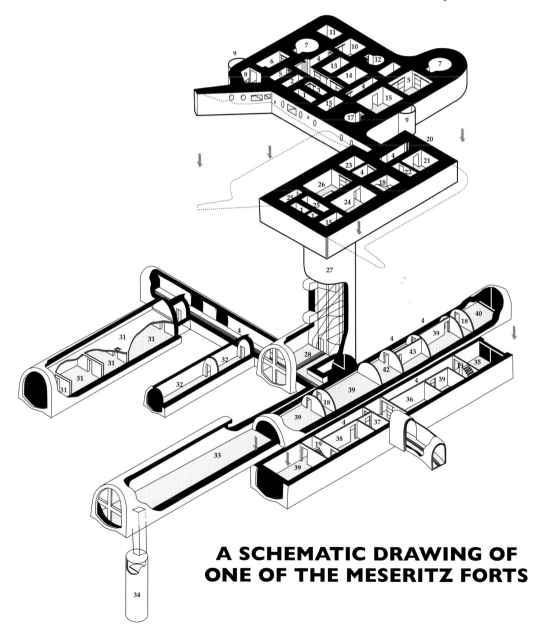

A SCHEMATIC DRAWING OF ONE OF THE MESERITZ FORTS

THE ACTION: In his capacity as commander of Army Group *Weichsel*, Himmler ordered SS-General Friedrich-Wilhelm Krüger of the Vth SS Mountain Corps based in the Meseritz area to try to block the Soviet advance on Berlin. Headquarters Vth SS Mountain Corps then had the 433rd and 463rd Reserve Infantry Divisions under command, deployed along the north–south line of the Odra River and the pre-war frontier defences against Poland known as the *Tischtiegel Riegel* (defensive belt), and was further reinforced by *Volkssturm* and other scratch units.

Massive though these partly completed *Maginot*-like defences were, they had long been stripped of their guns for the *Atlantic Wall*, and so failed to present the expected obstacle to the Soviet advance, being quickly overrun.

For German speakers, Berliner Unterwelt is currently offering one-day, weekend and 2^1/$_2$-hour tours.

One of the Meseritz forts today.

CHAPTER SEVEN

SEELOW TOUR F: THE SOVIET 33RD ARMY'S CEMETERIES AT CYBINKA (ZIEBINGEN)

OBJECTIVE: The Soviet 33rd Army's cemeteries at Cybinka, Poland.

LIMITATIONS: Ensure that your car insurance is valid for travel within Poland.

DIRECTIONS: From Seelow take the B-167 south to Lebus and turn right on the B-112 for Frankfurt/Oder, then follow the signs for **Slubice** (Polen) to cross the Oder. Upon arrival in Poland, turn right on Route 29 and drive 40 kilometres along

The entrance to the officers' cemetery, Cybinka.

THE SOVIET 33rd ARMY'S CEMETERIES

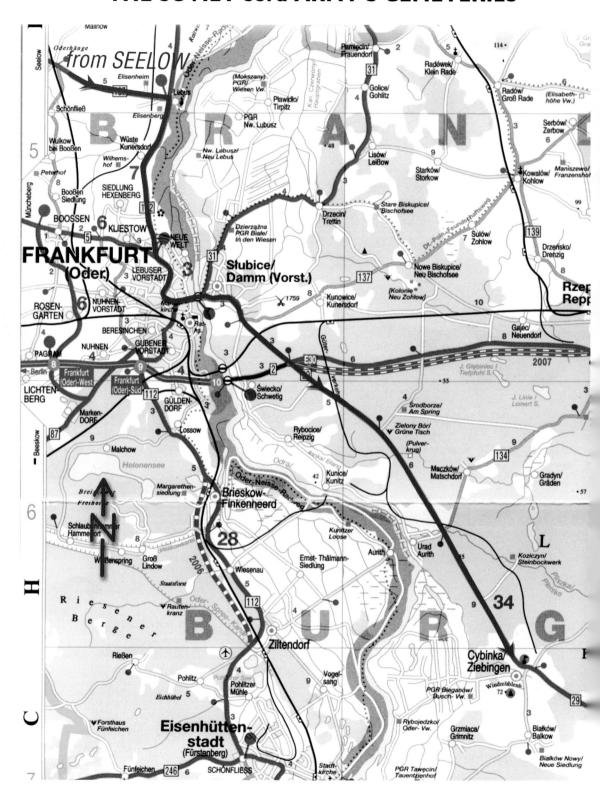

Officers' graves.

this road to **Cybinka**. The officers' cemetery is near the town church, on the site of the gardens of the former Schloss.

THE SITE: Cybinka (Ziebingen) held the headquarters and main field hospital of Colonel General S.D. Svetaev's 33rd Army. At the conclusion of hostilities, the 33rd Army Council apparently decided to gather all their dead here but then, curiously enough, chose to bury their officers and other ranks separately. The graves of 566

The entrance to the soldiers' cemetery.

officers, one warrant officer and one female soldier are located in what were the grounds of Schloss Ziebingen. The other ranks' cemetery is further out of town, denoted on the skyline by an obelisk visible from the officers' cemetery.

When the author originally visited Cybinka in about 1990, both cemeteries were in a sad state of neglect. The entrance to the soldiers' cemetery was flanked by massive self-propelled guns mounted on guardrooms. The soldiers had been buried in fours around mini obelisks engraved with their names. Both cemeteries have since been completely renovated.

The obelisk and some of the ground plaques giving the names of the 3,600 soldiers buried here.

CHAPTER EIGHT

SEELOW TOUR G: THE ADVANCE ON BERLIN

OBJECTIVE: This tour takes you back to Berlin from Seelow while covering some important aspects of the Soviet advance on the city.

STAND G1: DIEDERSDORF

DIRECTIONS: Take the B-1 for Berlin, and Diedersdorf is the first village you come to. On the way, as you reach the town boundary, you pass a well-preserved Prussian milestone on the right. The Prussian mile measured 4.8 kilometres, distances being taken from a milestone on Leipziger Strasse in Berlin. A copy of the original milestone is now located in the *Spittelkolonnaden* on the opposite side of that street.

THE SITE: The nature of the terrain made Diedersdorf a bottleneck and converging point for the Soviet forces first outflanking and then eventually passing through Seelow.

The manor house at Diedersdorf.

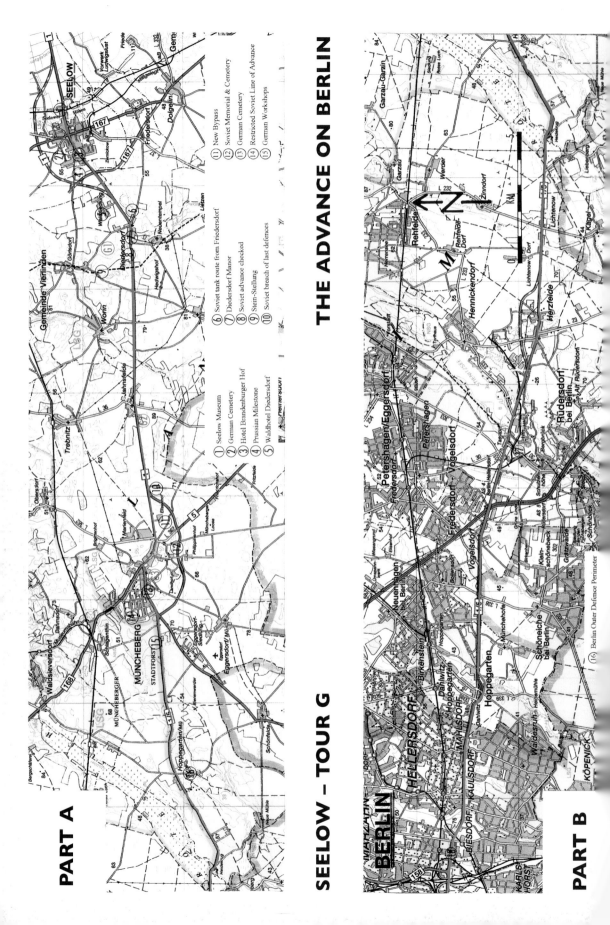

PART A

SEELOW – TOUR G

THE ADVANCE ON BERLIN

PART B

① Seelow Museum
② German Cemetery
③ Hotel Brandenburger Hof
④ Prussian Milestone
⑤ Waldhotel Diedersdorf

⑥ Soviet tank route from Friedersdorf
⑦ Diedersdorf Manor
⑧ Soviet advance checked
⑨ Stein-Stellung
⑩ Soviet breach of last defences

⑪ New Bypass
⑫ Soviet Memorial & Cemetery
⑬ German Cemetery
⑭ Restricted Soviet Line of Advance
⑮ German Workshops

⑯ Berlin Outer Defence Perimeter

THE ACTION: The road converging from the left as you enter Diedersdorf was the route used by the 1st Guards Tank Army following the Ludwigslust-Friedersdorf penetration of 16/17 April 1945. Further down on the left you pass the large manor house in which the commander of the 29th Guards Rifle Corps set up his command post on the night of the 17th. Here Colonel Babadshanian of the 11th Guards Tank Corps, while effecting his own liaison with the infantry, was witness to an interesting episode:

> After some bitter fighting at the Seelow Heights our troops reached the Third Defensive Strip in the Müncheberg-Diedersdorf sector.
>
> I drove to General Shemenkov's 29th Guards Rifle Corps command post with several officers of my own corps in order to coordinate further developments with him. His staff had set themselves up in a rather grand manor house. We went through several rooms until we finally came to the area in which this rifle corps' staff were working.
>
> As soon as he greeted me, Shemenkov informed me that he would not be able to attack at 0800 hours as ordered. He had postponed the time of attack to 0900 hours.
>
> 'That must be reported to Chuikov!' [I said], but Shemenkov paid no heed to me.
>
> Early in the morning Chuikov and Katukov appeared. 'Are the troops ready to attack?' asked Chuikov.

The scene of the Soviet defeat at Diedersdorf.

Shemenkov tried to explain why he had postponed the attack.

'What do you mean, postponed?' roared Chuikov.

How this exchange developed further, I cannot say, for Katukov took me aside and whispered: 'There is nothing more here for you to do. Drive back to your troops as quickly as possible. The order must be executed according to schedule!'[1]

Lined by trees, the B-1 winds out of the village in an S-bend to reach a belt of woodland, where you stop alongside a soccer pitch. Looking back, this is where the second belt of German fortifications began, known as the *Stein-Stellung*. A line of trenches is still clearly to be seen running just inside the leading edge of the woods. Backed up among the trees were two 88mm guns that engaged the advancing Soviet tanks as they emerged from Diedersdorf on the morning of the 18th with their last four remaining shells each.[2]

This prepared position relied on survivors from the forward lines to man it, such as Second Lieutenant Tams and a handful of his men, but the Luftwaffe joined in too. With their vehicles jammed nose to tail on the highway, the results were devastating for the Soviets.

This disaster, added to the formidable losses sustained in the previous two days, led Marshal Zhukov to order every last available man from his Rear Area to be rounded up and sent forward as reinforcements that day, and that evening he issued fresh orders governing the conduct of the battle, especially with regard to road movement in the advance on Berlin. This also involved the fusion of the 1st Guards Tank Army with the 8th Guards Army under General Chuikov for the next phase of the battle.

STAND G2: JAHNSFELDE

DIRECTIONS: Continue along the B-1 to the crossroads in **Jahnsfelde**.

THE ACTION: On the morning of 19 April 1945 the 3rd (Flak) Battalion of Artillery Regiment 18, consisting of the 7th, 8th and 9th Batteries of 88mm guns

The site of the last stand of the 3rd Battalion, Artillery Regiment 18. The slope rises over 20 metres to the line of trees in the dip on the skyline where the three batteries were hastily deployed when they encountered the Soviet advance along the main Seelow–Müncheberg highway.

and commanded by Captain Müller, was withdrawing south through Jahnsfelde when it was caught by some T-34 tanks. Second Lieutenant Werner Elsner of the regimental staff reported:

Just as I was bringing orders to Captain Müller from the battalion commander urging haste before daylight, the first light dawned. While following the 9th Battery, the first shot from a tank hit a gun and tractor, killing three. Captain Müller immediately deployed the battery left in front of a wood, bringing gun after gun into position. The gunners hastened to prepare their guns for firing. When I reminded the commander that this was not where he was meant to take up his position, he shouted: 'We will not be going any further! See for yourself!' and pointed left, where fifteen to twenty tanks, a mass of them with even more following, were appearing between the Jahnsfelde houses and rattling at top speed over the kilometre-long rounded but coverless slope up to the battalion, while already shells were exploding on the firing position. Lieutenant Baruth, the commander of the 9th Battery, fell. The T-34s were still at some distance, coming to within 800 metres, advancing fast, firing with their guns and machine guns.

As the 9th Battery arrived, the command was given: 'Tanks in front, 400 metres, fire!' against the wall of steel and fire rapidly getting nearer. The thunder of engines, rattling of tracks, roar of guns and bursting of shells rose to a combined powerful din. The dense pack of tanks was already illuminated with seven stopped burning on the slope, the others increasing the distances between them, shells bursting among them. The shots from the 7th Battery echoed hollowly across – there a flash as high as a house, a turret barrelled through the air, a hit in the ammunition! The tanks spread apart, one turning with a torn track – next target! But the number of casualties in the firing position was increasing. The 9th Battery had already lost its no. 4 gun with two dead while taking up position, and now the no. 2 gun had lost its gun-layer. Captain Müller ran to the 7th Battery, which had suffered the worst casualties. Second Lieutenant Rainer Zmerzly of the regimental staff commanded the 9th Battery in this fight and shot up one tank after another himself, the last at only 250 metres. When the commander of the 8th Battery fell, Captain Müller took over.

Captain Müller and his officers were sure that the battalion could not hold out for much longer. But they could no longer escape, and until help arrived . . . 'Even if we do have to sacrifice ourselves, this is it, we have no choice!' the battalion commander decided, but sent Second Lieutenant Tolk to Heinersdorf, where the 169th Infantry Division and some of the SS-Division *Nederland* were located, to ask for tanks or ground-attack aircraft. 'They will be here in an hour!' one comforted oneself as once more the call came: 'Tanks in front!'

In several rows and wide apart, over thirty tanks were attacking from Jahnsfelde making the ground shake. Their guns were firing relentlessly, the shells exploding in the crests of the trees behind the firing position. Second Lieutenant Zmerzly took the gun-layer's seat and gave the order: '800 metres,

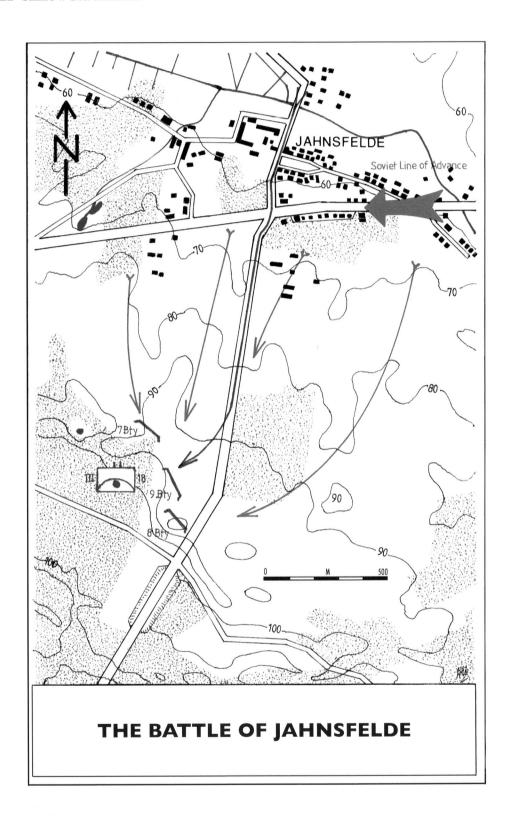

THE BATTLE OF JAHNSFELDE

fire!' Tank shells exploded around him as the guns fired. Suddenly he noticed eight to ten tanks pulling over to the right and stopping on the road. They wanted to outflank the firing position. If they succeeded, the battalion would have been completely lost. In order to get there, the tanks suddenly turned aside, exposing their vulnerable sides. The gun hastily swung round until the leading tank was in its sights. The first shot went wide. '700, fire!' Direct hit – clouds of smoke, bright flames. Second Lieutenant Zmerzly did not hear the second shot; a direct hit on no. 3 gun next to him: the barrel split, the ground plate shattered, the sights smashed and all the crew killed.

The tanks got closer to the road with undiminished speed. Correcting the sights, as within a flash the first shots rang out, Zmerzly shouted to the number two: '600 – wait a moment!' Then the gun loader shouted: 'Only six rounds left, sir!' The subaltern turned brusquely: 'Get some from the wrecked gun!' While he was following the diverging tanks, several had broken away from the main pack to the left, going past the battalion's arc of fire, and skilfully reached the edge of the wood near No. 7 Battery, which had destroyed many tanks. Now five T-34s were outside the arc of fire and were approaching the firing position from the left. The battalion commander was at the 8th Battery's flank gun, but could not help. The 7th Battery tried to train its guns round, the gunners swearing. Are these tanks faster? 300 metres – 250 metres – 200! The leading T-34 appeared at 150 metres with another two behind it, just driving on, ever closer, threateningly, unescapable, unstoppable! The battalion was in extreme danger; at the most only one of the two guns could aim, the second could not get round far enough. One gun against five tanks at minimum range – hopeless!

'Hollow-charges!' shouted Second Lieutenant Zmerzly at the ammunition carrier panting his way up, who ran away from the gun. The Russian mortar was taking a break. He could not see what was happening at the 7th Battery. He could only hear the guns and see black clouds of oily smoke. A hit! 'Carry on firing!' he ordered the neighbouring gun as he rushed past. Then the

The dip on the crest of the hill where the guns deployed.

ammunition carrier came back from the gun tractor with the hollow charges, five between his clasped fingers. The officer grabbed them out of his hands and ran to the edge of the wood, ducking under the fence to the right opposite the tanks in front of the 7th Battery. The situation here was precarious. One of the guns had managed to train round, the second was holding back. The leading tank was burning 70 metres away, but two of the gun crew had been killed by its machine gun in the exchange of fire. The gun was silent. 'Leave No. 2! Everyone to the other gun and bring up the ammunition!' he shouted, loaded and fired. The steel monster was hit and emitted smoke, stopping still. The remaining three increased speed, their machine guns raking away at the gun crew, then a direct hit on the gun, an ear-breaking crack and thick smoke. The battalion commander at the 8th Battery shouted: 'Tanks from the left, close defence!' as Second Lieutenant Zmerzly suddenly ducked under the trees and chased after the nearest tank. With their machine guns aimed forward, the three T-34s were driving so close together that they were no longer covering themselves from the firing position. Zmerzly jumped up on the wing of the tank behind the turret and placed the charge right over the casing, jumped off and threw himself into a crater. Metres-high flashes and an ear-blasting explosion! With a hollow charge in each hand he chased after the two remaining tanks that were driving on unperturbed – 15 metres, 10, 7 . . . then the main pack of 25 tanks broke over the brow of the hill, firing away at the firing position as they advanced at top speed, just as it was hit by a hefty mortar bombardment. This was the end. The Second Lieutenant collapsed under a cloud of yellowish smoke.

That evening Colonel von Gilsa divulged the shattering news that of the 3rd (Flak) Battalion, Motorized Artillery Regiment 18, the commander, regimental liaison officer, Second Lieutenant Zmerzly, three battery commanders, three battery officers and 163 men had fallen, over two-thirds of the battalion wounded, and all the guns lost.[3]

Soviet losses here have been estimated at about 100 tanks.

Some 3 kilometres further on you come to a sign on the left indicating a track to the *Elisenhof* farm. Although the *Wotan-Stellung* – the final line of defence in the form of an anti-tank barrier based on Müncheberg – held the Soviets in check for most of the day, by about 1700 hours on 19 April 1945, the fourth day of their breakthrough battle, sufficient Soviet forces had collected near the *Elisenhof* for them to punch their way through at last, although at a reported cost of about 60 tanks according to the German Army Group report that evening.

STAND G3: MÜNCHEBERG

DIRECTIONS: Just beyond the *Elisenhof* track junction turn right off the beginning of the bypass, take the original highway into **Müncheberg** and drive into the town.

THE SITE: The town centre was virtually obliterated in the fighting and had to be rebuilt, but you pass an ancient gate tower capped by a stork's nest and then the unusual church with its separate bell tower connected to the main body of the church by a common roof. You pass another ancient gate tower on the way out. On the left is a park with a small Soviet monument. The main road for Berlin then turns to the left and about 500 metres along there is a large Soviet monument, lined with graves, up some steps in the woodland to the left.

THE ACTION: Colonel General Chuikov of the 8th Guards Army described the taking of the town:

> The 242nd Regiment of the 82nd Guards Rifle Division did some fine fighting during the battle for Müncheberg. The regiment's commander, Colonel Ivan Sukhorukov, a veteran of the battle of Stalingrad, made a bold and carefully considered decision. His regiment approached Müncheberg by the road running from the Oder. The enemy had built numerous defence installations here. Leaving only one company in this sector, Sukhorukov ostensibly, in full

The Soviet memorial at Müncheberg.

The Soviet cemetery behind the memorial.

German soldiers' graves at Müncheberg.

view of enemy observers, pulled back his main forces, then swiftly entered the woods north of Müncheberg and from there attacked the town from the flanks and rear. His infantry, operating in small groups, was supported by tanks and self-propelled guns. Sukhorukov himself was with an infantry sub-unit in the centre of the regiment's battle order. House-to-house fighting lasted several hours. Carrying out their commander's orders, the troops tried to cut off the enemy's escape routes. They came to street intersections and, opening sudden fire, created the impression of having surrounded the place. The Germans panicked, which was exactly what Sukhorukov wanted. Launching an all-out attack with his main forces, he finished off the enemy. The town was thus captured with our side suffering only minimum losses.

When the fighting for Müncheberg was over, I learned from the regimental surgeon that Ivan Sukhorukov had been gravely wounded in the chest and leg. I had him promptly evacuated to hospital. On the recommendation of the Army Command, Colonel Sukhorukov was made Hero of the Soviet Union.[4]

Take the next turning right and then the second left to reach the town cemetery, where there is a large military section.

STAND G4: THE BRIDGE AT TASDORF

DIRECTIONS: Return to the main road and go on until you come to the traffic lights controlling the junction with the B-1 bypass; turn right for **Berlin**. The road now leads through two thick belts of woodland with a clearing at the village of **Hoppegarten**, where the German armoured workshops were located. These woods constricted the Soviet armour to the main road, where it was harassed from prepared positions and by *Hitler Youth* armed with *Panzerfausts* and mounted on bicycles. Traces of defence positions can still be found on either side of the road.

Continue through the villages of **Lichtenow** and **Herzfelde**. Emerging from the latter, you pass a vast cement manufacturing plant on the right. This is now British owned, but under East German rule employed labour drafted in from Angola and Mozambique in an arrangement with their governments. This labour force was accommodated in wooden huts hidden behind the trees on the left just before the railway bridge over the road. A little further on, on the crest of the hill on the left, was an East German prison factory for the manufacture of segments of the Wall, the prisoners being bussed in daily from prisons in the surrounding area. The road now dips down to a bridge over a canal, the site of the next stand.

THE ACTION: During the withdrawal of the LVIth Panzer Corps to Berlin, Captain Horst Zobel found himself guarding this bridge with a few tanks to enable its demolition by a captain of engineers. The demolition charge failed, entailing a death penalty for the distraught engineer, but fortunately, as he was reporting his failure, the news came through that the Soviets had just crossed the canal to the south of them, and the engineer was spared.

Beyond this point the road goes past the vast Rudersdorf chalk pits, where many of the German prisoners taken in the city were later assembled and sorted by their Soviet captors.

DIRECTIONS: Continue along the B-1 towards **Berlin**, crossing the Autobahn ring and passing through another Hoppegarten, a place that was famous for its horse-racing even under Communist rule. Pass the city boundary and continue straight on for **Alexanderplatz**.

The new bridge at Tasdorf across the last water obstacle before Berlin.

PART TWO

BERLIN BATTLEFIELD

CHAPTER NINE

INTRODUCTION TO BERLIN

Transport Services

Berlin has two main traffic hubs, **Alexanderplatz** and the **Zoo** (*Zoologischer Garten*), both linked by the S-Bahn, U-Bahn and bus services all run by the BVG, Berlin's traffic corporation, which also includes trams in the eastern part of the city. Tickets are available from machines located in the various stations, from special BVG information counters in Alexanderplatz railway station and at the entrance to the square outside the Zoo station. Instructions are given in English on all machines. Some hotels also stock them.

As a tourist, you are probably best off with an all-day or seven-day ticket for a combination of A and B zones. For a group of up to five, small group one-day tickets provide good value. The current (2007) rates are:

All-Day Tickets (*Tageskarte*), valid until 3 a.m. next day, cost €5.60.

Seven-Day Tickets (*Wochenkarte*), valid until 3 a.m. next day, cost €24.30.

Small Group One-Day Tickets (*Gruppentagekarte*), valid for 5 persons until 3 a.m. next day, cost €14.00.

Single Fare Tickets (*Normaltarif*), valid for two hours in one direction only, cost €2.00.

Short Hop Tickets (*Kurzstreckentarif*), valid for three U-Bahn or S-Bahn stops, or six bus or tram stops, cost €1.20.

Note: It is important to remember to validate tickets purchased from machines or your hotel as soon as you start using them; the red or yellow validation machines are to be found at the entrance to S-Bahn and U-Bahn stations and on buses. Those purchased from bus drivers are automatically date-stamped.

In this section I will be using the buses as much as possible, as they give a better impression of the city, and S-Bahn and U-Bahn routes only when a faster means of travel is more appropriate. **You will need a proper city map** to find your way around, and I would suggest the *Knick Mich!*, which as its name implies folds up in book form to fit into one's pocket, at €7.95.

When walking in Berlin, remember that the traffic and pedestrians keep to the right, the opposite to that in the UK. Watch out for cyclists coming from the rear: that red strip on the pavement is reserved for them. Also, jay-walking is not allowed: only cross on the green light.

A Potted History of Berlin

Berlin's history dates back to 1307, when the two villages of Berlin and Cölln which lay on either side of a ford across the Spree River combined in self defence to form a town. At the beginning of the fifteenth century the Hohenzollern family acquired the province of Brandenburg and built their residential Schloss in Berlin.

The town was of little consequence until the reign of Frederick William, the Great Elector (1640–88), whose reforms and foreign policy laid the foundations of the Prussian state. He gave refuge to 20,000 French Huguenots, built a new section of town north of today's Unter den Linden, and also created the Hohenzollern Canal, which linked the city with Hamburg and Breslau in Silesia and brought a great increase in trade. His son Frederick succeeded him and declared himself 'King in Prussia' in 1701, establishing his court in Berlin and attracting many artists, painters, philosophers and architects to the city. However, he left his country almost bankrupt.

His successor was the 'Sergeant King', Frederick William I, who spent all his resources on doubling the size and effectiveness of the Prussian Army, which was put to use by his son, Frederick the Great (1740–86), in a series of three wars that almost ruined the country before it stabilised and became recognised as a world power, with Berlin growing to a population of 150,000. However, twenty years later Prussia fell to Napoleon's invasion of 1806 and did not recover until the latter's retreat from Moscow in 1812 brought a revival of Prussian nationalism and participation in the defeat of Napoleon during the years 1813–15.

The nineteenth century failed to bring peace. There was a revolution in 1848 that came to nothing. In 1864 there was a brief war against Denmark to acquire territory, and another two years later against Austria. In 1867 Count Otto von Bismarck became Chancellor and began work on forming a North German League under the presidency of the King of Prussia, William I. Then in 1870 France declared war on Germany, which ended with William I being declared Emperor ('Kaiser') at Versailles the following year.

The reparations extracted from France enabled the financing of the subsequent development of Berlin as it rapidly industrialised with the establishment of such firms as AEG and Siemens. By 1900 the population had risen to 2,000,000. Then came the First World War with its disastrous results. The country had been run by the Army High Command, which did not deign to acknowledge its defeat to the populace, giving rise to the 'stab in the back' accusations that were to agitate the country's politics over the next generation, which also had to endure the Great Depression, and eventually gave birth to the Nazi movement that was to bring even more devastation in its wake.

It is estimated that 750,000 tons of high explosives alone were dropped on the city during the Second World War, plus an incalculable number of incendiaries. A single raid on 3 February 1945 killed 53,000 people. Overall civilian casualties have been estimated at between 110,000 and 125,000. Further damage was inflicted by the Soviet artillery during the fighting for the city, which left 1,500,000 people homeless, half the city's bridges destroyed (it has more than Venice), and over 60 per cent of the city centre destroyed.

Devastation from bombing and shelling in Kreuzberg.

The city was surrendered to the Soviets on 2 May 1945 and the final surrender of the German Armed Forces was made at Karlshorst on the night of 8 May.

Although the decisions on the division of Germany into zones of occupation and Berlin into sectors had been agreed previously, the positions in which the advancing Western Allied and Soviet forces had ended did not tally with the occupation plot, the Western Allies having to withdraw a considerable distance to the agreed boundaries before the Soviets would allow access to Berlin. Consequently it was

Field Marshal Sir Bernard Montgomery with Marshals Zhukov and Rokossovsky after presenting them with British awards.

not until 4 July that the Allied contingents arrived in the city to take over their sectors from the Soviets.

The French were not party to the original agreement, but demanded a share and eventually the British ceded the northern two districts of their sector to them. The Americans occupied the districts of Kreuzberg, Schöneberg, Neukölln, Steglitz, Tempelhof and Zellendorf, the British Spandau, Charlottenburg, Tiergarten and Wilmersdorf, the French Reinickendorf and Wedding, and the Soviets the rest.

The government of the city came under the Allied Kommandatura, located in the American sector, but the city also initially housed offices of the Allied military governments and military missions from all the nations that had been involved in the war against Germany.

Land access by means of the autobahn and railway linking Helmstedt in the British zone with Berlin was by prior agreement between the military commanders and was dependent upon the goodwill of the Soviets as regards supervision and maintenance of these routes. Only the use of the three flight corridors into Berlin was formally regulated by arrangement within the Control Council at the end of 1945, which established the Berlin Air Safety Centre. With representatives of all four nations, this unit functioned without a hitch till the very end of the Allied and Soviet occupation.

In the spring of 1948 the Soviets began impeding the road and rail access routes, and on 23 June imposed a full land blockade of the city over a dispute regarding currency reform in the western sectors. This led to the introduction of the Berlin Air Lift, which managed to sustain the garrisons and populations of the western sectors until the Soviets lifted their blockade at midnight on 12 May 1949.

A Sunderland flying boat on the Havel during the Blockade.

Meanwhile a Communist government had evolved in the Soviet zone under the guise of being a coalition of Socialist parties. To counter the bright lights of the Kurfürstendamm in West Berlin, construction work began on Stalinallee, part of the former Frankfurter Allee.

Then on 16 June 1953 masons and carpenters working on this project protested against a drastic increase of their expected job-performance quotas with a march from Strausberger Platz to the consortium of ministries housed in the former Air

Soviet tanks suppressing the workers' uprising.

Soviet tanks facing American tanks on Friedrichstrasse, 28 October 1961.

Ministry building on Wilhelmstrasse. Next day the remaining construction workers joined in and tens of thousands of workers flooded into the governmental district, and the Red Flag was torn down from the Brandenburg Gate. In panic, the East German government called on the Soviets for assistance and the local military commander declared martial law, using tanks to crush the uprising.

The ever-increasing flow of East Germans to the west was such that by 1961 over 2,500,000 had sought refuge via the Marienfelde refugee camp in West Berlin. On 13 August 1961 the East German government sealed off the western sectors from the outside and started building the Wall. Then on the 28th of that month came the Soviet–American tank confrontation at Checkpoint Charlie.

Following demonstrations in East Berlin and Dresden against a background of a collapsing Soviet Union, the Wall was eventually breached from the eastern side on 9 November 1989 after a fumbled performance by a member of the Politbüro at a press conference earlier that evening. The official opening ceremony then took place at the Brandenburg Gate on 22 December.

On 2 October 1990 the Western Allies formally handed over their residual powers to the city government and at midnight that day the ceremony of German Unification took place in front of the Reichstag.

The Soviets handed over their Reichstag War Memorial to the safekeeping of the city authorities immediately before Christmas 1992, and in 1994 the Soviet and Allied garrisons departed after a series of farewell ceremonies, ending with a torch-lit *Grossen Zapfenstreich* (Tattoo) by the *Bundeswehr* for the Western Allies on Pariser Platz on 8 September.

The Wall falls, 10 November 1989.

The chairman commandant, Major General R.J.S. Corbett CB, signs over Allied rights to the city government on 2 October 1990.

For a fascinating multi-media exhibition on Berlin's history, one should visit **The Story of Berlin** at the rear of a mall at 207–208 Kurfürstendamm; this is a good two-hour experience, and includes a tour of a vast Cold War nuclear bunker. To get there from the Zoo, take **U-9 Rathaus Steglitz** one stop to the **Kurfürstendamm**, then the **U-15 Uhlandstrasse** one stop to the end of the line. On emerging on to the Kurfürstendamm, look out for the *Maison de France* forming one of the corners of the street junction with Uhlandstrasse: that is the block in which the exhibition is located. Follow the Kurfürstendamm pavement until you come to an upright aircraft tail-plane indicating the entrance.

The Story of Berlin

Entry €9.30; open daily 1000–2000 hours.

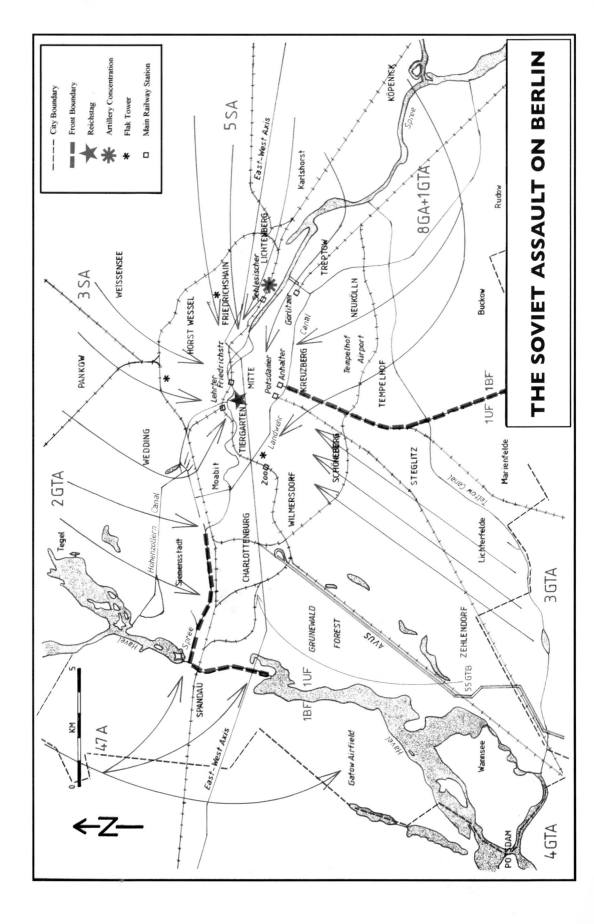

THE SOVIET ASSAULT ON BERLIN

CHAPTER TEN

THE BERLIN BATTLE SYNOPSIS

In early March 1945 a plan had been worked out for the defence of the city and much effort had gone into preparing trenches, barricades, anti-tank obstacles and the like, but, apart from the city's own *Volkssturm* units, many of which were sacrificed ineffectively in belated attempts to stall the Soviet breakthrough from the east, there were very few troops available to man these defences. Thus the unexpected arrival of General Weidling's LVIth Panzer Corps trying to swing south to rejoin the bulk of the 9th Army proved a godsend to the High Command, and Weidling was appointed Defence Commandant.

General Helmuth Weidling, GOC LVI Panzer Corps, Defence Commandant Berlin.

Volkssturm men digging an anti-tank ditch on the outskirts of Berlin.

German Formations Engaged in the Defence of Berlin

LVI PzCorps/Berlin Defence Area (Gen. Helmuth Weidling)
9th Para Div (Col. Harry Herrmann)
18th PzGr Div (Maj-Gen. Josef Rauch)
20th PzGr Div (Maj-Gen. Georg Scholze)
Müncheberg Pz Div (Maj-Gen. Walter Mummert)
11th SS, *Nordland* PzGr Div (SS Maj-Gen. Jürgen Ziegler/SS Maj-Gen. Dr Gustav Krukenberg)
23rd SS, *Nederland* PzGr Div (SS Maj-Gen. Wagner)
Berlin Garrison

A *Hitler Youth* undergoing training with a *Panzerfaust.*

The original Soviet plan for the taking of the city had Zhukov's two tank armies advancing quickly on Berlin in a classic pincer movement, closing in on the Reichstag from the north-east and south-east, followed by three of the combined-arms armies slicing through from east to west, while the fourth swung round north of the city to shield the operation from intervention on the western flank.

Soviet Formations Engaged in the Reduction of Berlin

1st Byelorussian Front (Marshal G.K. Zhukov)
1st Gds Tk Army (Col-Gen. M.Y. Katukov)
2nd Gds Tk Army (Col-Gen. I. I. Feduninsky)
47th Army (Lt-Gen. F.I. Perkhorovitch)
3rd Shock Army (Col-Gen. V.I. Kutznetsov)
5th Shock Army (Gen/Col-Gen. N.E. Berzarin)
8th Gds Army (Col-Gen. V.I. Chuikov)
3rd Army (Col-Gen. A.V. Gorbatov)
1st Polish Inf Div *Tadiuscz Kosciuszko* (Gen. Stanislaw Poplawski)
16th Air Army (Col-Gen. S.I. Rudenko)
18th Air Army (AVM A.Y. Golovanov)
Dnieper Flotilla (Rear Adm. V.V. Grigoryev)
1st Ukrainian Front (Marshal I.S. Koniev)
3rd Gds Tk Army (Col-Gen. P.S. Rybalko)
10th Gds Tk Corps (4th Gds Tk Army) (Lt-Gen. Y.Y. Belov)
128th Rifle Corps (28th Army) (Maj-Gen. P.F. Batirsky)
350th Rifle Div (13th Army)
10th Aslt Arty Corps (5th Gds Army)
25th Aslt Arty Div
23rd AA Arty Div
2nd Air Fighter Corps (2nd Air Army)

The rival Soviet Marshals Zhukov and Koniev.

However, the four-day battle at Seelow had exacted such a high price in men and armour that Zhukov had to make a hasty revision, in which the 1st Guards Tank Army was amalgamated with the 8th Guards Army under Colonel-General Chuikov's command to advance directly on Berlin and then swing across the Spree and Dahme Rivers to tackle the southern half of the city, while the 2nd Guards Tank Army was temporarily split, one corps going to reinforce the 47th Army, which would outflank the city from the north and cover the western flank, clearing the west bank of the Havel River. The other two armoured corps would bring the leading elements of the 3rd and 5th Shock Armies to their start lines on the edge of the city and then swing north to regroup and assume a sector of their own coming down from the north.

Soviet armour and artillery converging on Berlin.

Although Stalin had promised Zhukov the taking of Berlin, throughout the battle for the Seelow Heights he had been taunting him with his rival Marshal Koniev's success to the south, and now Stalin decided to remind them both that he was the master by using the lack of communication between them to play them off against each other in the taking of the city.

Berlin street scene.

The first troops across the city boundary were Zhukov's at Weissensee and Hohenschönhausen in the north-east on 22 April, but when Chuikov's leading elements reached Schönefeld airfield south of the city on the morning of the 24th they found some of Koniev's troops waiting for them; furthermore, Koniev's main forces were already launching a massive attack across the Teltow Canal west of an inter-front boundary that divided the southern half of the city in two and gave him the opportunity of competing for the Reichstag. Koniev was personally directing his 3rd Guards Tank Army, which he had heavily reinforced with infantry and artillery, and was concentrating his effort in a direct thrust on the Reichstag.

While the remainder of Zhukov's forces continued to deploy and converge on the city centre as planned, Chuikov's group concentrated on the Neukölln–Tempelhof sector, took the airport and closed up to the Landwehr Canal, but also thrust due west, south of the canal, straight across the inter-front boundary towards the German defensive position based on the Zoo Flak-tower. Consequently when Koniev launched an attack from just north of Schöneberg town hall on the morning of the 28th with the aim of getting into the Tiergarten by that evening, he soon found that he was attacking an area already occupied by his rival's troops. Soundly humiliated, Koniev returned to his command, leaving the 3rd Guards Tank Army to clear a much reduced area within a boundary redrawn by Stalin that left the field open to an already chastened Zhukov. The much-prized Reichstag was subsequently taken by the 79th Corps of the 3rd Shock Army coming in from the north through Moabit.

The converging Soviet forces gradually reduced the area occupied by the defence to a narrow sausage-shaped area extending from the banks of the Havel opposite Spandau in the west to Friedrichstrasse in the city centre.

Fighting conditions in a heavy smog of smoke and dust.

An SU-76 self-propelled gun providing close support in the streets.

Special tactics had to be developed for this street-fighting role in an already devastated city, in which it was difficult to find one's way, radios and compasses failed to function properly, and the exercise of command and control posed serious problems. These tactics involved forming combat teams of a mix of all arms working in close harmony. Errors were made and some new tricks learnt. Casualties were so high among the 2nd Guards Tank Army's infantry that the 1st Polish Infantry Division was called in to support them for the last couple of days.

Soviet Street-Fighting Organisation

The combat teams generally consisted of a platoon of infantry, one or two tanks, some sappers, some man-pack flame-throwers, a section of anti-tank guns, and two or three field guns, usually 76mm, but sometimes even 150mm guns or 203mm howitzers were used in this role when particularly strong positions had to be attacked.

For the mass artillery the main problem was finding sufficient open space in which to operate, and in some places the guns were packed so closely together it seemed that their wheels must be touching. The *Katyusha* rocket-launcher units found a solution to their problem by dismantling the frames from the truckbeds and reassembling them on convenient rooftops. All these artillery concentrations were protected by a profusion of anti-aircraft guns.

A pattern emerged by which all the artillery combined in a massive hour-long bombardment of the day's targets first thing every morning. This was first experienced at 0515 hours on 24 April and gradually increased in intensity as more guns were brought into play on subsequent days. At night the shelling did not actually stop but diminished considerably.

Howitzers in action on the city streets.

Soviet Street-Fighting Techniques

The street-fighting techniques used by the 1st Byelorussian Front were based on the principle that each street should be tackled by a complete regiment, with one battalion working down either side of the street and the third battalion in reserve and bringing up the rear. The frontage of a regiment was thus as little as 200 to 250 yards, while that of higher formations varied according to the terrain. Individual units were each day assigned immediate tasks, subsequent tasks and an axis for further advance, the depth of penetration expected of them varying according to the circumstances. Usually the troops did not advance down the streets themselves but mouseholed their way through the buildings at different levels, while the supporting artillery pushed its way through the back yards and alleys with engineer assistance. The light infantry guns and dismantled rocket-launchers were manhandled up into buildings and used with great flexibility. In attacking a heavily defended building the assault group would usually split into two, one part concentrating on quickly bottling up the enemy in the cellars, where they would normally have taken shelter during the preliminary bombardment, and the other clearing the upper storeys.

In this direct support role the guns advanced with their teams, firing over open sights at ranges of up to 400 yards down the axis of the streets. They would set themselves up under cover of smokescreens, or would fire at the blank walls of buildings to raise clouds of dust for the same purpose. At these ranges the gunners inevitably took casualties from infantry fire, and it was a particularly trying time for their observers with the leading infantry, who frequently needed relief from the strain and fatigue of their role.

A JS-2 heavy tank and Panje wagen at the rear of the Reichstag.

A *Sherman* of the 2nd Guards Tank Army, which was extensively equipped with Lend-Lease materiel, flies the regimental banner.

German and Soviet dead in the rubble.

It was only after Hitler had committed suicide, followed by Goebbels after his ineffective attempts to secure a truce, that General Weidling was at last able to order a surrender of the garrison on the morning of 2 May. However, this was done in such a way that those who wished to do so could attempt to break out before daylight. One group fought its way out northwards up Schönhauser Allee, heading for Oranienburg, and some survivors got through to the west, but nearly all those that tried to follow them later and those members of the much larger force that fought its way out to the west through Spandau were either killed or caught in the next two days. The break-out attempt from the *Führerbunker* and the city centre also ended in either death or capture.[1]

CHAPTER ELEVEN

BERLIN TOUR A: CENTRAL BERLIN

Stadtmitte – SS Panzergrenadier Division *Nordland*'s Last Stand – Checkpoint Charlie – Landwehr Canal – Anhalter Station – SA, SS and Gestapo HQ – Air Ministry – *Führerbunker* – Potsdamer Platz – Potsdamer Bridge – Bendlerblock – Zoo

AREA: This mainly walking tour covers the central part of the city.

DIRECTIONS: From the Zoo S-Bahn station take any of the following trains:
    S-3 Erkner
    S-5 Strausberg
    S-7 Ahrensfelder
    S-9 Flughafen Berlin-Schönefeld
    S-75 Wartenberg
four stops to **Friedrichstrasse.**
    Alternatively, from Alexanderplatz take any of the following S-Bahn trains:
    S-3 Westkreuz
    S-5 Spandau
    S-7 Potsdam Hbf
    S-9 Westkreuz
    S-75 Spandau
    two stops to **Friedrichstrasse.**
    Then descend to the U-Bahn and take the **U-6 Alt Mariendorf** two stops to **Stadtmitte.**

THE SITE: An empty carriage with smashed windows, no electricity and no telephone was the command post allocated to SS-Major General Dr Gustav Krukenberg, commanding the 11th SS Panzergrenadier Division *Nordland*, after the division withdrew from fighting in the Neukölln district to regroup on 26 April 1945 and was then assigned to the Central Defence Sector *Zitadelle*. The sector commander was Lieutenant Colonel Seifert, whose command post was in the cellars of the Air Ministry on Wilhelmstrasse, but as the sector contained the Reichs Chancellery and Führerbunker, Seifert was answerable to SS-Major General Wilhelm Mohnke, commander of Hitler's guard detachment, as well as to the Berlin Defence Commander, General Helmuth Weidling.

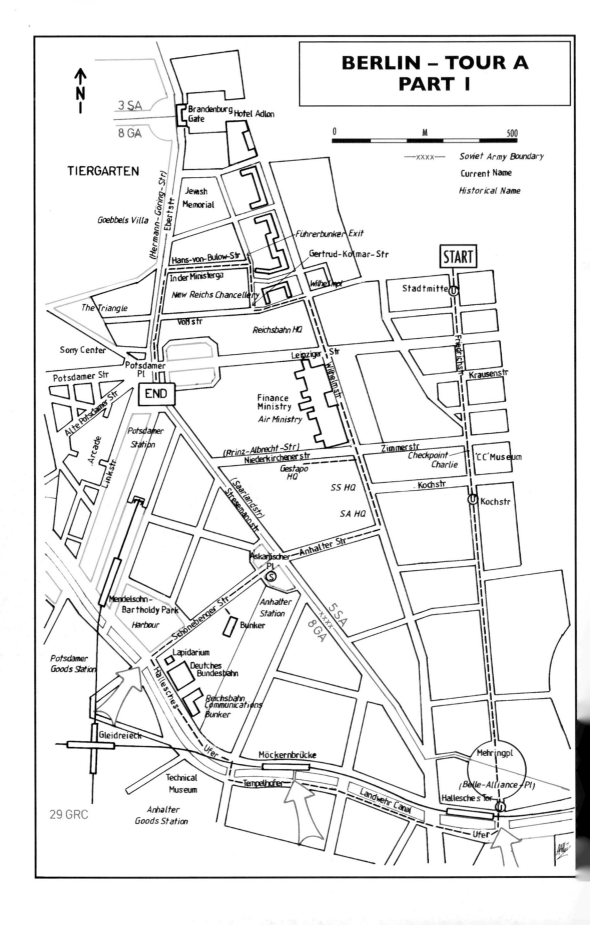

SS-Major General Dr Gustav Krukenberg.

Krukenberg went to see Seifert, who showed him a map marked with defensive positions and claimed that all was in hand. He wanted no assistance or advice, he refused to meet the regimental commanders, and was pointedly rude and arrogant. Krukenberg therefore sent his regimental commanders to reconnoitre the deployment area without consulting Seifert, and when they returned saying that there was no evidence of any of the installations Krukenberg had been shown on Seifert's map, Krukenberg went to the Reichs Chancellery to protest to Mohnke. Weidling appeared and agreed that Defence Sector *Zitadelle* should be allocated to Mohnke and split into two sub-sectors along the line of Wilhelmstrasse with Seifert responsible for the west side and Krukenberg the east. However, those *Nordland* troops that were already west of the line, almost a third of the division, would have to remain there until they could be relieved by other forces.

Krukenberg had no further communication from Weidling and his staff, nor could he obtain any reliable information about what was happening on his flanks. He therefore established his main line of defence along Leipziger Strasse with the Regiments *Danmark* and *Norge* facing south toward the Landwehr Canal, from where the main Soviet attack was expected. He then had his divisional artillery deploy in the streets debouching into the Unter den Linden to cover his rear and deployed volunteer reinforcements to cover his flanks. He then had the

Looking south down Friedrichstrasse, 1945.

Checkpoint Charlie site from the north. The US observation post was in the balcony window on the right above the Café Adler. A replica represents the original checkpoint building, the original and later versions now being located in the Allierten Museum in Dahlem.

regiments divide their units into three parts, placing one third in the rubble of the forward area up to the canal, and another third further back in prepared nests of anti-tank and machine guns. The last third was held in reserve at command post level as shock troops, ready to go forward quickly along passages knocked through the intervening buildings to repel any enemy penetrating the lines. The divisional dressing station was established in the air raid shelter of the Hotel Adlon on Pariser Platz.

Krukenberg also had with him some 300 men of the disbanded 33rd SS Volunteer Panzergrenadier Division *Charlemagne* who had volunteered to accompany him to Berlin, arriving as the last reinforcements to get through on 24 April. Specialists in combating tanks, they proved highly successful in this role, and on 29 April Krukenberg decorated Sergeant Eugéne Vaulat with the Knight's Cross for having destroyed two Soviet tanks in Neukölln and a further six in the city centre.[1]

Go up to street level on **Friedrichstrasse** and cross over Leipziger Strasse, from where the near corner of the Air Ministry building is visible on the right two blocks away beyond the prominent Post Office building with its globe on the parapet. Ahead you can see the portrait of an American soldier suspended over the centre of the street marking the **Checkpoint Charlie** site. The next cross-street, Krausenstrasse, marks the near end of the vast East German checkpoint that existed this side of Checkpoint Charlie until Unification. In contrast, the Allied checkpoint was maintained demonstrably as a temporary structure.

These crossroads provided the most dramatic scene of the Cold War when the East German government attempted to assert its authority and obtain the formal recognition of the Western Allies by demanding the showing of identity documents when passing through, contrary to prior practice. It so happened that General Lucius D. Clay, formerly commander-in-chief of the American zone of Germany, although retired from active service, had just been sent to Berlin by President John F. Kennedy, officially as adviser to the American Commandant but in fact as a boost to the morale of the Berliners, who trusted him.

On 27 October 1961 General Clay sent a State Department official into East Berlin escorted by soldiers with fixed bayonets and a military police jeep with a machine gun. The East German officials stepped back to let them through and the vehicle returned safely a few minutes later.

However, some ten minutes later Soviet tanks appeared on Friedrichstrasse and lined up in close echelon with their guns pointing down the street. A platoon of American tanks that had been held in close reserve then lined up facing the Soviets in similar formation, with guns levelled. It was some considerable

Confrontation at Checkpoint Charlie.

The bulls-eye of Belle-Allianz-Platz from the air with Friedrichstrasse running up the centre of the picture. Göring's Air Ministry can be seen top left.

time later before the leading Soviet tank raised its gun barrel and the Americans followed suit, leading to a gradual withdrawal by both sides. The Soviets had showed their backing of the East German government but were not prepared to go to war over it.[2]

The **Checkpoint Charlie Museum**, once impressive in displaying escapee attempts and equipment, has sadly become overblown with exhibits not so à propos. Part of the original checkpoint cabin and the final version can be found at the *Allierten Museum* in Dahlem (part of Berlin Tour D).

Continue along Friedrichstrasse to **Kochstrasse U-Bahn station**, where you take the **U-6 Alt Mariendorf** one stop to **Hallesches Tor**. Here the U-Bahn station is elevated above the street with the Landwehr Canal on the south side and the circular Mehringplatz on the north side. The latter was previously known as Belle-Allianz-Platz and formed a bull's-eye at the southern end of Friedrichstrasse, which was easily identifiable from the air and gave Allied bombers a useful aiming point. It also marks the southern end of Wilhelmstrasse, leading to the Reichs Chancellery and the *Führerbunker*.

After overrunning Tempelhof airfield from the south, Colonel-General Chuikov's combined 8th Guards and 1st Guards Tank Armies closed up to the Landwehr Canal on 27 April 1945 on a 3-kilometre front with their right flank here at the Hallesches Tor. To the north of them, and coming in from the east to converge on the Reichstag and Reichs Chancellery, was Colonel-General Berzarin's 5th Shock Army, so that the inter-army boundary here appears to have been the line of Saarlandstrasse (now Stresemannstrasse) running north-westwards from Belle-Allianz-Platz.

Chuikov decided to use the next day to rest his troops and prepare for the crossing of the Landwehr Canal, while leaving his artillery and mortars to keep the Germans occupied and sending forward reconnaissance parties to probe the German defences. Two Soviet tanks were knocked out at the Hallesches Tor that day, and another Soviet group that included two Czech-made tanks bearing German insignia penetrated the near end of Wilhelmstrasse before they too were knocked out.

With all the bridges blown in the immediate area, crossing the canal posed a considerable problem, and Chuikov took all of the 28th to make his preparations for the assault on the 29th. This did not just amount to deploying his troops and lining up his artillery and rocket-launchers in support, but also involved dealing with the problems of communication and control in the chaotic rubble of a city already devastated by bombing and artillery fire, and where radios and compasses failed to work. To ensure his orders were obeyed, Chuikov distributed Communist Party representatives evenly among his sub-units.[3]

Turn right and follow the **Tempelhofer Ufer** until you reach the elevated

The restored footbridge across the Landwehr Canal to the Möckern Bridge station.

Möckernbrücke U-Bahn station opposite. (The U-7 part of the station on the south bank is of post-war construction.)

This was the stretch of canal that Chuikov's troops had to cross on the morning of 29 April, making their way either singly or in groups, some swimming or using improvised rafts or other devices to keep them afloat, others trying to cross by the station footbridge under cover of a smokescreen. Others used sewers to provide concealed approach and exit routes, emerging behind the German lines. Note the footbridge leading across to the elevated station from a parallel underground line south of the canal.

Go past Möckernbrücke U-Bahn station and cross the canal by the Möckern Bridge to continue along the north bank on the **Hallesches Ufer,** where the rail tracks for the Anhalter station used to cross overhead. Opposite us, where the elevated U-Bahn tacks across the canal, is the Deutsches Technik Museum, which is well worth a visit on its own account. There is an especially interesting exhibition on the assassination of SS Obergruppenführer Reinhard Heydrich, who had presided over the Wannsee Conference (see Berlin Tour E), by Czech patriots in Prague in June 1942.

Deutsches Technik Museum

Closed Mondays, open Tuesday–Friday 0900–1730, weekends and holidays 1000–1800. Adults €4.50, Groups €3

The shattered U-Bahn tunnel under repair below the Landwehr Canal with the Reichsbahn bunker behind.

You now come to a large bunker, which was the Reichsbahn (State Railways) communications centre. Next to it is the Bundesbahn (Federal Railways) headquarters building. Somewhere below you is the safety bulkhead to prevent flooding of the S-Bahn tunnels passing under the canal at this point. This is where Waffen-SS engineers attempted to flood the underground system by blowing the roof of the tunnel under the canal, about which we will learn more shortly. This section of the canal had to be sealed off and drained after the war to enable repairs to the S-Bahn tunnel roof.

The next building along is the Lapidarium, an early pumping station, which now provides storage for statues recovered after the war that have not been restored to their original sites.

Now turn right up **Schöneberger Strasse**. The little park on the left was a canal harbour basin at the time of the battle and was filled in with rubble after the war.

The Reichsbahn communications bunker today.

On the right is a gateway with a sign to the *Gruselkabinett & Luftschutzraum* (Chamber of Horrors and Air Raid Shelter). As you enter the courtyard you can see the three-storey bunker that was built by the Reichsbahn as a shelter for travellers from the adjacent Anhalter railway and S-Bahn stations, to which it was connected by a tunnel. Painted on the front of the bunker is the slogan *Wer Bunker baut wirft Bomben* ('He who builds bunkers drops bombs'). The building has escaped

The post-war ruins of the Anhalter station with bunker in the foreground.

demolition because of the danger this would pose to the S-Bahn tunnel under the Landwehr Canal. The exhibition in the bunker is what one might expect, but a visit to the lower floor gives an idea of how these shelters were laid out and there is an exhibition of pictures and newspapers relating to the bombing of the city.

Gruselkabinett and Luftschutzraum

Open Tuesday–Sunday 1000–1900 hours.

Entrance Adults €7, Children €5

The bunker was cleared of the civilians sheltering there by Waffen-SS troops when the fighting closed in, but the passive nature of the building made it totally unsuitable for defensive purposes.

You now come to **Askanischer Platz** with part of the ruined façade of the Anhalter railway station on your right, the façade having been retained as a memorial to the bombing.

Second Lieutenant Kroemer of the Panzer Division *Müncheberg* recorded the events of 27 April in the S-Bahn station below:

The Anhalter railway station air raid shelter.

> The new command post is in the S-Bahn tunnels under Anhalter railway station. The station looks like an armed camp. Women and children huddle in niches, some sitting on folding chairs, listening to the sounds of battle. Shells hit the roof, cement crumbles from the ceiling. S-Bahn hospital trains trundle slowly by.
>
> Suddenly a surprise. Water splashes into our command post. Shrieks, cries and curses. People are struggling around the ladders reaching up the ventilation shafts to the street above. Gurgling water floods through the tunnels. The crowds are panicky, pushing through the rising water, leaving children and wounded behind. People are being trampled underfoot, the water covering them. It rises a metre or more then slowly runs away. The panic lasts for hours. Many drowned. Reason: on somebody's orders engineers have blown up the safety bulkhead control chamber on the Landwehr Canal between the Schöneberger and Möckern Bridges to flood the tunnels against the Russians. The whole time heavy fighting continues above ground.[4]

A post-war examination of the event reported few dead found, although the flooding reached beyond the Spree River to the north. Nevertheless a post-war Soviet film depicted soldiers and civilians struggling waist-deep in water.

Cross Stresemannstrasse (formerly Saarlandstrasse) and go up **Anhalter Strasse** to the junction with Wilhelmstrasse. The undeveloped area on your left contains the site of the Prinz Albrecht Palace, which faced the entrance to Kochstrasse and housed the *Reichssicherheitshauptamt* (RSHA) under Reinhard Heydrich from 1936 until his appointment as Deputy Reich Protector of Bohemia and Moravia in 1941. This palace combined the headquarters of the Gestapo, Criminal Police and Security Service (SD) under his command. A display board outside gives the history of the building.

The building that stood on the corner next to the palace, as you turn left into **Wilhelmstrasse**, housed the Berlin-Brandenburg headquarters of the *Sturmabteilung* (SA), the rivals of the SS. Nothing remains of these two buildings, which were severely damaged in the last days of the war in desperate close-quarter fighting. But the next corner with Niederkirchnerstrasse (formerly Prinz-Albrecht-Strasse) accommodates the remains of the Berlin Gestapo headquarters, consisting only of part of some of the cells that were constructed in the building's cellars. These have been turned into a photographic exhibition named *Topographie des Terrors*. Turn in here and walk along the top path to the far end before descending to the exhibition.

Askanischer Platz following the devastating air raid of 3 February 1945 that left 100,000 Berliners homeless.

The ruined Gestapo headquarters before demolition.

Topographie des Terrors

Open daily, 1000–2000 hours in summer, or until nightfall in winter.
Entrance is free, and publications in English can be obtained from the site office.

Returning to the Wilhelmstrasse end of the exhibition, turn left and stop on the street corner. Threadbare remains of the infamous Wall line the back of the exhibition opposite Göring's *Luftministerium* (Air Ministry). The state of the Wall in this area was the result of its being chipped away by people who became known as *Mauerspechte* ('Wallpeckers').

Göring's Air Ministry building, built in 1936, stands on the site of the former Prussian War Ministry, which he took over in May 1933, and now houses the Federal Ministry of Finance, having previously accommodated a consortium of East German ministries.

Continue past the Air Ministry building to the paved area at the far end next to the junction with Leipziger Strasse. Any remaining empty sites to your right were probably formerly Jewish-owned, whose ownership the post-war Supreme

Hermann Göring taking the salute at a parade outside his Air Ministry.

The *Topographie des Terrors* exhibition.

Restitution Court, instituted by the Allies, presumably failed to establish during the Cold War period.

Looking back at the building, you can see the East German murals depicting happy workers under the Communist regime, as well as a photographic display showing the brutal suppression of the uprising. A display board in the corner of this little square gives a potted history of the building.

On 16 June 1953 the East German government announced a 10 per cent increase in the work norm for the workers engaged on the construction of Stalinallee (now Karl-Marx-Allee/Frankfurter Allee). The next morning some 100,000 workers protested outside this building. The East German government called on the Soviets for support and a tank unit duly arrived, but the troops, having been indoctrinated as defenders of the workers, could not understand when they were asked to open fire on them. Nevertheless, some 200–400 demonstrators were killed outright. Another 21 were later executed, along with 18 Soviet soldiers who had failed to obey the order to open fire; their unit was then isolated until it could be disbanded. The West Berliners erected a monument to these executed soldiers on the centre strip of the Potsdamer Chaussee where it crosses the autobahn leading into the Avus at the Kreuz Zehlendorf, close to the later location of Checkpoint Bravo.

Returning to the 1945 battle, it was from the Air Ministry cellars here that Lieutenant Colonel Seifert, the sub-sector commander, established contact with the Soviets to enable General Hans Krebs, Chief of Staff of the

Demonstrators stoning Soviet tanks on 17 June 1953.

Oberkommando des Heeres (Army GHQ), to conduct ceasefire negotiations on behalf of Josef Goebbels following the death of Hitler. A local ceasefire was arranged to enable Krebs to cross into the Soviet lines on the night of 30 April, accompanied by Colonel Theodor von Dufving, Weidling's chief of staff, and an interpreter. When von Dufving returned first with a message from Krebs for Goebbels, he found that Seifert had meanwhile been replaced by SS-Major General Krukenberg. The Waffen-SS soldiers who met him knew nothing about his mission and he had difficulty in explaining himself, to the extent that SS-Major General Mohnke had to come from the Reichs Chancellery to rescue him. Krebs's mission had been a failure, for the Soviets insisted upon unconditional surrender. He later committed suicide.

It was also here in the cellars that the last French *Charlemagne* volunteers, who had fought on the west side of Wilhelmstrasse as a tank-destroying unit, were captured, being so exhausted after the fighting that they failed to post sentries.

Now cross **Leipziger Strasse** and continue northwards along **Wilhelmstrasse**. The first block on the left used to contain the *Reichs Verkehrsministerium* (Reichs Traffic Ministry) and the head offices of the Reichsbahn. You next come to the

Wilhelmplatz in the mid-1930s before the construction of the New Reichs Chancellery, with Hitler's balcony overlooking the square.

The Borsig Palace on the corner of Voss-Strasse and Wilhelmplatz, showing the double entrance to the Ehrenhof of the New Reichs Chancellery and Hitler's balcony on the Old Reichs Chancellery next to it.

junction with **Voss-Strasse** on the left and Mohrenstrasse on the right. The former Wilhelmplatz was bisected by Mohrenstrasse, but the East German government transformed this area in the 1970s with the new prefabricated buildings that you can see around, and Wilhelmplatz ceased to exist.

A statue of the Fürst Leopold von Anhalt-Dessau has recently been erected on the street corner opposite Voss-Strasse, replacing one that stood here along with others of Frederick the Great's field marshals before the end of the Second World War. A little further down is Mohrenstrasse U-Bahn station that used to be incorporated in the Hotel Kaiserhof, after which it was named at the time.

Since Unification, display boards have been erected along Wilhelmstrasse giving the historical background of the government buildings that used to stand here.

A model of the New Reichs Chancellery showing how the Borsig Palace and Old Chancellery were incorporated into the structure.

The ruins of Hotel Kaiserhof showing the exposed U-Bahn tunnel used in the breakout from the Reichs Chancellery on the night of 1/2 May 1945.

Albert Speer proudly showing Hitler around the New Reichs Chancellery.

The ruined New Reichs Chancellery with the 'Garden of the Dead' behind.

Looking across the Mosaiksaal and Runder Saal to the Marmor Gallery inside the ruined New Reichs Chancellery.

Walk down Voss-Strasse as far as the kink in the road, which marks the end of the Borsig Palace site and the beginning of the New Reichs Chancellery site, which extended as far as Hermann-Göring-Strasse (today's Ebertstrasse). Albert Speer constructed the New Chancellery in the remarkable time of just less than one year for Hitler's diplomatic New Year reception on 10 January 1939.

Continue along Voss-Strasse and turn right into Gertrud-Kolmar-Strasse, until you come to the first street off on the left. As shown on the accompanying drawing, the approximate site of the *Führerbunker* exit into the Reichs Chancellery garden is about 20 yards beyond this junction, although tourists are often shown the children's playground in the corner to the right as the actual site. The upper *Vorbunker* was completely destroyed in 1988, as was the roof of the *Führerbunker*, leaving just the floor and walls covered in concrete debris well below ground level.

The exit to the *Führerbunker*, outside which Adolf and Eva Hitler's bodies were burnt after committing suicide, and where Josef and Magda Goebbels later committed suicide.

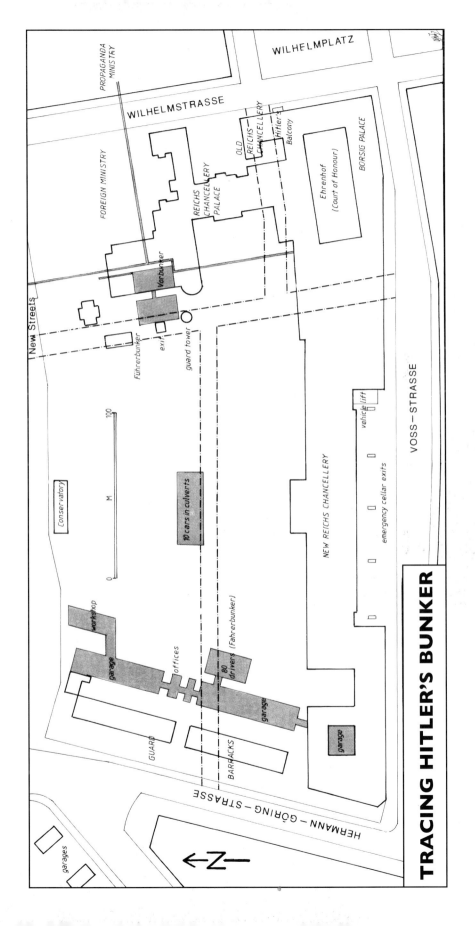

TRACING HITLER'S BUNKER

It was here in Hitler's command post that the last dramatic incidents of the Second World War in Europe took place in an oppressive atmosphere of noisy air conditioning and sweating concrete walls, with no distinction between night and day. The only communications facilities consisted of a one-man switchboard, a radio transmitter and a radio-telephone, the latter dependent upon an aerial suspended from a small balloon. Here Adolf Hitler married his mistress, Eva Braun, then both committed suicide and had their bodies burnt in this garden.

Goebbels then took over and made a vain attempt to negotiate with the Soviets. He and his wife then committed suicide in turn after murdering their six children. So many corpses were found here when the Soviets eventually captured the site that they called it the 'Garden of the Dead'.

Looking ahead you can see the rear of the Hotel Adlon across an area that used to be a series of gardens to the government ministerial buildings fronting Wilhelmstrasse, and the approximate route Hitler used to make his way discreetly to Speer's offices next to the Hotel Adlon. The area now incorporates the Jewish Memorial opened in 2005 and contains below ground an excellent information centre on the Nazis' extermination policy between 1933 and 1945.

Memorial to the Murdered Jews of Europe

Open daily 1000–2000 hours.

Admission free.

You now turn into **Hans-von-Bulow-Strasse** between the representative houses of the German *Länder* (counties) erected after Unification, coming to Ebertstrasse with the **Tiergarten** on your right and the corner of the newly developed *Triangle*

The site of Goebbels' villa uncovered in the excavations for the Jewish Memorial.

The Wall exhibition on Potsdamer Platz.

on your left. Opposite, on the corner of the Tiergarten, there used to be two bomb-proof garages, from where the petrol was taken for the burning of the bodies of Hitler and his wife.

The Wall ran down the east side of the street, with the area behind swept bare as far as the buildings lining Wilhelmstrasse. The *Triangle* opposite belonged to Mitte district and, being outside the Wall, became a sort of no-man's-land that miscreants made full use of until the West Berlin government purchased it from the East German government for an exaggerated sum shortly before Unification.

Turn left down **Ebertstrasse** (formerly Hermann-Göring-Strasse), passing the sites of the two Leibstandarte-SS *Adolf Hitler* barrack blocks on your left before coming to the junction with Voss-Strasse. It was here that the *Fahrerbunker* (Drivers' bunker), part of the underground garage system beneath the Chancellery garden, was discovered in 1990 and later destroyed.

We now come to **Potsdamer Platz,** which provides all the facilities for a welcome break. The architecture is of some interest here, particularly the 'cocked hat' of the Sony Center, whose frame spans the glassed-in old Hotel Esplanade with its *Kaisersaal*, one of only two buildings in this area to survive the war intact. On the pavement at the near end of the Sony Center block there is an exhibition about the Wall, and if you look down you will see the line of the Wall traced in bricks, as it is elsewhere, such as in front of the Brandenburg Gate. There are restaurants on both sides of Potsdamer Strasse, and even more eating places and bars in the shopping arcade on Alte Potsdamer Strasse half right.

An aerial view of the area across from Potsdamer Platz during the latter part of the Cold War with the octagonal outline of Leipziger Platz, Leipziger Strasse running through it and Voss-Strasse parallel above.

Potsdamer Platz and the Potsdamer station in 1945.

The site of Potsdamer railway station is now occupied by the open, grassy area leading to the Landwehr Canal. Beneath this is the S-Bahn station, where SS-Sergeant Major Willi Rogmann set up his command post for the battle of the Reichstag and accommodated his bandsman of the Leibstandarte-SS *Adolf Hitler* with their rockets and mortars, using the destroyed steps of one of the exits as a launching pad.[5]

Resuming your tour, from Potsdamer Platz follow the right-hand side of the railway station site along **Linkstrasse** as far as the **Landwehr Canal** and turn right along the **Reichpietschufer**. The next bridge you come to is where the new underpass leading north under the Spree River to beyond the new Hauptbahnhof (Main) railway station begins.

You next come to the **Potsdamer Bridge**, which is a post-war reconstruction, having formerly consisted of two separate structures with a gap in between. Traces of the old bridge can still be seen on the edge of the embankments.

This is where the alleged incident occurred involving Guards Sergeant Nikolai Masalov of the 220th Guards Rifle Regiment. With the intention of improving morale, the carrying of unit standards into battle had been introduced by the Soviets for the Berlin Operation and Masalov was the official standard bearer of his regiment. The story goes that in the intense quiet that preceded their attack across the canal, he and his two assistants heard the sound of a young child crying for its mother on the far side of the bridge, which was still intact but clearly mined for demolition. Having obtained permission from his commanding officer, Masalov then crawled across the bridge under covering fire from his comrades and found a 3-year-old girl lying in the rubble next to her dead mother. As soon as the artillery barrage opened up, he dashed back across the bridge with the child in his arms. He is now immortalised by a statue at the focal point of the Soviet cemetery in Treptow Park, where he symbolically smashes a swastika with a sword while holding a female child in his arms.[6]

By this stage of the battle the Soviets had developed some ingenious methods of protecting their tanks from the prolific German anti-tank weapons. Their tanks were festooned with sandbags, bedsprings, sheet metal and other devices to cause the projectiles to explode harmlessly outside the hull, and it was one of these devices that was used to trick the Germans. First the Soviet sappers had to clear the demolition charges while working under heavy machine-gun fire. Initial attempts to cross were checked by a dug-in *Tiger*, but then someone came up with the idea of pouring oil over a tank and adding smoke canisters so that it appeared to be on fire and out of control as it drove across. This worked and the bridge was secured.[7]

The area to your right is now known as the Kulturforum and includes Scharoon's yellow-clad Philharmonie and Staatsbibliothek (State Library).

Continue along the embankment towards the unusual GASAG building (originally the Shell Building) with its vertically rippled frontage, opposite the Bendler Bridge. The next block along today contains the Berlin Office of the Federal Ministry of Defence, but was the *Oberkommando der Wehrmacht* in the Second World War, when it was better known as the **Bendlerblock**. It was in the wing at the rear of the car park and adjoining the street off to the right, Bendlerstrasse (now Stauffenbergstrasse), that the 20 July 1944 plot against Hitler was planned, and the *Gedenkstätte Deutscher Widerstand* (Memorial Museum to the German Resistance) is now located here.

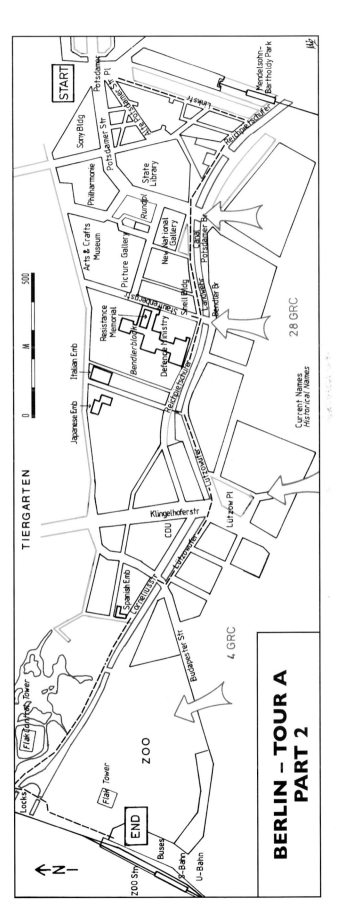

BERLIN – TOUR A
PART 2

Gedenkstätte Deutscher Widerstand

Open Monday–Friday 0900–1800 hours, weekends 1000–1800 hours.
Admission free.

In the courtyard in which the summary executions took place was the signals bunker in which General Helmuth Weidling set up his headquarters as Defence Commandant of Berlin on 26 April 1945. From here, after the failure of General Krebs's mission to the Soviets and Goebbels's suicide, Weidling sent his Chief of Staff, Colonel Theodor von Dufving, to negotiate the surrender of the garrison on the night of 1 May 1945. A radio-message was broadcast and acknowledged beforehand announcing the intention.

The courtyard in which the conspirators were executed.

The Bendler Bridge across the canal had been blown, but some pipes and cables that it had carried still remained and these had enabled the Soviets to get some troops across to the north bank. Von Dufving related:

Escorted by an interpreter, an officer and two soldiers to carry the white flag, we went along Bendlerstrasse. As it was dark, we signalled with our torches. I can no longer remember if there was heavy firing going on at this point or not, however, I do remember shouting out in the dark street: 'Hold your fire! We are parliamentarians acting on behalf of the military commander!'

But from some building or other on the German side came calls like: 'A German never surrenders!' or 'You are traitors!'

Without being shot at by the Russian side we approached the former bridge that had extended across the Landwehr Canal from Bendlerstrasse. The Soviets had already established themselves on the near [north] bank of the canal even though the bridge had been destroyed, and built a kind of barricade of cobbles, stones and rubble. As we clambered over it, hand-grenades thrown from the German side burst and flashed all around us!

I saw some dark shapes in front of me ducking down. I jumped over the barricade and found myself standing in a group of Soviet soldiers. A hullabaloo broke out on the Russian side with everyone shouting and crowding in on us. One bleeding, small Red Army soldier wanted to knock me down with the butt of his sub-machine gun, but I was able to defend myself against him and several others until the Russian major in charge intervened on the prompting of our interpreter.

This Russian major re-established order with a lot of shouting, which proved effective. Meanwhile I saw several Red Army soldiers armed with *Panzerfausts* go over the barricade and try to cross the street into the neighbouring buildings, and firing flared up again on both sides.

Gradually our interpreter managed to explain to the major that we had come as fully authorised parliamentarians. The major then asked of me, and I of him, that there should be a complete ceasefire at the crossing point. I therefore had to tell him that his men had to remain behind the barricade and not try to gain ground, as was happening at the moment.

After a few minutes of discussion it was agreed that there would be, firstly, a total ceasefire from both sides at the crossing point. In order to achieve this, I would return to the German side and he would recall his men.

Colonel Theodor von Dufving, Chief of Staff to General Weidling.

I went back and summoned the company and battalion commanders in charge to explain to them what was going on. . . . Then I set off once more. An officer reported to me in the Bendlerstrasse: 'Everything is in order, all Germans have been briefed.'

It really was quiet. I met our interpreter at the barricade again. He informed me that meanwhile a Soviet reception party was now waiting for me with a vehicle on the other side of the canal, having apparently first gone to the Potsdamer Strasse Bridge by mistake.[8]

Shell Haus and the remains of the bridge where von Dufving crossed to negotiate the German surrender to the Soviets.

Continue along the **Reichpietschufer**, passing the main entrance to the Federal Ministry of Defence, the old building still bearing its original naval decorations of swags of rope from when it was the Kaiser's Admiralty.

The residential part of the Tiergarten to your right is now mainly occupied by embassies, as originally intended in the plans for Albert Speer's *Germania*. The Nazis' Axis friends, the Italians, Japanese and Spanish, appear to have been provided with buildings in grandiose fascist style that survived the bombing, although damaged, when they were transferred from the Diplomatic Quarter next to the Reichstag.

Cross the canal by a footbridge and follow the pavement on the south side until you come to **Klingelhöferstrasse**. On your left is the little park of Lützowplatz, which served as an exclave for the mortars of Defence Sector *Zitadelle* during the battle. The building diagonally opposite the crossing houses the headquarters of the Christian Democratic Union and has been aptly dubbed by the Berliners as 'The sinking ship!'

The Flak-tower control tower, HQ 1st *Berlin* Flak Division.

Use the underpass to cross the road and continue along the south bank, the **Lützowufer**, to the junction with Stülerstrasse, where you cross over the bridge and switch to the north bank along **Corneliusstrasse**.

The last building on the right is the Spanish Embassy. Continue along the **Tiergartenufer** footpath. Up ahead a footbridge connects a section of the Berlin Zoo on this side of the canal with the main part to the south. Next to it is another footbridge connecting the embankment paths. Some 300 yards further on to the right was the location of the headquarters of the 1st *Berlin* Flak Division and the control tower for the Zoo Flak-tower.

Walk on to the next bridge across the canal, where you turn left and head for the Zoo station. In the corner of the Zoo grounds on your left was the site of the Zoo Flak-tower.

Harry Schweizer, a 17-year-old Flak Auxiliary with the *Hitler Youth*, wrote of his experiences here:

Flak Auxiliary Harry Schweizer.

The Zoo Bunker was the more comfortable of the three big flak-towers in Berlin. It was well equipped with the best available materials, whereas the interior fittings of the Friedrichshain and Humboldthain Bunkers had been skimped, only the military equipment being first rate. The Zoo Bunker's fighting equipment consisted of four twin 128mm guns on the upper platform, and a gallery about five metres lower down with a 37mm gun at each corner, and a twin barrelled 20mm gun in the centre of each side flanked by solo 20mm guns left and right. The twin 128s were fired optically (by line of sight) whenever the weather was clear enough, otherwise electronically by remote control. The settings came from the smaller flak bunker nearby, which only had light flak on its gallery for its defence, but was especially equipped with electronic devices. A long range *Blaupunkt* radar was installed there and our firing

An aerial view of the Zoo area with the Zoo Flak-tower and its shadow seen to the right of the white cloud and the control tower at 2 o'clock from there. Top left is the Technical University and bottom, the Kaiser Wilhelm Memorial Church.

The Zoo Flak-tower, in course of being dismantled, en from across the Landwehr Canal.

settings came from a giant *Wurzburg* radar as far away as Hannover. That bunker also contained the control room for air situation reports and was responsible for issuing air raid warnings.

Our training went along simultaneously with action with the heavy and light artillery pieces. We also received some basic training on radar and explosives. We suffered no casualties from air attacks, but comrades were killed by gun barrels exploding and recoils. The shells for the 128s relied on the radar readings for their fuse settings and were moved centrally on rubber rollers up to the breech. If there was only the slightest film of oil on the rollers, the already primed shell would not move fast enough into the breech and would explode . . .

The 128s were used mainly for firing at the leading aircraft of a group, as these were believed to be the controllers of the raid and this would cause the others to lose direction. Salvos were also fired, that is several twins firing together, when, according to the radar's calculations, the circle of each explosion covered about 50 metres, giving the aircraft in a wide area little chance of survival.

When we were below on the gallery with the 37s or 20s driving off low-flying aircraft, we would hear the din and have to grimace to compensate for the pressure changes that came with the firing of the 128s. We were not allowed to fasten the chinstraps of our steel helmets so as to prevent injury from the blast.

Later when we fired the 128s at clusters of tanks as far out as Tegel, the barrels were down to zero degrees and the shock waves were enough to break the cement of the 70cm high and 50cm wide parapet of the gallery some five metres below, exposing the steel rods beneath.

The 37s and 20s were seldom used against British and American aircraft as they flew above the range of those guns, and low-flying aircraft seldom came within range. It was different when the Russians sent their low-flying aircraft against the tower. The magazines of the 37s were normally filled with eight rounds of tracer but, as the Russian

Hitler Youth Flak Auxiliaries with their twin-mounted 128mm guns.

machines were armoured, this was changed to red tracer and green armour-piercing shells. These aircraft attacked almost ceaselessly in April to try to weaken the 128s, which were already firing at ground targets. The towers had considerable firepower and many aircraft were shot down. We had no protection like a shield on our guns and, when the wings of the attacking aircraft spurted fire at us and the shells whistled over our heads, it was not a nice feeling. The firepower of the three towers was quite noticeable and we could see that after the first salvo following units would turn away to get out of firing range.

The fighting bunker had been built with an elastic foundation to take the shock of the discharge of the 128s. Two twin 128s firing alone would have been sufficient to break a rigid foundation. The bunker had its own water and power supplies along with an up-to-date and well equipped hospital in which, among others, prominent people like Rudel, the famous *Stuka* pilot, could be cared for. Rudel had a 37mm cannon mounted in his aircraft, but we had later versions of the gun on the tower and he often came up to the platform to see the weapons in action during our time there. Normally only the gun crews were allowed on to the platform, but our superiors made an exception in his case.

During the last days the hospital was completely overcrowded and the wounded were even lying in the passageways, the orderlies and doctors only being able to attend emergency cases. Our beds were removed from our accommodation for them and, as we had little time for sleep anyway, sacks of straw sufficed.[9]

As the Soviet troops closed up to the **Zoological Gardens**, they encountered some of the animals that had escaped from their cages as a result of the

A 37mm
Flak gun.

shelling, giving rise to some ribald comments about having been at the vodka when they reported back, but they found the massive flak-tower impenetrable to their guns and came up against strong resistance from the troops dug in around it.

A 20mm quadruple Flak gun.

Of 1 May 1945 Harry Schweizer wrote:

The Russians were now quiet and packages of explosives were being thrown down on them from the gallery and being replied to with mortar fire. There were now about 25,000 people in the Zoo Bunker, including all kinds of servicemen, and it was a complete mix up. . . .

At about 2300 hours on the evening of the 1st May an announcement came over the loudspeakers to prepare for a break-out from the tower. We quickly put our things together. There was not much, just a haversack, waterbottle, weapon and ammunition, and an emergency ration of chocolate that could only be opened in a true emergency. We three waited together until several thousand had left the tower, not wanting to be among the first to leave, as we did not know what awaited us outside. Several of the older soldiers, some of them highly decorated, remained behind as they said it was all the same to them if they met their fate there or elsewhere.

As we mixed in the stream of people and emerged outside, it seemed to be quite peaceful with only the occasional shot nearby coming out of the dark night, and we were not fired at. We could not understand how we could get out of the bunker so easily. Somehow this stream of all kinds of servicemen, without any leadership, found its way to Spandau via the Olympic Stadium. Apart from a few shots at the Olympic Stadium, we reached a newly built part of Spandau without any interference from the enemy.

On the morning of the 2nd May, combat teams were formed to fight their way over the Charlotten Bridge through the Russians occupying Spandau to the Elbe River in the west. We joined one of these teams, as we were determined to get through to the Americans. Our propaganda had made us afraid of falling into Russian hands.[10]

Our tour ends here at the **Zoo station** complex.

Civilians leaving the Zoo Flak-tower after an air raid. Note some masonry visible between the heads in the centre. The Nazis now accepted the permanence of these structures and proposed embellishing them with cladding as shown.

BERLIN – TOUR B – EAST

Current _Historical_

0   500   1000   1500
M

CHARLOTTENBURG

Spandauer Damm

27 Apr

Hitler's 50th Birthday Parade
20 Apr 39

Technical
University

Ernst-Reuter-Pl
Am Knie

2 Pol IR
1 May

START 1
Bus X34

Flaktower

Zoo Stn

Breakout
1/2 May

Savignypl

Vehicles

Pedestrians

Weimarer Str

Kantstr

Bismarckstr

EAST WEST AXIS

SS GTB
checked
28-30 Apr

Lietzensee

Boundary of 29 Apr

2 GTA

N

Postwar
Autobahn cutting

1UF 1BF

Königin-Elisabeth-Str

Barracks

SS GTB
30 Apr
-2 May

Tramsheds

Haus des Deutschen Rundfunks

International
Congress Centre

Assembly Point

Kaiserdamm

Theodor-Heuss-Pl
Adolf-Hitler-Pl

Reichstr

WESTEND

Steubenpl

26 Apr

HQ British Control
Commission Germany

Funkturm
Exhibition Halls

Counterattack 28 Apr

Alexander
Kaserne
(HQ Defence Sector F)

Haus des deutschen Sports

Rifle
Ranges

Waldbühne

Glockenturm

Olympic Stadium

Olympiapl

Trakehner Allee

Flatowallee

Flak & Fd Arty

Maifeld

Jesse-Owens-Allee

Passenheimer Str

Heerstr

28 Apr

START
Bus 149

2 SPGs

SS GTB

Am Postfenn

GRUNEWALD

CHAPTER TWELVE

BERLIN TOUR B: WESTERN BERLIN

Zoo – Olympic Stadium – Spandau – Gatow Airfield – Heerstrasse – Commonwealth Cemetery – Technical University – Zoo

LIMITATIONS: Spandau Citadel is closed on Mondays.

AREA: This tour of the western parts of the city includes the break-out from the Zoo Bunker, a visit to the 1936 Olympic Stadium, an overview of the Reichssportfeld playing fields and buildings that recently housed the British Sector Headquarters, the German break-out over the Charlotten Bridge in Spandau, Spandau Citadel, the von Seeckt Kaserne (*Brooke* and *Wavell Barracks*), Spandau Allied Prison, Gatow Airfield and the Luftwaffen Museum, the defence of the Frey Bridge by a *Hitler Youth* Regiment, the British Commonwealth War Graves Cemetery on the Heerstrasse, and the Polish attack on the Technical University.

DIRECTIONS: Start at the **Zoo bus terminus**, taking **Bus X-34** for **Alt Kaldow**. This takes you up **Kantstrasse** as far as **Theodor-Heuss-Platz** and was the route taken by the armoured and other vehicles used in the break-out from the Zoo on

The Haus des Rundfunks today.

the night of 1 May 1945, while those on foot used the U-Bahn tunnels to reach the Olympic Stadium area.

Kantstrasse ends on a bridge overlooking the inner autobahn and S-Bahn ring, coming to the vast International Congress Center on the left. The bus crosses over into Masurenallee with the Funkturm (Radio Tower) in the main exhibitions grounds on the left and the Haus des Rundfunks (Broadcasting House) on the right. Although it was in the British sector, the Haus des Rundfunks was occupied by the Soviets until the late 1950s, the director at one time being Marcus Wolf, later head of the East German Secret Service, but then posing as Major Michael Sturm of the Red Army.

Lothar Loewe, then a member of the *Hitler Youth*, described the scene on the morning of 2 May 1945:

> The big assembly point for the break-out from Berlin to the west was on the big square between the Haus des Rundfunks and the Exhibition Halls. It was the morning of the 2nd May. The last tanks, self-propelled guns, fire engines of the Berlin Fire Brigade from the Suarez and Ranke stations, military stragglers, BVG double-decker buses, three-wheeled delivery vans, all in a tangled muddle. Mothers with prams were hoisted on trucks, whose woodgas generators burned smokily. Elegant ladies swung rucksacks over fur coats. Paymasters, army veterinary surgeons, SA and Party leaders, *Gold Pheasants* in brown uniforms, paratroopers and the remainders of still passably organised units, set off. The last German attack in Berlin, that was to cost thousands of lives in the course of the day, had begun.[1]

The lack of Soviet interference at this stage was due to two main factors. First, May Day had been duly celebrated the night before, and secondly, Colonel David Dragunski's 55th Guards Tank Brigade that had been operating in this area (and had penetrated Kantstrasse as far as Savignyplatz before being recalled on the night of 29 April as a result of a change of operational boundaries) had since withdrawn into the tramsheds and barracks on Königin-Elisabeth-Strasse two blocks away to the right.

Alight on the northern side of **Theodor-Heuss-Platz**, then known as Adolf-Hitler-Platz, although Hitler had plans to rename it after his chum Mussolini. Behind you

The Funkturm and Exhibition Halls before which the vehicular breakout element assembled on the night of 1/2 May 1945. The building on the right became the seat of the British Military Government in Germany.

The view down the Kaiserdamm towards the Brandenburg Gate.

is the Kaiserdamm leading back to the Brandenburg Gate; the Kaiserdamm was part of the east–west axis broadened by Albert Speer and still adorned by his twin lampposts. The east–west axis continues as the Heerstrasse on the far side of the square, while Reichsstrasse forks off to the right.

Look across to the far side of the square. The main building opposite housed the headquarters of the British Military Administration (Control Commission Germany) in the immediate post-war years. The building flanking it on the left was known as Edinburgh House during the British occupation of the city and was used as a transit hotel. Down the alley behind it was the British Officers' Club, now the International Club Berlin.

The tall structure to the right of this was the original NAAFI complex and cinema, later replaced by the Britannia Centre on the site of Spandau Allied Prison when the latter was demolished after the death of Rudolf Hess.

Josef Goebbels had an apartment on the left-hand side of the apartment block overlooking the square between the Heerstrasse and Reichsstrasse, where he was entertaining Hitler on the evening of 27 February 1933 when the news came that the Reichstag was on fire.

Cross the street to the U-Bahn station entrance and take the **U-2 Ruhleben** two stops to **Olympia-Stadion**, where the line emerges into the open. It was through these same U-Bahn tunnels that on the night of 1 May 1945 the troops and accompanying civilians made their way in total darkness all the way from the Zoo to Spandau, where they met up with the vehicular element for the break-out attempt in Spandau, which we will come to later. The vehicles had tried to use the Heerstrasse to cross the Havel but found the vital bridge blown and had to turn north to find an alternative crossing place.

From the station follow the pedestrian route, **Rossiter Weg**, to Olympiaplatz and you will come to the 1936 Olympic Stadium, which was recently modified to meet

(*Opposite*), an aerial view of the Olympic Stadium area, showing the rifle ranges of *Alexander Kaserne* below the cloud top centre, the *Waldbühne* with the *Murellenschlucht* gully where the executions took place coming into it from the right, the pencil-like shadow of the *Glockenturm* on the *Maifeld*, and the *Reichssportschule* in the top right-hand corner of the sportsfields. The numerous platforms of the S-Bahn can be seen below the stadium, car parks and *Olympiaplatz* above the station, and then the U-Bahn station. Reichsstrasse runs parallel to the right-hand side of the picture leading down to the Adolf-Hitler-Platz, from where the Heerstrasse runs diagonally across the picture. The partly completed War Academy, now buried under the 13 million cubic metres of rubble of the *Teufelsberg*, can be seen at the bottom left.

the requirements of the 2006 Football World Cup. The stadium was originally designed by Werner March as a structure in steel and glass, but Hitler rejected this idea, and the project was only saved when Albert Speer suggested using stone cladding. Despite its lack of height, the stadium could seat 65,198 people and take another 31,682 standing, this being accomplished by hollowing out the arena. On non-event days the stadium is open to visitors for a small fee.

The stadium and adjacent Reichssportschule and their facilities served as a depot for *Volkssturm* units and also as a base for anti-aircraft and field artillery during the fighting for the city, and towards the end of the Second World War the cellars of the stadium housed a **Blaupunkt** radio

The 1936 Olympic Stadium in 2006.

The interior of the 1936 Olympic Stadium in 2006.

Alexander Kaserne

Ranges

Murellenschlucht

Waldbühne

Sports Academy

Glockenturm

Maifeld

Olympic Stadium

U-Bahn

Olymplapl

Reichsstr

S-Bahn

Heerstr

Grunewald

War Academy

Adolf-Hitler-Pl

Exhibition
Grounds

factory and another factory. The structure was then later used as a temporary barracks by British troops when they first arrived in the city on 4 July 1945.

Walk round to the left of the stadium along Trakehner Allee past the S-Bahn station, to where the competitors were also brought in by train from the Olympic Village, which was

An 88mm gun alongside the Olympic Stadium.

established outside the city to the west in the German Army's training area at Döberitz.

Cross **Flatowallee**, which was renamed after the war in honour of a German-Jewish participant in the 1936 games, who was disposed of after the games, like other German-Jewish athletes, once he had served his purpose. Next you come to **Jesse-James-Allee**, named after the black American athlete who won several gold medals. The story goes that Hitler refused to shake hands with him because he was black, but in fact that was not the case. Hitler had begun by shaking the hands of all the victors after their events, but then he had been called away on state business, whereupon the Olympic Committee told him that he should either greet all the victors or none of them, and consequently he never got to meet Jesse James, but was said to have admired his performance.

Mussolini, Hess, Ciano, Göring and Hitler before the speech.

At the end of this avenue turn right into Passenheimer Strasse and continue past the Reitertor (Riders' Gate) to the **Glockenturm**, the Olympic bell tower. On the first-floor landing as you face the structure are memorials to the *Langemarck* student divisions that suffered tremendous casualties in the First World War. Symbolically Hitler started the opening of the 1936 Olympic Games by laying a wreath here, then walking across the *Maifeld* polo field to the stadium escorted by only two others; he was greeted by tumultuous applause upon his arrival.

Hitler's friend Mussolini, who was a fluent German speaker, did not do so well when he came to address a vast audience on the *Maifeld* one evening in September 1937. The heavens opened up during his speech, and the drenched but disciplined crowds listened dutifully until he had finished. He then drove back to his hotel in the city centre in an open limousine only to find that the hot water boiler in his hotel had broken down!

Take the lift up to the top of the **Glockenturm** (admittance in 2007 cost €2.50

per adult, €1 per child and €2 per person for groups). The lift stops below a copy of the original bell, which was damaged during the battle for Berlin when one of the *Hitler Youth* gunners manning an anti-aircraft gun on the *Maifeld* accidentally hit it. The top of the tower had to be replaced after the war, and the pulpit below over the entrance on to the *Maifeld*, from which Mussolini had addressed his paraded audience, was removed.

German guns on the *Maifeld*.

Reaching the top of the tower, you can look down on the Olympic Stadium and the sports fields of the former *Reichssportschule* half left, which later accommodated the Headquarters of the British Sector, British Military Government Berlin, BRIXMIS (British Commander-in-Chief's Mission to the Group of Soviet Forces in Germany) and the Headquarters of the Berlin Infantry Brigade.

The buildings and sports fields were commissioned by Carl Diem, Secretary General of the Reichs Physical Exercise Committee and later of the Olympic Games, work commencing in 1928. Towards the end of the Second World War several *Volkssturm* battalions were based on the stadium area, and Diem was appointed adjutant to one under the command of Karl Ritter von Halt, the *Reichssportführer*. On the afternoon of 21 April 1945 the 400-strong battalion, along with three others, was taken out by bus to just beyond Erkner, east of Berlin, in a vain attempt to try to stop the Soviet breakthrough reaching the city. In the subsequent chaos about 100 members of the battalion made their way back to the stadium, leaving only 40 men in the field. Diem and Halt went back to collect the others, but by then the Russians had advanced even further and they were told to remain where they were, by which time the stadium area was already under Soviet artillery fire from the north.

Looking left from the *Reichssportschule* complex you can see the site of the former German Army School of Musketry with its ranges modernised by the British. The ranges include the remains of *Ruhleben Village*, an area specially built for the training of troops in fighting in built-up areas (FIBUA).

Some of the original buildings of the former German Army's *Alexander Kaserne* are also visible, with some more buildings forming today's Berlin Police School. It was from here that Helmut Altner participated in a counterattack to drive encroaching Soviet forces back across the playing fields on 28 April, an action in which several hundred *Hitler Youth* members were caught in crossfire coming from the *Reichssportschule* complex.[2]

Beyond and further left is the ancient town and district of Spandau, with the woods and water of the Havel River and its lakes beyond. The radio tower on the southern horizon is still within the city boundary off the road from Wannsee to Potsdam, which may also be visible in the far distance. The mass of woodland to

The Teufelsberg.

the south is the Grunewald with the great hump of the Teufelsberg with its radar domes looming out of it.

The Teufelsberg took 22 years to construct from rubble brought on miniature railways from the bombed city. Once it was complete, the Americans set up a radio and radar intercept station on the crest to keep an eye and ear on the Eastern Bloc forces, an operation in which the Royal Air Force also took part. It was here that the concept of e-mail is said to have originated. The buildings are now derelict but the main dome houses today's air traffic control radar, replacing a former service operated from Tempelhof Airport that was eclipsed by the construction of tall buildings at Potsdamer Platz after Unification.

Below at the back of the Glockenturm is the *Volksbühne* amphitheatre, seating 20,000 spectators. In the gully leading into it from the right were three posts used for military executions during the latter part of the Second World War. It is estimated that some 300 soldiers were executed here.

Every year during the Allied Occupation the Queen's Birthday Parade was held on the *Maifeld*, usually reviewed by members of the royal family, Her Majesty the Queen attending twice. The three infantry battalions would march out from under the colonnades on either side of the Olympic Stadium behind a massed band to form up on the polo ground. They would be followed by columns of Landrovers and scout cars, the fourteen tanks of the armoured squadron having been previously manoeuvred into position at the rear with the aid of steel matting. Two thousand honoured spectators were seated by name, with the general public permitted on either flank of the central spectator stands. The saluting party would then appear on horseback or in a carriage from the left, escorted by a troop of mounted Berlin Police.

Go back down by lift. It was on the steps leading up to spectator tribunes that Werner

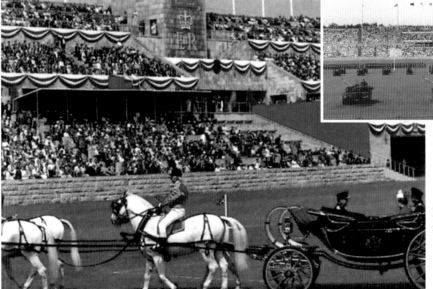

A Queen's Birthday Parade on the *Maifeld*.

HM The Queen reviewing the parade.

BERLIN – TOUR B – WEST

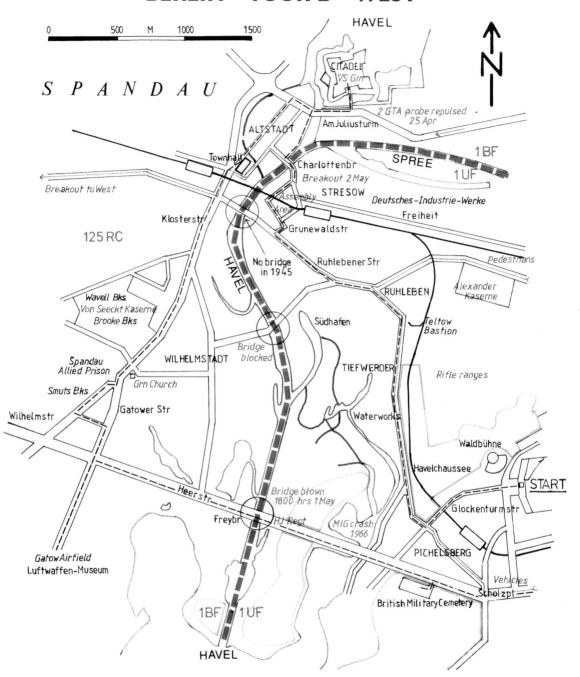

Mihan slept on the night of 26 April, only to discover the Soviets attacking across the playing fields next morning.

Following Mihan's escape route down Glockenturmstrasse, turn right on the Havelchaussee, passing the waterworks on the left where Mihan occupied an earthen bunker with his comrades, and then an old bastion of the Spandau defences on the right, before you come to Ruhlebener Strasse, where you turn left for Spandau.

Follow Ruhlebener Strasse to where Grunewaldstrasse turns off on the right. This was the limit of Ruhlebener Strasse in 1945, for the bridge ahead across the Havel had yet to be built. This was also the route taken by Helmut Altner in the break-out from the *Alexander Kaserne*. On the right are the allotment gardens where Altner previously hid with the idea of deserting before being obliged to go back to barracks.

Nearby next on the right is the old Prussian barrack block that once accommodated *Garde-Grenadier-Regiment 5* of the Kaiser's army, a reminder that Spandau was a garrison and fortress town with military facilities of considerable importance until the discovery of dynamite in the late nineteenth century. Grunewaldstrasse then leads to an underpass under the railway. Ahead you can see the tower of Spandau town hall, from where Soviet fire was directed on the hordes of soldiers and civilians attempting to break out along this route. The underpass and Stresowplatz beyond offered them some cover, but when they turned left to approach the Charlotten Bridge they were met by devastating ground-fire and air attack.

The break-out was led by the newly promoted Major Horst Zobel, who rode in an open-topped armoured personnel carrier as observation would have been too difficult from his tank. Helmut Altner gives his account:

> We pass under the S-Bahn bridge and then there are some burnt-out buildings and ruins alongside the street. In front of us is a mass of people unable to move, and I can hear sharp infantry fire. There are women among the soldiers carrying bags and rucksacks, some holding children by the hand. Most are people from outside the city who had fled in from the west or are afraid of the Russians. Some soldiers disappear into the buildings. Suddenly I see our company sergeant major with his wife behind him looking after the boys. The lieutenant's face also appears for a second and I make my way towards him, elbowing my way through, but the streets are fully blocked, so I press close to the buildings. The sea of people is dammed up behind a barricade. A mobile four-barrelled flak gun sends a burst to the Spandau town hall, from where

---

Väter der Bundeswehr

Oberst aD Horst Zobel (1918–1999)

Hochausgezeichneter Panzerführer und Inspizient der Panzertruppe der Bundeswehr

3. PzDiv

von Ralf Schumann

Am 6. 5. 1918 in Bromberg/Posen geboren, zählt Horst Zobel zu jenen Angehörigen der Panzertruppe, die während des Zweiten Weltkriegs Erfahrungen sammeln und diese dann an junge Soldaten der Panzertruppe der Bundeswehr weitergeben konnte. Somit zählt auch er zu den Vätern der Bundeswehr.

Nach dem Besuch der Schule in Bromberg, trat Zobel am 1. 10. 1936 in das PzRgt 6 der brandenburgischen **3. PzDiv** in Neuruppin ein. Die Division, die im Oktober 1935 in Berlin gegründet wurde, nahm am Einmarsch ins Sudetenland und Böhmen und Mähren teil, kämpfte zu Beginn des Zweiten Weltkriegs in Polen und Frankreich, wo Zobel als Zugführer und dann als Ordonnanzoffizier Verwendung fand und am **21. 6. 1940** mit dem **EK II** dekoriert wurde. Im Rahmen der Heeresgruppe Mitte von Juni 1941 bis Anfang 1942 an allen großen Schlachten des Russlandfeldzuges beteiligt, nahm sie dann am Vormarsch auf den Kaukasus teil. Zobel fand im Feldzug gegen die Sowjetunion als Adjutant einer Panzerabteilung, später als Kompaniechef und dann als Kommandeur der PzAbt in der PzDiv „Müncheberg" (Heeresgruppe Weichsel) Verwendung. Als Hauptmann war ihm am **14. 4. 1945** noch das **Ritterkreuz des Eisernen Kreuzes** verliehen worden. Bei Kriegsende auch mit dem **Panzerkampfabzeichen der II. Stufe** dekoriert, ging für ihn der Krieg zu Ende.

Als 1956 die Bundeswehr aufgebaut wurde, war er einer der Ersten, die sich wieder zu den Waffen meldeten. Am 22. 11. 1956 trat der hochausgezeichnete ehemalige Hauptmann der Panzertruppe in die Panzertruppenschule der Bundeswehr in Munster ein. Hier Hörsaalleiter, konnte er seine im Krieg gesammelten Erfahrungen an die jungen Panzerbesatzungen weitergeben.

Nach zweijähriger Verwendung als stellvertretender Kommandeur des PzLBtl 93, Munster, übernahm er wieder seine Tätigkeit als Hörsaalleiter. Hier hatte er eine vorbildliche Aufbauarbeit für die Panzerwaffe geleistet. 1962 erfolgte seine Ernennung zum Kommandeur des PzBtl 354 in Hammelburg.

Von 1966 bis 1973 in verschiedenen Verwendungen im Heeresamt Köln, wurde seine militärische Laufbahn 1973 mit der Ernennung zum **Inspizienten der Panzertruppe** gekrönt. Hier konnte er als verlässlicher und fürsorglicher Staatsbürger in Uniform seinem Heimatland erneute vorbildliche Dienste leisten.

Am 30. 9. 1977 erfolgte seine Versetzung in den Ruhestand. Seine militärischen Leistungen fanden in Verleihung des **Bundesverdienstkreuzes I. Klasse** noch ihre entsprechende Würdigung. Dieser in Krieg und Frieden hoch bewährte Offizier, der, seinem Vaterland in zwei Armeen gedient und sich aufs höchste bewährt hatte, starb am 2. 10. 1999 in Weilerswirt bei Bonn/NRW.

KA 7/8-2003

Major Horst Zobel, who led the breakout over the Charlotten Bridge, seen here as a Colonel of the Bundeswehr.

shots are ripping into the barricade. A bridge across the Havel has been blown and lies in the water.

On the right the S-Bahn tracks from Spandau main railway station pass between the buildings, and behind the barricade is an underpass. The enemy fire has eased off a bit as the flak gun sends its deafening salvos across the river. I jump over the barricade and dive down the street. There are some dead lying on the pavement and in the roadway. Machine-gun bursts and rifle shots whip past and strike the walls.

At last I am standing in the underpass and can breathe out again. Behind me the street is almost empty, except that one can see soldiers' steel helmets showing above the barricade. The odd man jumps across successfully or stumbles, collapses and remains lying.

Shots ring out ahead again. Several soldiers have gathered under the bridge, their faces wet with sweat.

Werner Mihan.

Our company sergeant major and his wife have got through safely, and the boys too are standing there trembling. Suddenly a truck comes out of a sidestreet and races over the dead and wounded. Its windscreen is splintered, the driver's face distorted and determined. He races past and we jump out of cover and run across to the pavement opposite. All hell has broken loose. Machine-gun salvos hit the walls, grenades explode and walls collapse, then we are through and fall exhausted into a quieter place.

The covered pedestrian approach to the Charlotten Bridge with two flights of steps leading up to the roadway.

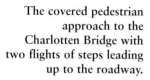

The Charlotten Bridge seen from Spandau town hall with the Deutsche-Industrie-Werke buildings on the right.

There are ruins left and right. The flood of people has eased off, pressed tight under cover in a dead angle against the barricade. Only the odd soldier, woman, civilian or child is getting through alongside the buildings, and others are sitting down in the rubble resting. I have put on my steel helmet and stare at the street, listening to the sounds of combat. The buildings look as if they have been sawn off, mostly at the first storey and their cellars have collapsed and, amid their broken brickwork, people are struggling through to us, through the ruins and the streets with only one aim, one hope; to get to the west to the Wenck Army, away from Berlin's rubble waste, this vast cemetery. Everyone runs, racing through the fire. The dance of death has begun and the big reaper is mowing his broad swathes through the rows of women, children and soldiers.

The street ends and a big road junction appears with house façades and ruins, in which hundreds of people are crowding. On the left the street rises gradually up to the bridge. The street looks swept clean, but people are crouching on the steps leading up to the bridge, and soldiers are pressed behind the walls of the ruins leading to the Havel embankment. Occasionally a few people jump up out of the shelter of the steps and run across the bridge. The mass of people growing behind us in the dead angles begins to spill over. Beside me among the soldiers are women with babies in their arms, old women, children and young teenagers of both sexes. I look carefully over the top step. Shots are racing across the bridge, and the horror hits me for the bridge is swimming in blood.

They are calling from below and pressing forward. I take another deep breath and jump up and run into the tacking of the machine-gun bursts, throwing myself into the death mill as the bullets strike all around. The road surface is slippery with blood and there are bodies lying around and hanging over the bridge railings. Vehicles and tanks race across grinding the bones with a crack. I dive forward, not seeing any more, just driven by the thought of getting over.

Then I throw myself down and slide behind a pillar. There is a dead man alongside me. A smashed truck has driven into the bridge superstructure and is stuck in the roadway, and a soldier and a woman are seeking cover between its wheels from the fire. Now shells are hitting the bridge. I jump up again. I can see figures ahead of me running and stumbling as if through a fog. I am without feeling and run, jumping over the dead and trampling on the wounded. Everyone is for himself and has no time to think of others. Then I reach the end of the bridge and crouch down behind the barricade, gasping for air. Shots wing over my head and hit the bodies. The number of figures on the bridge is increasing. Women with babies in their arms and holding children by the hand, *Hitler Youths*, girls, civilians, old men and women, fall to the ground, dragging down others with them, riddled with bullets and streaming with blood. Death plays his dance, mowing his bloody path. Tanks roll over the bridge, over people, squashing them to pulp, churning them up with their tracks and a wide street of death and blood, of bits of corpses and torn bodies spans the river murmuring beneath the bridge.

I run across to the shelter of the buildings, for only the bridge is under fire. A Luftwaffe General is already gathering soldiers and flak auxiliaries to him. There is a sudden explosion on the bridge and an ammunition truck blazes red like a torch in the roadway. People run past it as it sparks and bangs. The bridge superstructure has been destroyed and people are falling into the river from the opposite bank of the Havel and swirling away. All Hell has opened up.[3]

Spandau town hall from under the Charlotten Bridge.

Go forward along the lower road to reach the riverside below the bridge. It was here that Altner was sniped at from the town hall tower while guarding the bridge on 27 April and witnessed an elderly couple commit suicide by jumping into the river hand in hand.[4]

The Havel and Spree Rivers here formed the inter-front boundary between Marshal Zhukov's 1st Byelorussian Front and Marshal Koniev's 1st Ukrainian Front. Consequently, Zhukov's 47th Army, which had come round the north of Berlin to secure the western flank of his operation, was confined to the west bank of the Havel, and his 2nd Guards Tank Army coming through Siemensstadt was similarly originally confined to the north bank of the Spree. Of Koniev's forces in Berlin, only Colonel Dragunski's 55th Guards Tank Brigade was operational in this area but did not penetrate further west than the *Alexander Kaserne*, Koniev's main concern being to beat his rival to the Reichstag.[5]

Cross over the Charlotten Bridge and turn right along the river embankment, the **Lindenufer**, towards the next bridge. On your right you can see the remains of the *Deutsche-Industrie-Werke* that features so much in Helmut Altner's account, with the mouth of the Spree flowing into the Havel next to it. The next stretch is the area in which Werner Mihan had his searchlight and was engaged with Soviet *Sherman* and T-34 tanks of the 2nd Guards Tank Army coming from Siemensstadt on 25 April.[6]

Go across the main road, **Am Juliusturm**, and walk to **Spandau Citadel**. This moated fortress at the junction of the Spree and Havel Rivers dates back to the sixteenth century, but stands on the site of a much earlier Slav settlement of the twelfth century.

In April 1945 the fortress was occupied by a small military garrison, which was responsible for the destruction of the Soviet tanks outside with *Panzerfausts*, but also sheltered several hundred civilians and a field hospital. It also contained a *Wehrmacht* laboratory set up in 1935 for the testing of the effects of poison gases

The entrance to Spandau Citadel with the Juliusturm on the left.

on military equipment. The fortress entrance had been blocked by an old tank, and when Soviet emissaries arrived to negotiate the surrender of the garrison on 2 May, they had to climb up a rope ladder to reach the balcony of the commandant's residence above.

There are some interesting museums within the citadel, including one on the history of Spandau in the Kommandantenhaus above the gate.

Zitadelle Spandau

Open Tuesdays–Sundays, 1000–1700 weekdays, 0900–1700 weekends.

Museum entrance tickets available from the gatehouse.

The 30-metre-high Juliusturm dates back to the thirteenth century. Following the 1870–71 war against France, the tower was used to store the reparations money of 120 million gold marks extracted from the French. The coin was held here from 1874 until 1919, and was used to finance the vast expansion of Berlin at the end of the nineteenth century.

Go back into the old town of **Spandau**, which officially dates back to 1282, although traces of earlier settlements on this site dating back to the Stone Age have been found. It is thus older than Berlin, into the metropolis of which it was incorporated in 1920 as a district.

Turn left at St Nikolai Church and walk through Schurzstrasse to the town hall. Ahead of you now is the railway bridge, capped by new station buildings, over Klosterstrasse, through which those breaking through from the Charlotten Bridge made their way after passing around the back of the town hall. The new buildings to the right between the bridge and the crossroads replace the former railway sidings that filled this area in 1945. The break-out route continued to the right down Brunsbüttler Damm to Staaken.

Led by Major Horst Zobel and commanded by Luftwaffe Major General Sydow, the main body reached just north-west of Brandenburg before the survivors were finally rounded up, including Helmut Altner, who had been wounded in the meantime.[7]

A few actually reached the Elbe, among them Major Zobel, who got across naked, although he was unable to swim, but still armed with his pistol. He forced a local *Bürgermeister* to provide him with civilian clothing and a chit authorising him to visit his wife in the unnamed 'next village'. This enabled him to pass through American-occupied territory until he found and joined his wife who was working for the British Army in Braunschweig.

Werner Mihan's group was caught in Soviet fire while still on the Brünsbuttler Damm and the survivors subsequently split up. Mihan took shelter in a garden colony, where the last of his female charges died on 4 May 1945. Next day he reported to the Soviet Kommandatura in Potsdam and was discharged as a civilian, but not long after he and all other men of military age in the area were rounded up and sent off to a labour camp in the Soviet Union as part of the security preparations for the Potsdam Conference.[8]

Continue straight on along **Klosterstrasse**. Behind the school on your right is the *von Seeckt Kaserne*, which was built between the two world wars and housed two British infantry battalions during the Allied Occupation as *Brooke* and *Wavell Barracks* respectively. On the left is the old garrison church.

Coming up on the right is the site of the military prison that became **Spandau Allied Prison** after the Nuremburg Trials of 1947, housing only seven prisoners. The first building in distinctive Prussian hard-baked military brickwork you come to was used as the governors' mess, the others as warders' quarters.

An aerial view of Spandau Allied Prison.

A Soviet guard
preparing to take
over the prison.

The old military prison was demolished in 1987 following Rudolf Hess's death by suicide on 17 August, and only those buildings that stood outside the prison walls remain. The site was converted into the Britannia Centre for the British garrison, providing a cinema, shopping centre and facilities for various welfare organisations. The entrance to the site was railed off in keeping with the frontage and a new entrance established on the left-hand side. The two trees that stood in the prison courtyard can still be distinguished in the centre between the former warders' accommodation blocks.[9]

Continue down Wilhelmstrasse, passing a smart barrack block on the right that served as the Education Centre for the British garrison and has a First World War memorial just inside the railings. Turn left on Am Omnibushof to Gatower Strasse and take a **134 Hottengrund** bus eight stops to **Alt Gatow**, where you change buses to a **334 Siedlung Habichtswald**, which takes you to the **Luftwaffen Museum** at Gatow Airfield.

The museum, housed in a hangar and the former station headquarters, contains some very interesting exhibits of both world wars and the Cold War, and there is a magnificent display of NATO and Warsaw Pact aircraft on the now disused airfield.

Luftwaffen Museum der Bundeswehr

Open every day, 0900–1700 hours.

Entry free.

Gatow Air Base was established in 1935 as the Luftwaffe's Academy, Staff College, Aeronautical Engineering School and Air Training Centre. In an attempt to disguise its importance, it was given a Potsdam address even though it was located within Berlin's boundaries, and was omitted from contemporary maps.

On 21 April 1945 an aircraft delivery pilot by the name of Beate Uhse landed at Gatow in an *Arado* 66 with the object of rescuing her 2-year-old son and his nanny from their home in Rangsdorf. When she returned with them next day, she found that her *Arado* had been destroyed by shellfire. However, she knew an aircraft mechanic on the base, who told her of a twin-engined five-seater *Siebel* 104 belonging to some general that was in a hangar there. She managed to persuade the colonel in charge of the airfield to let her have some fuel for it to enable her to return to her unit at Barth and flew out with her son, his nanny, the mechanic and two wounded soldiers. After the war she founded a successful chain of sex shops, renowned throughout Germany.

The establishment came under Soviet ground attack on 23 April and held out until the 28th, during which time Luftwaffe Colonel General Robert Ritter von Greim and his mistress, the famous aviatrice Hanna Reitsch, landed here and switched aircraft to fly on to the east–west axis west of the Brandenburg Gate, in answer to a summons from Adolf Hitler.

The airfield was used by the British delegation to the Potsdam Conference, and the base was taken over by the Royal Air Force and played a prominent role during the 1946–7 Air Lift. Flying boats, bringing in corrosive cargoes such as salt, landed on the Havel nearby and a pipeline was laid between there and the airfield using material taken from the cross-Channel *Pluto* resources.

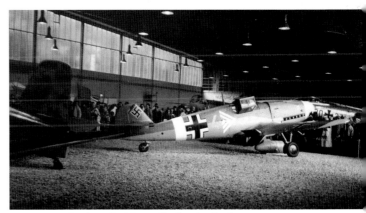

The base is now non-operational, much of the old airfield having been taken over by

A Messerschmitt Bf 109 on display in the hangar.

housing development, but it still accommodates the Headquarters of the 4th Air Division under the title *General-Steinhoff-Kaserne*.

Return by bus **334 Kankenhaus Hohengatow** three stops back to the Kladower Damm, where you change to bus **134 Spandau Wasserwerk** eight stops to the **Heerstrasse** (Army Street), which was so named because the troops marched along it from the Döberitz training area west of Berlin to participate in parades, such as Hitler's 50th birthday parade on 20 April 1939. Here you change to bus **149 Bf. Zoo** for three stops.

This takes us across the Havel by the Freybrücke, which was defended by a *Hitler Youth* Regiment on the far side in expectation of the arrival of General Wenck's 12th Army coming to the relief of the city. A chance shell hit the bridge's demolition chamber on the evening of 1 May. As previously explained, the Havel formed the inter-front boundary, so there was no question of the Soviet troops that were occupying Spandau crossing here anyway, not that the Germans would have known. Captain Boldt described the scene here on 29 April:

> The *Hitlerjugend* lay alone or in pairs with their *Panzerfausts* at irregular intervals in the trenches on either side of the Heerstrasse in front of the

The destroyed Freybrücke.

Pichelsdorf bridges. The dawn was sufficiently advanced to be able to distinguish the dark shapes of heavy Russian tanks against the even darker background, their guns pointing at the bridge. We found the leader of the combat group, who told us what had happened to his people: 'When the fighting started here five days ago there were about 5,000 *Hitlerjugend* and a few soldiers available to take on this desperate struggle against overwhelming odds. Inadequately equipped with only rifles and *Panzerfausts*, the boys have suffered terribly from the effects of Russian shelling. Of the original 5,000 only 500 are still fit for combat.'[10]

The bus next goes across a bridge where the Havel on the right connects with the Stössensee lake on the left. Alight at the **Stössensee Brücke**.

On 6 April 1966 two Soviet airmen deliberately crashed their YAK-25 *Firebar* into the Stössensee lake on orders when their engine failed. British Sector HQ immediately cordoned off the area in anticipation of the arrival of Soviet troops and organised a salvage team of sub-aqua club members operating from a raft provided by the Royal Engineers, while BRIXMIS, the British liaison mission to the Soviet Commander-in-Chief, fended off Soviet intervention. The bodies were recovered and handed over two days later, but the wreckage was not handed over until the radar and other vital elements of this new Soviet aircraft had been surreptitiously removed and examined in the UK, much to the fury of the Soviets.[11]

Go back across the road at the traffic lights and make your way up the slip-road on the right to reach the gates of the **British Commonwealth War Graves Cemetery**, where over 3,500 Commonwealth servicemen are buried. The majority of these are airmen. Their bodies, found between Berlin and the Oder/Neisse River line were concentrated here immediately after the Second World War. (A cemetery for the British Commonwealth dead of the First World War can be found in the

The British Commonwealth War Cemetery.

Waldfriedhof at Stahnsdorf just outside the Berlin city boundary, not far from Wannsee.)

Continue up the slip-road to **Scholzplatz**, where Am Postfenn comes in from the right. This is where Colonel Dragunski's 55th Guards Tank Brigade emerged from the Grunewald forests and turned right up the Heerstrasse after capturing two *Ferdinand* self-propelled 88mm guns guarding this corner. The brigade started fighting its way through the residential areas on either side of the Heerstrasse against increasing opposition. Colonel Dragunski described the advance with his tanks in column about 100 metres apart, scouts out on the flanks and sub-machine-gunners across their front, and engineers, artillery and assault groups following the tanks so that they could see what was happening. All resistance was smothered with heavy concentrations of fire, while long-range artillery shelled the areas yet to be penetrated. By nightfall they had overrun the ammunition dump in the unfinished War Academy (now buried under the Teufelsberg) and occupied the Eichkamp area. Brigade Headquarters remained on the edge of the woods under heavy guard, as nothing was known about the enemy forces in this area.

Colonel Dragunski, Commander of the 55th Guards Tank Brigade, pictured some thirty years later as a retired general.

Take bus **149 Bf. Zoo** for six stops. Along the Heerstrasse the route passes through what was developed as a British officers' married quarters area on either side. The tall building on the left was the British Military Hospital, the top storey of which was reserved for Rudolf Hess while he was at Spandau Allied Prison. At the crest of the hill you pass Heerstrasse S-Bahn station on your right and continue along to **Theodor-Heuss-Platz**. Alight here and cross over to the central island.

Leading off the square half left is Reichsstrasse, where Colonel Dragunski's brigade experienced some difficulty in penetrating toward the Olympic Stadium. Apart from rubble-blocked streets, the troops found that neither their compasses nor their radios would work, owing to the amount of metal in the wreckage.

Enter the nearest U-Bahn station and take the **U-2 Pankow** five stops to **Ernst-Reuter-Platz**. Unfortunately there is no direct bus service on this route under the east–west axis because the U-Bahn provides the necessary service, but it was through these tunnels that Helmut Altner and his comrades from the *Alexander Kaserne* experienced a terrifying walk from the Olympia-Stadion station to Wittenbergplatz beyond the wrecked Zoo U-Bahn station on 28 April 1945. At that time only a short spur of the U-7 track had been completed between Bismarckstrasse station and Richard-Wagner-Platz to the north, an area already occupied by the 2nd Guards Tank Army, which had penetrated as far as Sophie-Charlotten-Platz and the Deutsches Opernhaus on the East–West Axis above, so that fighting was going on above and below ground as far as the Knie (today's Ernst-Reuter-Platz).[12]

The dug-in *Panther* that Altner encountered on Sophie-Charlotten-Platz upon his return to Ruhleben above ground. It had clearly fought a hard battle.

Hitler taking the salute on his 50th Birthday Parade. (The diminutive chap in a bowler on the right is President Hocha of Hungary, who was completely overawed by the occasion.)

At Ernst-Reuter-Platz U-Bahn station take the tunnel leading under the line to emerge on the **Technische Universität** side of the street, heading for the **Strasse-der-17. Juni**, the street named after the 1953 workers' uprising in East Berlin. On the right a post-war building, flanked by older ones, blocks off a street that used to run through the heart of the university. Further on is the main university building on this street, which has slight projections at either end that have more modern frontages than the other parts of the building. It was midway opposite that Hitler's podium was situated for the parade held in honour of his 50th birthday on 20 April 1945.

Some 50,000 troops took part, coming all the way from the Döberitz training area west of Berlin. The street had been specially widened for the occasion under Albert Speer's direction. Preparations included the demolition of some older buildings facing the university, except for one set further back than the others, and the rebuilding of the wings of the Charlottenburg Gate to allow wider passage either side.

The 2nd Guards Tank Army fighting in this area was so depleted of infantry, with up to 95 per cent casualties in some units, that the 1st Polish Infantry Division was brought in from the 1st Polish Army fighting in the Oranienburg area north of Berlin to help out. The sheer width of the street here was a tremendous obstacle for the infantry attacking the university site. The Polish gunners dismantled some of their guns and reassembled them in the upper storeys of the sole surviving building across the way to provide covering fire. The Soviet armour was also vulnerable in

Wrecked Soviet armour near the Charlottenburg Gate.

these circumstances, and some appears to have been deliberately sacrificed to provide a steel screen behind which the infantry could cross the road.

Go on to the **Charlottenburg Gate**; on the far side are the statues of the Great Elector and his wife Charlotte, for whom he had built the original Charlottenburg Palace, a model of which she is holding in her arms. Unusually for the senior aristocracy in those days, he was genuinely in love with his wife and gave her the palace as a present. It was later greatly expanded and today contains a number of interesting museums.

Go on to the **Tiergarten S-Bahn station**, which was the last military objective

Soviet troops celebrating their victory before the Siegesäule.

captured by the Poles before they hoisted their flag on the **Victory Column** (*Siegesäule*) further down the street. From here you can take any of the S-Bahn trains going one stop to the Zoologische Garten station. Alternatively, you can continue down the Strasse der 17. Juni to the Victory Column and take bus **100 Bf. Zoo** back to the start point.

This stretch of the road was used for the Allied victory parades at the time of the Potsdam Conference and later by the Western Allies for their annual parades demonstrating their support of the West Berlin population. The Victory Column originally stood directly in front of the Reichstag, but was moved here in 1937 as part of the grand design for *Germania* in time for the celebration of the city's 700th anniversary. Hitler found the column too short for its new surroundings, so Albert Speer had another section, the second one down, inserted. The column commemorates the Prussian victories over the Danes (1864), Austrians (1866) and French (1870–71), with the mosaic

The French Spahi contingent on one of the annual Allied Forces Day parades.

insert under the minor columns depicting the French surrender at Sedan. The bronze plaques on the four sides of the base were removed after the Second World War at the request of the French military authorities and taken to Les Invalides in Paris, but were returned in 1987 for the city's 750th anniversary.

On the northern side of the roundabout are statues of the famous Prussian generals Moltke and Roon, with Bismarck set back in the centre. Behind them are the offices of the Federal President (*Präsidialamt*) and his official residence Schloss Bellevue, outside which you can take bus **100 Bf. Zoo** back to the start point.

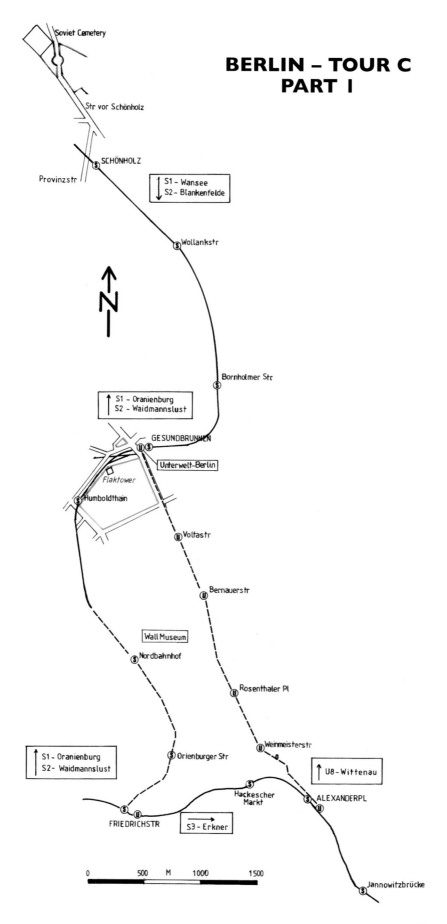

Soviet Cemetery

Str vor Schönholz

Ⓢ SCHÖNHOLZ

Provinzstr

S1 – Wansee
S2 – Blankenfelde

Ⓢ Wollankstr

N

Ⓢ Bornholmer Str

S1 – Oranienburg
S2 – Waidmannslust

GESUNDBRUNNEN
Ⓤ Ⓢ

Unterwelt-Berlin

Flaktower

Ⓢ Humboldthain

Ⓤ Voltastr

Ⓤ Bernauerstr

Wall Museum

Ⓢ Nordbahnhof

Ⓤ Rosenthaler Pl

S1 – Oranienburg
S2 – Waidmannslust

Ⓤ Weinmeisterstr

U8 – Wittenau

Ⓢ Orienburger Str

Ⓢ Hackescher Markt

Ⓢ ALEXANDERPL
Ⓤ

Ⓢ Ⓤ FRIEDRICHSTR

S3 – Erkner

Ⓢ Jannowitzbrücke

0   500   M   1000   1500

**BERLIN – TOUR C
PART I**

CHAPTER THIRTEEN

BERLIN TOUR C: EASTERN BERLIN

Humboldthain Flak-Tower – Pankow Soviet Cemetery – Karlshorst Museum – Treptower Soviet Cemetery – Advance of the 5th Shock Army – Fate of the 'Siemensstadt' *Volkssturm* Battalion – Friedrichstrasse Break-out.

LIMITATIONS: Prior contact with the Berlin Unterwelten Association is advisable for weekend visits to their bunkers. Karlshorst Museum is closed on Mondays, and the German Historical Museum on Wednesdays.

AREA: This tour covers the eastern part of the city, including the sole remaining Flak-tower, the two main Soviet cemeteries and Karlshorst Museum, where Field Marshal Keitel signed the final surrender of the German armed forces, then traces the advance of the 5th Shock Army and the fate of the 'Siemensstadt' *Volkssturm* Battalion, and finally the break-out at Friedrichstrasse station.

The air war was an important part of the battle for Berlin, so this excursion starts with a visit to **Humboldthain Flak-tower**, one of the three massive gun platforms that dominated the Berlin skyline during the Second World War. Only the northern half of it still remains. These flak-towers, originally equipped with four single-mounted 105mm ship's anti-aircraft guns, later carried four twin-mountings of 128mm anti-aircraft guns and were ringed with a lower platform carrying twelve 20mm four-barrelled and 37mm single-barrelled guns for dealing with low-flying aircraft.

The other flak-towers were located at the Zoo and in Friedrichshain Park, but the former was

The badly battered Humboldthain Flak-tower during the construction of an artificial hill of rubble in the park behind it.

completely demolished after the Second World War and the latter was blown up and buried under debris taken from the destroyed buildings in the neighbourhood.

If you can fit this into your programme and you can speak German, or are with an English-speaking group, you are strongly advised to take part in a tour of the interior of the tower arranged by the **Berliner Unterwelten** Association, which operates out of the Gesundbrunnen U-Bahn station, and offers regular tours every Saturday at 1200, 1400 and 1600 hours. Special arrangements can be made for English-speaking groups on other days. However, for safety reasons, numbers are limited and the lower age limit is set at 18, except for children aged 14 and over escorted by their parents or legal guardians. Tickets cost €9 (concessions €7) and should be obtained from the office at least 15 minutes before the tour commences.

> **Berliner Unterwelten e.V.**
> Brunnenstrasse 108a, D-13355 Berlin
> Tour information phone: 030-4991-0518
> info@berliner-unterwelten.de
> www.berliner-unterwelten.de

The association also offers tours of air raid shelter bunkers built into the station complex and has its own museum in one of them.

DIRECTIONS: From the Zoo station take any of the following S-Bahn trains:
   S-3 Erkner
   S-5 Strausberg
   S-7 Ahrensfelder
   S-9 Flughafen Berlin-Schönefeld
   S-75 Wartenberg
   four stops to **Friedrichstrasse**, where you switch to either of the following:
   S-1 Oranienburg
   S-2 Weidmannslust
   four stops to **Gesundbrunnen**.
Alternatively, from Alexanderplatz take the **U-8 Wittenau** five stops to **Gesundbrunnen**.

From the S-Bahn platforms descend to the lower level and turn left to link up with the U-Bahn station, proceeding to the far end where a long escalator takes you up to street level. As you turn right, the offices of **Berliner Unterwelten** are immediately on your right. Outside on the pavement are two two-man concrete shelters. Cross Brunnenstrasse and follow the signs to the *Flakturm*.

As you ascend the winding path leading to the gun platforms, you pass the northern face of the tower, which bears the scars of shelling at point-blank range by Soviet artillery when the 3rd Shock Army converged on this bastion and then had to contain it while its forces bypassed it on either side, the railway cuttings below forming an effective dry moat against a frontal assault.

Several attempts were made to remove this tower after the war, but the risk to the railway lines below saved it from complete destruction. The face of the tower

The scarred remains of the Humboldthain Flak-tower today.

also bears the scars of internal explosions, which caused it to squat down somewhat. As you wind your way up to the surviving gun platforms you can admire the view. Across the park, to the south of the gun platform, was its control tower, which has since been completely demolished. From there the main guns could be controlled automatically, the only manual task being loading the 28kg shells on the fuse-setters. The maximum height the guns could reach was 14,800 metres (48,500ft), forcing Allied bombers to fly at extreme heights, and they fired at a rate of ten to twelve shells per minute. The control tower would select a 'window' some 250 metres square for the guns to fire at, through which no aircraft could pass unscathed.

Wolfgang Karow, an infantry NCO on leave in Berlin who mustered into an ad hoc unit based on this flak-tower on 23 April 1945, later wrote of his experiences here the following day after an abortive excursion by his unit to engage the Soviets about a kilometre away:

So we . . . made for Humboldthain Flak-tower. There we were put into reserve and were able to get to know the interior of this vast bunker. We experienced the violent shaking when all eight 128mm anti-aircraft guns fired a salvo at the Russians, feeding them a violent form of respect.

The artillery fire was particularly fierce against the walls of the bunker since the infantry could not get in. The brave gunners were being killed mercilessly at their posts, and they were nearly all young Flak Auxiliaries, 14- to 16-year-olds. These brave gunners continued to serve their guns fearlessly, and several were felled before our eyes.

An assault group was formed from our reserve combat team, and I also belonged to it. We were ordered to try to get some sweets from the Hildebrand Chocolate Factory in Pankestrasse, which was nearby in no-man's-land, so we put on some large Luftwaffe rucksacks and set off. We arrived without any trouble, but then had to detain an NSDAP [Party] official, who tried to prevent us entering at gunpoint. We were able to fill our rucksacks with chocolates and return to the bunker without suffering any casualties, and were warmly received by our comrades.[1]

Like the others, this Flak-tower also provided shelter for some 12,000 people but probably held far more during the fighting. It also provided shelter for scientific departments of the AEG and Telefunken concerns studying captured British and American radar and locating equipment.

Return to the Gesundbrunnen complex and take either the **S-1 Oranienburg** or the **S-2 Waidmannslust** three stops to **Schönholz**. Emerging from the station, turn right along Provinzstrasse and then left on the Strasse vor Schönholz. Either take bus **150 S-Bf. Buch** from this junction to the next stop, or walk it. You will come to a small roundabout in the park with Pankow Soviet cemetery to your left.

Although this is not the cemetery that was used for formal parades as at Treptow, it compares very favourably, being impressive in its own right. The 13,200 dead buried here appear to be commemorated with their individual names on bronze unit plaques, whereas at Treptow the unnamed graves are concealed under ground ivy and extracts from Stalin's speeches take precedence.

Return to Schönholz S-Bahn station and take either the **S-1 Wannsee** or the **S-2 Blankenfelde** seven stops to return to **Friedrichstrasse**. Here you switch to the **S-2 Erkner** and travel nine stops to **Karlshorst**, sitting on the **right-hand side** of the train. On the way beyond Alexanderplatz you come to **Jannowitz** station, immediately beyond which the track turns away from the riverbank at the point where SS-Sergeant Major Willi Rogmann, whom we met in Berlin Tour A, set up the mortars of the band of the Leibstandarte-SS *Adolf Hitler* to engage the Soviet tanks approaching from the Schlesischer station (today's Ostbahnhof). During a break while his men were sheltering below, Rogmann lost all but two of his mortars to Soviet counterfire.[2]

The imposing entrance to Pankow Soviet Cemetery.

Beyond the Ostbahnhof you pass through some of the extensive railway sidings where the Soviets massed their main artillery for the assault on Berlin. The vital railway bridge at Küstrin had been knocked out by German aircraft on 16 April but was reopened to traffic seven days later. Having meanwhile adapted the German gauge to suit their rail stock, the Soviet railway wagons were able to deliver ammunition directly to the guns. The Stavka Reserve artillery, originally intended only for the breakthrough battle at Seelow, had been reassigned to the 1st

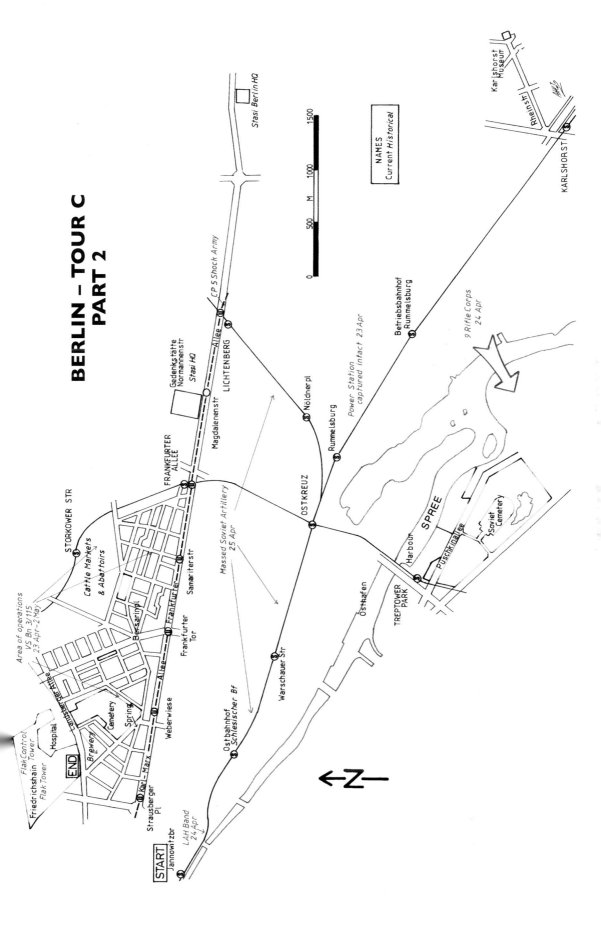

BERLIN – TOUR C
PART 2

NAMES
Current *Historical*

Karlshorst Museum
Rheinstr
KARLSHORST

Stasi Berlin HQ

CP 5 Shock Army

Gedenkstätte Normannenstr
Stasi HQ

Magdalenenstr
LICHTENBERG

FRANKFURTER
ALLEE

Nöldnerpl

Rummelsburg

Power Station
captured intact 23 Apr

Betriebsbahnhof
Rummelsburg

STORKOWER STR

Cattle Markets
& Abattoirs

Massed Soviet Artillery
25 Apr

OSTKREUZ

9 Rifle Corps
24 Apr

SPREE

Area of operations
VS Bn 3/115
23 Apr–2 May

Bersarinpl

Samariterstr

Frankfurter
Tor

Harbour
Puschkinallee

Soviet
Cemetery

TREPTOWER
PARK

Osthafen

Flak Control
Tower
FlakTower
Friedrichshain

Hospital

END

Brewery
Cemetery
Spring
Weberwiese

Landsberger Allee

Frankfurter Allee

Karl-Marx

Warschauer Str

Ostbahnhof
Schlesischer Bf

Strausberger Pl
Jannowitzbr

START

LAH Band
24 Apr

—N→

0   500   M   1000   1500

Karlshorst Museum.

Byelorussian Front when it was realised that the requirement for such a reserve no longer existed, and additional firepower was provided by some German siege artillery captured in the Crimea that had been brought forward by rail. Colonel-General Berzarin, in whose 5th Shock Army's sector these railway sidings lay, later commented: 'The Allies dropped 65,000 tons of bombs – we fired 40,000 shells in two weeks!'

At **Karlshorst** descend the station steps to street level, turning right on to Stolzenfelsstrasse, then turn left up to Treskowallee, turn right again to cross Ehrenfelsstrasse and take Rheinsteinstrasse out of the far corner of the little square. Follow Rheinsteinstrasse to the far end. As you cross over Waldowallee and Köpenicker Allee, you can glimpse former Soviet barrack blocks a few yards off to your right.

Facing you at the end of the street is the **Deutsch-Russisches Museum**, once the officers' mess of the German Fortress Engineers and later the Red Army Museum.

Deutsch-Russisches Museum Berlin-Karlshorst

Open free 1000–1800 hours, Tuesday–Sunday.

Entering the main door, turn sharp right to descend to the cellars, where there is a cloakroom, bookshop and toilets, as well as some exhibits. Then return up the same staircase to the first floor, where you are greeted by the contents of a Soviet field surgeon's medical pack. Turn left to Room 1, where there are photographs showing German troops in the Ukraine in the First World War and then others illustrating the secret exchange of training facilities under the Rapallo Pact of 1926, which enabled Soviet staff officers to train in Germany (not that it did them much good, for they were all subsequently executed as spies by Stalin) and provided tank and aircraft training facilities on the Russian steppes for the Reichswehr.

Room 3 contains some interesting material on the German–Soviet Non-Aggression Pact of 1939, showing German–Soviet military cooperation in the division of Poland, the delivery of supplies vital to the German military economy, and the compulsory resettlement of *Volksdeutsche* (ethnic Germans) in the captured territories that went with it.

Room 4 shows the battle plan for Operation Barbarossa, the 1941 invasion of the Soviet Union, while the next two rooms show pictures and videos of the fighting and life behind the front from both sides. Note the Red Army uniform in Room 6 with a two-coloured ribbon on the breast. This denoted the kind of non-Russian language the soldier spoke, for not all Red Army soldiers spoke Russian.

Room 7 contains records of various German detention, concentration and prisoner-of-war camps, while Room 8 contains exhibits relating to the siege of Moscow, the German occupation of Soviet territory and the incorporation of certain ethnic units into the Wehrmacht. Of particular interest is a map, together with scale models, showing the ultra-broad-gauge railway the Germans intended to use to connect their conquered territories with the homeland. Room 9 contains exhibits from the slave-labour camps.

From here you descend a staircase to the ground floor, where you come to some exhibits relating to the battle for Berlin. In the next passage is a panorama of the battle of the Reichstag, together with busts of the two Heroes of the Soviet Union that hoisted the flag of the 150th Rifle Division on the Reichstag. The next passage contains photographs of some of the various Soviet cemeteries to be found in the eastern part of Germany.

You now come to a room whose focal point is a three-dimensional model of Berlin made by Red Army engineers to help plan the battle. In fact, as the various Soviet armies converged on the city, with all that could aiming for the Reichstag, one can imagine that it must have been very useful for Zhukov and his staff in their headquarters at Strausberg in determining army boundaries. The contents of this room also pay tribute to the contribution made by the Western Allies, such as the D-Day landings, and the vital element of Lend-Lease, upon which so much of the

Field Marshal Wilhelm Keitel saluting the assembly with his baton.

Red Army effort depended, in the form of canned food, trucks, jeeps, tanks, locomotives, railway wagons and aircraft.

The next room you come to, the main reception room of the former fortress engineers officers' mess, is where the final surrender ceremony took place on the night of 8 May 1945. As it was followed by a feast and a party in which all the original furniture was smashed, only the few items displayed on the top table are original. The carpet is believed to have come from the Reichs Chancellery. A vast plaque on the end wall commemorates those Red Army units that excelled themselves in the battle for the city.

Marshal Zhukov, Colonel-General Sokolovsky and Foreign Minister Vishinsky and his staff look on aghast at Keitel's form of salute.

The story of the surrender ceremony is a complicated one. Colonel General Alfred Jodl had signed the unconditional surrender of the *Wehrmacht* at General Eisenhower's headquarters in Reims on 7 May. Unfortunately, Eisenhower's chief of staff, General Walter Bedell-Smith, forgot that he had in his safe the approved draft document for this purpose, one that had been worked on for months in London by representatives of the major powers, and instead drafted one of his own. The signing of this document fully satisfied Eisenhower, but not Stalin's national pride. Nor did the British government want a repeat of what occurred at the end of the First World War, when no formal surrender of the German Armed Forces had occurred. Stalin demanded a repeat surrender ceremony presided over by Marshal Zhukov, ordering Andrei Vyshinsky, his First Deputy Commissar for Foreign Affairs, to organise the event.

General Stumpf, Field Marshal Keitel and Admiral von Friedeburg hear the terms of unconditional surrender.

As the latter had been the chief prosecutor in the trials that had purged the leadership of the Red Army in 1937–38, and Zhukov knew that Stalin was gunning for him, this could not have been an easy situation for him.

The Western Allied and German representatives were flown in to Tempelhof Airport and then driven out to Karlshorst though streets deserted except for Red

Air Chief Marshal Sir Arthur Tedder (UK), General Spaatz (USA) and General de Lattre de Tassigny (France) with Marshal Zhukov presiding.

Army traffic police. The German delegation was put into a house across the road from today's museum, where they had to wait a long time before they were called, while the Allied delegation was entertained by Marshal Zhukov within the main building.

Various matters delayed the proceedings. The Moscow delegation had first to translate the vital document from English, and then four lines were found to be missing, which had to be sent on from Moscow. The Western Allied flags had been cobbled together by local housewives and the French tricolour was found to have been made with horizontal instead of vertical stripes. Lastly there was an argument over who would sign the surrender document apart from Marshal Zhukov. Air Chief Marshal Sir Arthur Tedder was there as Eisenhower's representative and therefore could sign for the Western Allies, but General Carl Spaatz of the United States Strategic Air Force and General Jean de Lattre de Tassigny of the 1st French Army, who regarded themselves as national representatives, were finally obliged to sign as mere witnesses.

It was nearly midnight when the German delegation was marched in, the principals being Field Marshal Wilhelm Keitel, Luftwaffe General Hans-Jürgen Stumpf and Admiral Hans-Georg von Friedeburg, who had just come from the ceremony at Reims after previously having negotiated a surrender to Field Marshal Sir Bernard Montgomery on Luneberg Heath, and was so depressed by the whole business that he committed suicide shortly afterwards.

The display behind the Deutsch-Russisches Museum.

The whole ceremony was over in about ten minutes, during which midnight had struck unnoticed, and the German delegation marched out. Photocopies of the original surrender documents are on display, and there is a running slide-show shown from the gallery above. In the next room you can see the original Stars and Stripes flag used at the surrender ceremony.

Go on to Zhukov's office in which he entertained the Western Allies. One of his uniform jackets is on display with his four stars of Hero of the Soviet Union, the first of which he was given for his victory over the Japanese at Kharkin Kol in Mongolia, the second for Moscow, the third for Berlin, and the fourth for his 60th birthday!

Before leaving, it is worth having a look at the Soviet armour and artillery on display behind the museum.

Return to Karlshorst S-Bahn station and take the **S-3 Westkreuz** three stops to **Ostkreuz**, where you can switch to any of the following lines taking you one stop to **Treptower Park**:

S-6 Zeuthen

S-9 Westkreuz

S-8 Grunau

S-46 Königs Wusterhausen

To do this, you have to turn back down the platform you alighted on and ascend the stairs to the platform on the railway bridge above.

At **Treptower Park** descend to the riverbank where there are landing stages for several of Berlin's pleasure-boat companies. Go past these and along the riverbank as far as the rose garden, where you turn right and go through to the main road, where a pedestrian crossing gives access to the Soviet Cemetery, where the Russians' farewell parade was held in 1994.

Go through an entrance gateway, which is balanced by another one on the far side of the park.

Mother Russia mourns her fallen sons.

The symbolic approach to the cemetery.

The main cemetery.

The monument depicting Guards Sergeant Masalov.

Midway between them is the statue of Mother Russia mourning the loss of her sons. During the Communist regime it was customary for newly-wed East German brides to lay their bouquets at her feet. Around the statue are trees imported from Russia, some of which have had to be replaced because of disease. A broad ramp leads upwards between rows of weeping birches to a platform between two dipped Red Flags with the bronze statue of a guardsman kneeling before each, one young, one old, the focus being on a monument at the far end of the cemetery.

This monument depicts the story of Guards Sergeant Nikolai Masalov, standard bearer of the 220th Guards Rifle Regiment, whose story was recounted in Berlin Tour A. He is shown holding a German child in his arms while symbolically slashing a swastika with his sword.

As you reach the top of the ramp, the imposing cemetery opens out before you. There are five squares of grass, hedged with low bushes, and each containing a large horizontal bronze wreath on a concrete base. It was once thought that each square contained 1,000 dead soldiers, with the odd hundred or so buried in the mound beneath the statue, but this is not so; the dead are buried in individual graves under the trees on either side of the central rectangle, the graves being covered with ivy and unmarked.

One grave immediately in front of you is said to contain a colonel, a captain, a sergeant and a private, as representatives of the rest. A naval wreath on the first square represents the Dnieper Flotilla naval contingent that brought their gunboats to Berlin. The eight white marble blocks on either side of the rectangle are carved with reliefs depicting different aspects of the Great Patriotic War and representing the then sixteen republics forming the Soviet Union. Extracts from Stalin's wartime speeches are carved in German on one side of the rectangle, and in Russian on the other.

Going up the steps of the monument to the barred gate at the top, you can see the mosaics around the interior depicting mourning representative figures from the sixteen republics and above a copy of the Order of Victory fashioned from the lens of a German searchlight.

Return via the gateway by which you entered and make your way across to the riverbank. On the far side you can see the massive industrial complex that includes the Rummelsburger power station, the capture intact of which earned Colonel Shishkov of the 301st Rifle Division the Order of Suvarov.

Further along to your right, where there is now an amusement park, the 9th Rifle Corps of the 5th Shock Army conducted an assault river crossing into Treptow Park with the assistance of part of the 1st Brigade of the newly arrived Dnieper Flotilla during the early hours of 24 April. Ten gunboats, described as hydrofoils, had been brought in by road, and these, together with 50 pontoons, 100 guns and mortars, 27 tanks and 700 supply trucks were brought across the Spree under fire. According to Soviet accounts, the crossing was opposed in strength, but in fact the defence consisted only of the local *Volkssturm*, reinforced by the engineer battalion of the SS Panzergrenadier Division *Nordland*.

Go back past the harbour to the Treptower Park S-Bahn station and take the **S-9 Westkreuz** (**anti-clockwise!**) one stop back to Ostkreuz.

From the train as it starts off you can see the **Osthafen** on your left where the Soviets found barges to help them get across the river further downstream at the Mühlendschleuse locks in the city centre. At **Ostkreuz** descend to the lower platform to take any of the following trains two stops to **Bahnhof Lichtenberg:**

S-5 Strausberg

S-7 Ahrenfelde

S-75 Wartenburg

From Lichtenberg station make your way to **Alt-Friedrichsfelde**, the eastern extension of Frankfurter Allee. Here on the junction of Frankfurter Allee with Rosenfelder Strasse (above what is now a florist's shop) was the command post of Colonel-General N.E. Berzarin (spelt Bersarin in German), Commander of the 5th

A close-up of one of the sixteen reliefs quoting Stalin.

Shock Army and the first Soviet city commandant of Berlin. Due to his measures to help feed the captured population he became quite popular. He was killed while riding his Lend-Lease Harley-Davidson motorcycle when he ran into the back of one of his unlit trucks at night.

Facing you down the main street to the right is a tall building with two vertical tower-like projections. This was the new *Stasi* (State Secret Police) headquarters complex that opened shortly before Unification. Its sheer size indicates the volume of spying being conducted against the civilian population in both sides of the city under the East German regime. In the opposite direction you can see another tall building with a revolving sign on its roof advertising the German Railways with the initials 'DB'. This was also part of the *Stasi* national headquarters operating under the pseudonym 'Normannenstrasse', the name of the

Colonel-General Berzarin's command post during the 5th Shock Army's advance down Frankfurter Allee.

street behind it. The complex included the offices of *Stasi* General Erich Mielke, head of the organisation, together with a prison, armoury, hospital and bank, for *Stasi* personnel were more highly paid than normal citizens and their accounts had to be kept secret. The complex was stormed on 15 January 1990 by irate citizens demanding to see their files, since when it has become a memorial to *Stasi* victims, with displays of spying equipment, interrogation and punishment cells, and the like.

Forschungs- und Gedenkstätte Normannenstrasse

Open weekdays 1100–1800 hours, weekends 1400–1800 hours.

If you would like to visit 'Normannenstrasse' on this excursion, return to the **U-5 Alexanderplatz** and go one stop to **Magdalenstrasse** and then turn right up Ruschestrasse to the entrance. Otherwise take the same **U-5 Alexanderplatz** two stops to **Frankfurter Allee**, where you go up to the street and turn right up an alley running parallel to the S-Bahn tracks to the S-Bahn station. Take either the S-4 Bernau or the S-8 Birkenwerder one stop to **Storkower Strasse**, from where you take the long footbridge leading to Eldenaer Strasse.

The cattle markets seen from the footbridge before the area was redeveloped.

This footbridge crosses the site of the former central cattle market, now under redevelopment, where the 'Siemensstadt' *Volkssturm* Battalion 3/115 was engaged on 23 and 24 April 1945. It should be noted that this battalion was exceptionally well-trained and equipped in comparison to most, mainly due to its Siemens connections, and that it had already been in action since the 21st with engagements at Kaulsdorf and Friedrichsfelde-Ost. The adjutant, Dr Gustav-Adolf Pourroy, later recorded:

> At about 0300 hours the commanding officer and adjutant made a reconnaissance of the new position around and in the Central Cattle Market.
> According to the regiment, the battle line was that of the S-Bahn, which, as it was in a cutting, appeared a good one, but in fact the Russians had already crossed over and secured themselves in the extensive area of the market, had installed several heavy tanks in the allotment gardens north of the S-Bahn and were firing with these tanks, anti-tank guns and even artillery without pause

VOLKSSTURM BATTALION 3/115
CENTRAL CATTLE MARKET
23-24 APR 45

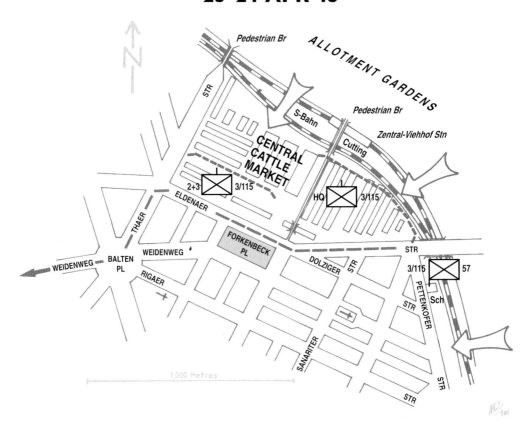

at the northern and north-eastern fronts of the market buildings.

The battalion command post was established in the school on the corner of Pettenkoferstrasse and Eldenaer Strasse, where the school bordered on the market and the S-Bahn. The Russians had already flooded across the railway tracks into the market, making it impossible to occupy positions along the S-Bahn as ordered. When the troops arrived from Lichtenberg town hall at dawn, they were deployed on the north and north-eastern edge of the market and further back in the market buildings in order to cover the open spaces and streets between the buildings, with Headquarters Company on the right and the other two companies, Nos 2 and 3, on the left.

After daybreak the commanding officer discussed the layout in detail with the company commanders, and it was clear that it would soon be a matter of all-round defence. It was also obvious that the area was too big for the battalion, so a detachment of police troops was inserted between the battalion's two combat groups after discussion with the regimental commander. However, there was unfortunately a big row with the police within the next few hours when the police commander asked for orders to allow him to withdraw. As the regiment could not be reached for the moment, an almighty row broke out between the commanding officer and the police commander. Even with their pistols drawn, the commanding officer and adjutant were unable to stop the police leaving. It would have meant opening fire, and the commanding officer did not want that.

The police detachment moved out soon afterwards, leaving a dangerous gap in our lines, which the Russians immediately infiltrated and started shooting in all directions. Russian infantry with light and heavy weapons were pouring into the market by the long footbridge leading across the S-Bahn, and were able to form a wedge between Headquarter Company and the other two, which was hardly surprising considering the complexity of the market with its numerous buildings, some of which had been shot to pieces and were on fire.

The companies tried with all their might to defend themselves, but the Russians quickly set up their mortars

Captain Gustav-Adolf
Pourroy as a subaltern
with Iron Cross First
and Second Class in the
Maikäfer Garde Fusilier
Regiment in the First
World War.

and were also firing anti-tank guns down the market streets from across the S-Bahn, and so were able to slowly push our lines back close to Eldenaer Strasse.

Here we mounted a counterattack from the command post with a handful of men that had been held back as a reserve. Led by the commanding officer and the adjutant, the counterattacking force burst out of the command post at the last moment and charged into the market complex in support of the hard-pressed companies.

Meanwhile the Russians had been pressing forward without pause and especially hard close-quarter fighting developed, taking a dramatic form with firing from man to man in the open spaces, on the streets, between the buildings and especially in the wide halls, with ricochets whistling around everywhere, and shells bursting in a shed filled with hanging hams and sausages. Men jumped from cover to cover and shot at anything that indicated the presence of the enemy, ahead, behind and on both sides. Small pockets of resistance formed, dissolved and melded with others. This kind of fighting was particularly hard on the *Volkssturm* men, but it was simply a matter of self-defence: him or me.

VOLKSSTURM BATTALION 3/115 RICHTHOFENSTRASSE & LÖWEN-BÖHMISCH BREWERY 25 APR – 2 MAY 45

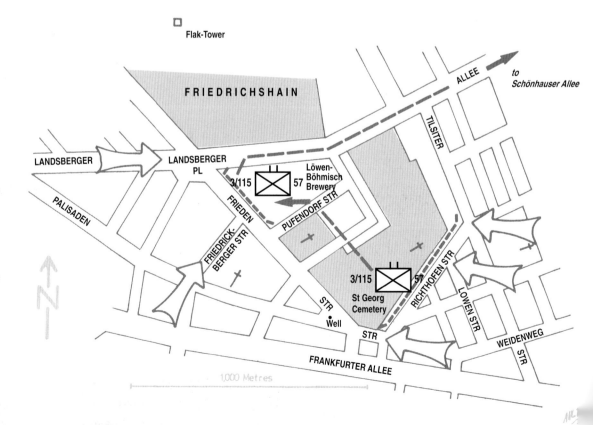

The main thing the battalion lacked was heavy weapons to counter the Russian mortars and anti-tank guns, and the situation became more and more untenable. Company Commander Treutner was severely wounded and had to be carried off after an emergency dressing. Company Commander Dr Weinholdt was reported missing but, as was later established, he too had been severely wounded, and both were to die of their wounds at the dressing station. . . .

Extraction from the market complex while under constant pressure from the Russians was a risky business, but the battalion managed to assemble, taking the walking wounded with it. The severely wounded had to be left behind in the school on Pettenhoferstrasse.

By this time the commanding officer, adjutant and the last remaining company commander, Gebhardt of Headquarter Company, were the only senior officers to have come out of the heavy fighting unwounded. The commanding officer had had his cap shot off his head, the adjutant had had a scratch to his shoulder, and only Gebhardt remained totally unscathed.

So that afternoon we marched across Forkenbeckplatz and along Thaer Strasse and Weidenweg to Baltenplatz [now Bersarinplatz], where we stopped for a break. It was only a short break, for then the battalion received orders to go back up to Frankfurter Allee immediately.[3]

The battalion was ordered to hold the line of Samariter Strasse between Dolziger Strasse and Frankfurter Allee, which it did until the morning of 25 April 1945, so you can see this position before following the earlier line of withdrawal across Bersarinplatz. Dr Pourroy wrote:

In crossing Liebigstrasse, where we had to go above ground into daylight to reach Weidenweg, Wehrmacht Corporal Donath distinguished himself by standing in the middle of the street with a light machine gun at his hip and firing so accurately at the Russian tank and escorting infantry firing at us from Frankfurter Allee that they stopped firing, and we were able to dash across the street safely and reach Baltenplatz. For this act of heroism, Corporal Donath was later awarded the Iron Cross First Class.[4]

You now follow the battalion's route to Richthofenstrasse (named after the First World War fighter ace and now called Auerstrasse) via Weidenweg and Löwestrasse. (Note on the way Richard-Sorge-Strasse, formerly Tilsitstrasse, which

The fountain used by civilians and combatants of both sides during the fighting. The wall of the St Georg Cemetery can be seen behind.

The site of the Löwen-Böhmisch Brewery today. The building on the right is all that remains of the original brewery complex, which occupied the core of the vast block on the left between Pufendorfstrasse, Friedenstrasse and Landsberger Allee.

was named after a famous German spy working for the Soviet Union in Japan during the Second World War; he sent Stalin advance warning of Operation Barbarossa which was ignored at the time, but subsequently appreciated.) Here the battalion, now down to about fifty rifles and only two machine guns, but supported by stragglers of other *Volkssturm* units and the Wehrmacht, held out until the afternoon of 26 April 1945.

One extraordinary feature of the fighting in this area was the use by the troops of both sides, as well as civilians, of the natural fountain on the corner of Pallisadenstrasse and Friedenstrasse for obtaining water without interfering with each other, as if it were neutral ground. The fountain is still there in a more modern setting.

From here follow Friedenstrasse past the cemeteries and then the church on the right until you come to a renovated part of the Löwen-Böhmisch Brewery, in which complex the battalion holed up until the morning of 2 May 1945. Dr Pourroy described the scene:

> Entering the brewery proved a tricky business. An unnatural quiet reigned, and immediately at the entrance was a long flight of cellar steps leading down. By the faint light of a pocket torch, and with drawn pistols and hand-grenades

at the ready, we went down the steps and suddenly saw six white oxen walking quietly towards us.

We then discovered that hundreds of civilians were sitting tightly pressed together in the brewery's capacious cellars, where they had already been waiting for days for the fighting to end. There was ample food for cooking, and an emergency medical service, children were being born, and a group of brewery employees under a very understanding brewmaster had set up a small brewery in a corner, which proved highly welcome to our starving troops.

In addition, the SS had a truly vast depot there, filled to the roof with wines of the best quality, French champagne and cognac. This special depot was clearly highly dangerous under the circumstances, and the brewery manager immediately asked us to provide armed guards to secure these cellars straight away.

From the remains of the battalion, now down to about 30 rifles and the two light machine guns, three combat teams were formed to cover the front along Friedenstrasse and Pufendorfstrasse, with Schrade's on the right, Gebhardt's in the middle and Müller's on the left. They then improvised defensive positions in the cellars of the brewery buildings and adjacent ones, providing alternative firing positions for the light machine guns.

On 27 April the Russians pressed forward on the brewery, starting from Landsberger Platz and from Friedrichsberger Strasse. Singularly, no attack came from Pufendorfstrasse. Gebhardt's team managed to knock out a Russian anti-tank gun with a *Panzerfaust*. The Russians realised that they would be unable to take the brewery that easily, and during the following days and nights every attempt to break through was met with fire by the few men available, now well fed from the brewery cellars.

Mounds of rubble cover the ruins of the flak-towers in the Friedrichshain Park.

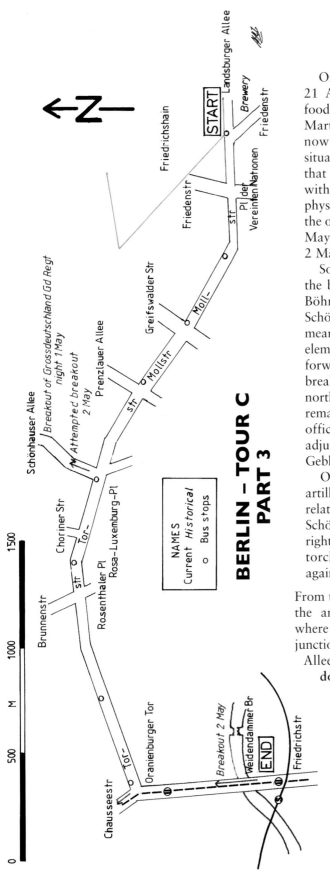

←–N–→

Landsburger Allee

Friedrichshain

Friedenstr

Friedenstr

START

Brewery

Friedenstr

Pl der Vereinten Nationen

Moll- str

Greifswalder Str

Mollstr

str

Prenzlauer Allee

Breakout of Grossdeutschland Gd Regt night 1 May

Attempted breakout 2 May

Schönhauser Allee

Choriner Str

Tor-

str

Brunnenstr

Rosenthaler Pl

Rosa-Luxemburg-Pl

NAMES
Current Historical
o Bus stops

**BERLIN – TOUR C
PART 3**

Oranienburger Tor

Tor-

Chausseestr

Breakout 2 May

Weidendammer Br

END

Friedrichstr

1500

1000

M

500

0

On 27 April, for the first time since 21 April, there was plenty of warm food again, and with it issues of French Martell cognac. However, everyone now realised from the general situation, whatever the news might be, that the end was in sight. The troops, with the best of wills, were both physically and mentally spent. Thus the orders, received at 2230 hours on 1 May for a break-out at 0230 hours on 2 May, came as a relief.

So at dawn on 2 May the remains of the battalion set off from the Löwen-Böhmisch Brewery to march to Schönhauser Allee. We were by no means alone. A growing stream of elements of all kinds of units surged forward with the aim to try to either break through or break out to the north from Berlin. In this the battalion remained relatively intact with the last officers, the commanding officer, adjutant and Company Commander Gebhardt in the lead.

On the morning of 2 May the artillery fire on the city centre was relatively quiet, and there was none on Schönhauser Allee. But to the left and right the buildings were burning like torches, collapsing and flaring up again.[5]

From the end of Friedenstrasse you can see the artificial hill in Friedrichshain Park where the flak-tower was buried. From the junction of Friedenstrasse and Landsberger Allee take bus **340 U-Bf. Mierendorffplatz** eight stops to **Oranienburger Tor**. The fourth stop is at the entrance to Schönhauser Allee, where the remainder of the 'Siemensstadt' *Volkssturm* Battalion was finally obliged to surrender, as Dr Pourroy related:

The leading elements of the big

stream of mixed units, including the remains of *Volkssturm* Battalion 3/115, had reached about level with the elevated Schönhauser Allee S-Bahn station when the first Russian resistance was encountered. Rifle and machine-gun fire ripped into the ranks, followed by an exceptionally heavy mortar bombardment, the bombs bursting among the struts and supports of the elevated railway with increased explosive effect. The results were devastating. Within seconds some 30 to 50 dead and wounded were strewn across the street. It was a miracle that none of the remaining members of the battalion was hit.

Everyone scattered, seeking shelter in the surrounding buildings and side-streets. The battalion stayed together and was taken in by a friendly tailor, who, despite his own distress, immediately sought to give everyone something to eat and something warm to drink.

It was now obvious to everyone that there was no longer any chance of breaking out to the north from Schönhauser Allee, for the Russians were sweeping the street with their rifle and machine-gun fire.[6]

Others had preceded them on this route, which was why the Soviets were alerted, as this extract from *The History of the Grossdeutschland Panzer Corps* records:

Major Lehnhoff gave orders to this combat team of the *Grossdeutschland* Guard Regiment to assemble at 2300 hours on the 1st May in Kastanienallee to break out to the west via Rathenow.

The remaining vehicles were tanked up, millions of Reichsmark coins were shared out among the men, the last rations issued, and then away. The break through the Soviet lines was made at the Schönhauser Allee station, where *Stalin-Organs* and tank fire inflicted heavy casualties. With five tanks and 68 men Major Lehnhoff broke out of the city toward Oranienburg, where unfortunately the tanks had to be blown up because of breakdowns. Divided into four groups the men then pushed on toward the Elbe and Schleswig-Holstein.[7]

Alight at the Oranienburger Tor and take the **U-6 Alt Mariendorf** one stop to **Friedrichstrasse**, where you ascend to street level. Turn towards the river and go on to the Weidendammer Bridge across the Spree, which is where the break-out from the *Führerbunker* by the troops in the city centre took place on the night of 1/2 May 1945.

SS-Major General Wilhelm Mohnke, who was in charge of the *Führerbunker* group, failed to liaise with SS-Major General Dr Gustav Krukenberg commanding the 11th SS *Nordland* Panzergrenadier Division in this area, so considerable confusion resulted.

SS-Major General Wilhelm Mohnke.

Amazingly, Mohnke's break-out group was turned back by the watchmen guarding these doors to the tunnel under the Spree.

The *Führerbunker* group, which was split into ten smaller groups, had set off at ten-minute intervals with the intention of following the U- and S-Bahn tunnels as far as the Stettiner railway station (now the Nordbahnhof) some 1,200 metres due north of the Spree. From there they would march as far as the Gesundbrunnen station, another 2,000 metres, and there split up to make their individual way to find the German forces via Neuruppin.

However, when the leading group under Mohnke, which included Reichsleiter Martin Bormann, reached the level of the Spree, they found their way blocked by a waterproof steel door guarded by two railway men, who refused to let them through. The door was regularly locked between the last train at night and the first in the morning, and although no trains had passed for a week, the watchmen were sticking to their orders. Amazingly, the group complied, turning back to emerge above ground at the Friedrichstrasse station.

The Weidendammer bridge was blocked by a German anti-tank barrier and was being shelled by the Soviets, so they cut their way through the barbed wire blocking the footbridge integrated under the near side of the still intact railway bridge and made their way across the river. Following an encounter with Soviet troops at Lehrter station (site of the present Hauptbahnhof), Martin Bormann and his companion, SS Colonel Dr Ludwig Stumpfegger, committed suicide, realising the hopelessness of their situation. Their remains were not found and identified until 1972.

Meanwhile other groups started arriving at the Friedrichstrasse station, some having come above ground, and attracted Soviet attention, so that searchlights and

The footbridge incorporated into the railway bridge at Friedrichstrasse station used by Martin Bormann and others in the break-out.

artillery fire were directed at the crossing. SS-Major General Krukenberg had been caught unprepared and decided to use those of his troops immediately available to force a break-out. A *Königstiger* with a damaged turret led the way, smashing through the anti-tank barrier on the bridge, closely followed by five armoured personnel carriers and then a mass of soldiers and civilians. However, by then the Soviets were waiting in ambush for them. All the armoured vehicles were destroyed and hundreds of people killed. Only a few survivors managed to get through with Krukenberg. SS-Sergeant Major Willi Rogmann wrote:

> Meanwhile we were all waiting for Mohnke in vain. I went around the crowd and met some people I had not seen for years, but it was no time to chat, we were all too concerned with what might await us.
>
> Then at last there was some movement. A lone *Königstiger* tank rolled up noisily with a defective track. I crossed the Spree and stopped a short distance behind the barricade there, whose right-hand side was open. Then a self-propelled gun and an armoured personnel carrier drew up behind it side by side. Next five armoured personnel carriers drew up and lined up behind the others. In the second one I could see a figure in a cap and overcoat, whom in

the darkness I took to be Mohnke. . . .

The officer I had taken for Mohnke was in fact SS-Major Ternedde, commander of the *Norge* Regiment of the *Nordland*, and all the vehicles were from that division. . . .

The armoured vehicles started moving forward and we formed up right across the street beyond the barricade. The first rank consisted of machine gunners with their weapons on slings, all carrying 50-round drum magazines. Apart from my machine gunner, I and my men followed in the second rank.

The armoured vehicles speeded up. We followed in quick time, but could not keep up and soon lost contact. We then came under infantry fire from the windows of the buildings on the right side of the street and all the machine gunners returned the fire,

SS-Sergeant Major Willi Rogmann.

spraying the front of the buildings. The din caused by a hundred machine guns firing simultaneously was enough to burst one's eardrums. Now tanks opened up on us from either side. . . .

There was no sense of leadership in this mob. There were no responsible officers. My men only obeyed me because they knew me and trusted me. They had only to catch my eye and signal, for shouting was no good in this din, to follow my orders. Literally thousands of people were thrusting blindly forward behind us. I had never seen such a primitive form of attack, being used to an empty battlefield in modern warfare. This was utter nonsense.

They were not just Waffen-SS behind us, and not just soldiers, but even officers with their wives, even my former company commander SS-Lieutenant von Puttkamer with his heavily pregnant wife.

Meanwhile we had reached the level of Ziegelstrasse on our right, which was now full of Russian tanks that must have been alerted to our impending break-out by their scouts. With our incomprehensible long waiting we had given them plenty of time to form up, although the tank had been able to slip through, if a bit damaged. But the self-propelled gun and one of the armoured personnel carriers had been shot up as the other armoured vehicles passed through, as I saw no other wrecks around.

The Russians fired into our packed ranks as we stumbled forward without regard for our dead and wounded. My group was now in the lead. Then we came under fire from tanks in Johannisstrasse on our right, and the effect of high explosive shells bursting in our ranks was simply terrible. The advance came to a halt and thousands of people started streaming back. I had never seen such a fiasco.

However, we did not go with them. It was obvious that there would be another attempt, so we vanished like lightning into the buildings on our left, where we were safe. As we had been right in front, no one could prevent us stepping aside as we did. We were right in front because in an attack that is the safest place to be, as experienced front-line soldiers know.

So far my own men had suffered no casualties and were still sticking together. We waited for the inevitable second attempt, which was preceded by an armoured personnel carrier firing on all sides as it raced toward us, but it was only hastening to its fate, for it stopped and burst into flames, blocking the street for the other armoured vehicles following.

As those on foot reached us, we jumped out to resume the lead. The street now lay full of dead and wounded, the armoured vehicles racing over them. While under cover in the buildings, we had met up with some experienced men from the *Nordland* and even some parachutists. Enemy tanks appeared in front of us again and we tried to creep up under their fire to knock them out in order to get past, but fresh tanks appeared behind them from the right and sprayed those in front with machine-gun fire, the ricochets causing heavy casualties among us. Practically the whole of my platoon was hit by this fire, which broke up the attack, sending the masses streaming back again.

We pulled our wounded into the cover of the buildings and bandaged them

A Hanomag armoured personnel carrier of the SS *Nordland* Panzergrenadier Division wrecked in the break-out north of the Spree.

up as best we could. I used my bottle of schnapps to pour courage into them. I realised that the whole business was hopeless. The Russians had been reinforced and when another crowd moved up they were slaughtered before my eyes.

We did not take any further part in this massacre. I worked out that the leadership had driven off, abandoning us, so I owed them no further allegiance and must save my own life and those of my few remaining unwounded men. We had to leave our wounded behind, which made my heart bleed, for it was for the first time in this war.[8]

CHAPTER FOURTEEN

BERLIN TOUR D: SOUTHERN BERLIN

Allied Control Council – Teltow Canal – Tempelhof Airport – Chuikov's HQ – Schöneberg Town Hall – Allied Kommandatura – Allied Museum – Fehrbelliner Platz

LIMITATIONS: The Allied Museum is closed on Wednesdays.

AREA: This tour encompasses events and places of historical interest in the southern part of the city, involving the Allied Control Authority, the Soviet assault across the Teltow Canal, Tempelhof Airport, Chuikov's headquarters, the *Germania* concept, Schöneberg Town Hall as the centre of West Berlin in the Cold War, Koniev's thwarted attempt to reach the Reichstag, the Allied Kommandatura, US Sector HQ and the Allied Museum commemorating the Allied Occupation.

Goebbels calling for total war in the Sportspalast.

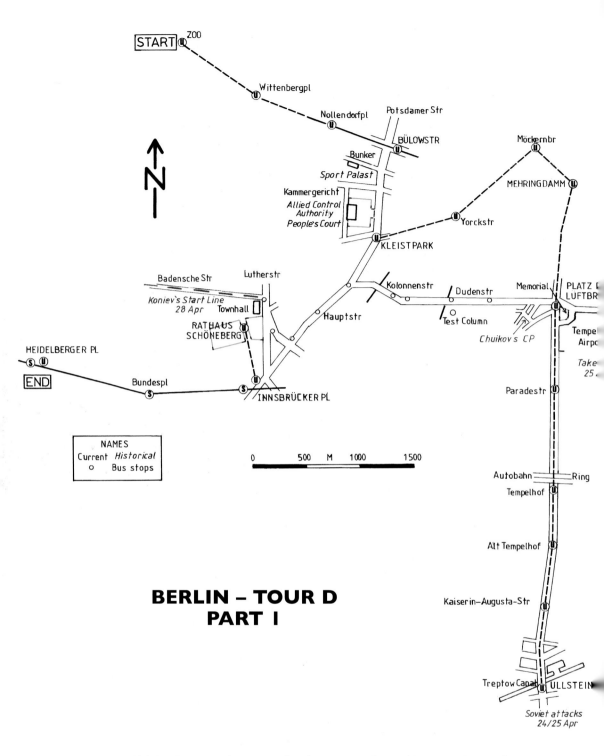

BERLIN – TOUR D
PART I

DIRECTIONS: From the Zoo take the **U-2 Pankow** three stops to **Bülowstrasse**, then walk south down Potsdamer Strasse along the right-hand pavement. The next street on the right is Winterfeldstrasse, astride which is an apartment block that also spans an enormous concrete air raid shelter. Behind the next block of buildings once stood the Sportspalast, where Dr Josef Goebbels gave his famous speech after the fall of Stalingrad calling for total war.

Cross over Pallasstrasse and you will come to the Heinrich von Kleist Park on your right. Leading off the street into this park are the *Königskolonnaden* (King's Colonnades), which were moved there from the Königsbrücke at Alexanderplatz in 1910. The large building behind was built as the Prussian Court of Appeal between 1909 and 1913. During the Second World War it accommodated the notorious *Volksgericht* (People's Court), where Roland Freisler conducted a parody of justice before the cameras (note the hole in the Swastika behind) in his trials of those

accused of participating in the plot against Hitler on 20 July 1944 and other alleged cases of treason. It was then used by the Allied Control Council, whose four flagpoles are still splayed above the entrance, and also housed the quadripartite Berlin Air Safety Centre throughout the Occupation, but has since reverted to its original role as a court of appeal.

The next street corner was the scene of heavy fighting on 26 April when elements of the 28th Guards Corps came up against a strongpoint here.

Roland Freisler conducting one of his notorious trials.

From the Kleistpark U-Bahn station take the **U-7 Rudow** three stops to **Mehringdamm,** where you switch to the **U-6 Alt Mariendorf** for six stops to **Ullsteinstrasse,** where you emerge on the Stubenrauch Bridge over the Teltow Canal next to the old Ullstein printing works.

This is where Colonel General Vassili Chuikov's combined 8th Guards and 1st Guards Tank Armies attacked on 23 April 1945, as Colonel Wolfgang Skorning commanding the 2nd Battalion, Fortress Regiment 60, reported. This was an ad hoc unit composed mainly of army ammunition technician trainees reinforced by *Volkssturm.*

> I immediately drove to the Mussehl Bridge, where I found great uproar. The engineer sergeant responsible for blowing the bridge was drunk and had shot himself in the foot while playing about with a *Panzerfaust* and had to be carried off. One Soviet tank had already taken up position behind the Klinger factory and was firing at the Mussehl Bridge, although to little effect because of the flat trajectory of its gun and the poor aim of the Russians. Certainly it was not out to destroy the bridge, but its fire was demoralising.
>
> With a few men of my battalion quickly brought forward, I formed a bridgehead, which was reinforced by soldiers, *Reichsarbeitsdienst* Flak gunners and *Volkssturm* streaming back, who had to be forced to stay at

The Allied Control Council building.

gunpoint. As these stragglers were known neither by name nor personally, the bridgehead garrison dwindled during the night.

The battalion command post was set up in a restaurant on the Gottlieb-Dunkel-Strasse/Germaniastrasse crossroads. No. 2 Company – reinforced by *Volkssturm* found on the Teltow Canal mainly in positions at the cemetery north of the Mussehl Bridge – took over the sector between the railway bridge and the beginning of the Krupp-Druckenmüller factory, where Second Lieutenant Werner's platoon was sited. This continued on the left with No. 3

The harbour on the Teltow Canal across from the Ullstein building.

Company, reinforced by *Volkssturm* Company 3/311. I discovered that during the retreat to the Teltow Canal, Captain Zwicker commanding No. 3 Company had been severely wounded. He died after having a leg amputated and was buried in the Heidefriedhof, Alt Mariendorf. To my knowledge Second Lieutenant Werner took over this company, as Lieutenant J. Schulz had been reported taken prisoner.

The Russians pressed forward during the night under heavy fire, the Soviet tank in the end standing directly south of the Mussehl Bridge and the little bridgehead garrison north of the bridge. I had the bridge blown shortly after midnight, which was only done with difficulty because of the drunken engineer sergeant. The railway bridge refused to blow despite the demolition charges that had been laid, and the noise of battle abated. An attempt by the Russians at dawn to cross over to the Krupp-Drukenmüller factory by inflatable boats failed. The single-track railway bridge, which was kept under machine-gun fire, was avoided by the Russians because of its narrow approach and structure rendering it impassable.

On 25 April the Russians tried to soften the defence with mortar fire. But apart from several assault troops' attempts at dawn that we were able to repel, the rest of the day was quieter. I was wounded in an artillery barrage on the afternoon of the 25th (shrapnel in the right hand and neck) and was taken to the previously mentioned Reserve Field Hospital 122 [today the Wenckebach-Krankenhaus]. Cavalry Captain Döbrich took over command of the remains of the battalion – one could no longer talk of a combat group. During the afternoon the Russians constantly fired on the hospital, where an end of the world atmosphere reigned, and I left on foot to rejoin my battalion. I found my deputy very upset, the Russians having managed to cross the Teltow Canal, and he wanted to commit suicide. He had an artificial leg and by now was completely exhausted. I had the remains of the battalion, as much as could be contacted by runner, assemble at the Landes-Frauenklinik on Mariendorfer Weg, a conspicuous place, but then had a frightful argument with the doctor, who understandably forbade soldiers to come on his territory. I had the wounded taken off by official car, together with the completely exhausted Captain Döbrich. They were supposed to drive across a bridge over the S-Bahn to the Oderstrasse stadium, but fell into the hands of the Russians, who, according to the same source, immediately shot them, including an NCO of my battalion who had the Ritterkreuz.[1]

Walk back up the Tempelhofer Damm, past the little harbour on your right, five blocks to the junction with Albrechstrasse, where you take bus **184 Flughafen Tempelhof** three stops to **Tempelhof U-Bahn** station, where you take the U-6 **Alt Tegel** two stops to the **Platz der Luftbrücke**.

The buildings on this square were all constructed as part of the Tempelhof Airport facility, and in the little park there is the Air Lift Memorial commemorating the eleven-month Soviet blockade of the city in 1948/9. The names of the 39 British, 31 Americans and 5 Germans who lost their lives in providing 1.7 million tons of food, fuel and other necessities with 212,621 flights are inscribed on the pediment.

Unloading aircraft at Tempelhof during the Air Lift.

The airport was built in the form of a quadrant during the period 1936–9, replacing an earlier structure, on what had been the Berlin garrison's exercise and parade ground. From above it takes the form of a spread-winged eagle, which makes the building uniquely distinguishable even from space.

The airfield was attacked by the 28th Guards Rifle Corps, supported by two tank brigades of the 1st Guards Tank Army late on 25 April 1945 following the crossing of the Teltow Canal. The infantry advanced across the airfield with one division in the centre and one on either flank, using artillery fire to keep the runways clear. As the Soviets did not know the exact location of the underground hangars and their exits, some combat groups were tasked with ensuring that no aircraft should escape. During the course of the first day the Soviets overran the two local defence lines and encroached on to the airfield, but it took until the following afternoon for them to secure it.

The unveiling ceremony of the Air Lift Memorial on 10 July 1951.

The airport played a critical role in the Berlin airlift, but the proximity of tall buildings has since decreased its value for civilian air traffic and its future remains a subject of debate. The airport buildings now also house the city's police headquarters (*Polizei Präsidium*), including a small police museum.

Polizeihistorische Sammlung

Free entry: open Mondays to Wednesdays, 0900–1500 hours.

Cross over the Tempelhofer Damm to the left-hand side of Dudenstrasse for one short block then left turn down Burgherrenstrasse to the Schulenburgring facing

General Hans Krebs with his interpreter, SS-Lieutenant Neilands of the SS 15th *Latvian Fusilier Battalion*, disguised as an Army 'Sonderführer' outside Colonel General Chuikov's command post.

you. A plaque outside **No. 2 Schulenburgring** commemorates its use as the command post of Colonel-General Vassili Chuikov, commander of the combined 8th Guards and 1st Guards Tank Armies in the attack on Berlin. It was here that General Hans Krebs, escorted by Colonel Theodor von Dufving, was brought to meet Chuikov when Goebbels sent him over to try to arrange an armistice on the night of 30 April 1945.

Colonel von Dufving and General Helmuth Weidling, the Berlin Defence Area commander, were brought here separately on the morning of 2 May following the garrison's surrender. Colonel von Dufving later recorded:

I recognised the building, for it was the place where General Krebs and myself had been taken for the negotiations 25 hours earlier. We were taken into the anteroom, and I could hear General Weidling's voice nearby. He appeared and beckoned us in. Refior, Knappe and the others complied, but I did not go with them, perhaps because I was somewhat switched off and thought that it was the others' turn to do something.

Meanwhile Weidling had prepared his appeal [for the troops to lay down their arms] with the help of Refior and Knappe in the room next door. The door to the negotiating room was opened and it was announced that German officers

Colonel Theodor von Dufving under interrogation after the surrender.

would take the appeal, which the Russians had turned into an order, informing the troops of the cessation of the fighting.

Weidling, the other generals, Refior, myself and some other staff officers, were led into another room, where the table was laid and eating had already begun. We were amazed at this hospitality, which happened to other German officers, even members of the SS, at this time, being astonished at our victors' reconciliatory behaviour.

We were then taken to another building in which campbeds and mattresses had been set out. I lay down and slept and slept. Later I was told by Refior and Weidling that several attempts had been made to wake me without success. It seems that I was completely exhausted, which was not surprising, for I had been in action for 16 days without a break. I had not stopped and the last days had been physically the most demanding. Weidling later said something to me reproachfully: 'Since we couldn't wake you up, they kept coming for me!'[2]

Return to Dudenstrasse, where the Soviets had a strange encounter on 26 April. According to Colonel General Chuikov, men of the 28th Guards Corps were amazed to see advancing openly down Dudenstrasse towards them a group of about 400 boys, not older than fifteen, wearing *Hitler Youth* uniforms and armed with *Faustpatronen* mounted on metre-long poles. The soldiers fired yellow flares to warn the boys off, but they kept coming and started releasing their *Faustpatronen*, inflicting casualties on men and horses, giving the Soviets no option but to mow them down with machine-gun fire.

Cross the road to take bus **104 Neu-Westend/Brixplatz** seven stops to **Rathaus Schöneberg** at John-F-Kennedy-Platz. Immediately ahead of you there is a bridge across a railway line where Dudenstrasse becomes Kolonnenstrasse, and on the left there is a strange concrete pillar of vast proportions. This was a testing device to see how the ground in this area would withstand the weight of the Triumphal Arch that was personally designed by Hitler for the north–south axis of *Germania*.

Schöneberg town hall was the seat of the West Berlin government following the split with the East Berlin authorities. It was from the balcony above the main entrance that President John F. Kennedy addressed the population on 26 June 1963,

Hitler's design for the Triumphal Arch on the north-south axis.

President Kennedy addressing Berliners from the Schöneberg town hall balcony.

The weight-testing column.

announcing: 'Ich bin ein Berliner!' I don't think anyone could have told him this colloquially translates as 'I am a doughnut!'

The street to the left beyond the Rathaus is Badensche Strasse, which constituted the front line for Marshal Koniev's 3rd Guards Tank Army when he launched his bid for the trophy of the Reichstag on the morning of 28 April 1945, the immediate objective being the crossing of the Landwehr Canal by nightfall. It was not until fairly late in the morning that it was discovered that some of the ground ahead of him was already occupied by Colonel General Chuikov's troops, who had either accidentally or deliberately crossed Moscow's designated inter-front boundary.

The exact consequences of this episode in the rivalry between Marshals Koniev and Zhukov have not been made public, but one can imagine the fireworks! Moscow ordered a revised inter-front boundary swinging away to the north-west toward Savignyplatz, and Marshal Koniev left Berlin in high dudgeon to return to his front headquarters.[3]

Now go through the little park to the left of the Rathaus to the Rathaus Schöneberg U-Bahn station on Innsbrucker Strasse, where you take the **U-4 Innsbrucker Platz** on its final stage and there transfer to the **S-9 Westkreuz** two stops to **Heidelbergplatz**, where you switch again to the **U-1 Krumme Lanke** five

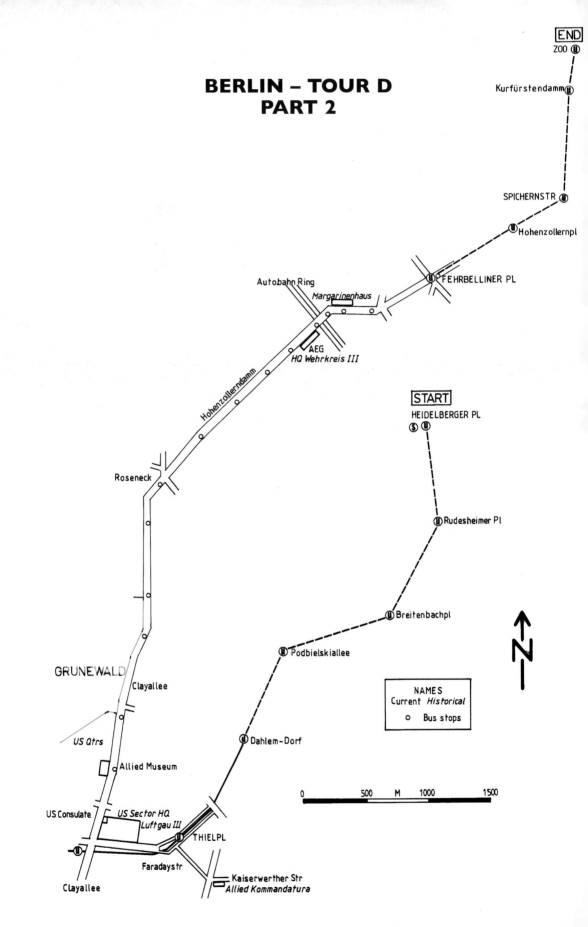

BERLIN – TOUR D
PART 2

END
ZOO

Kurfürstendamm

SPICHERNSTR

Hohenzollernpl

Autobahn Ring

Margarinenhaus

FEHRBELLINER PL

AEG
HQ Wehrkreis III

Hohenzollerndamm

START
HEIDELBERGER PL

Roseneck

Rudesheimer Pl

Breitenbachpl

Podbielskiallee

GRUNEWALD

Clayallee

NAMES
Current *Historical*
o   Bus stops

N

US Qtrs

Dahlem–Dorf

Allied Museum

0   500   M   1000   1500

US Consulate

US Sector HQ
Luftgau III

THIELPL

Faradaystr

Kaiserwerther Str
Allied Kommandatura

Clayallee

The closing ceremony at the Allied Kommandatura.

stops to **Thielplatz**. Here you go up to Brümmerstrasse and take **Faradayweg** to the junction with Thielallee. Across the road on the corner of Kaiserwerther Strasse is the insurance company building used as the **Allied Kommandatura**, which functioned as a four-power institution until the Soviets walked out in June 1948, after which it continued operating under the three Western Allies. The flags were lowered here after the final session before the Allied signatories moved on to Rathaus Schöneberg for the formal handover of powers on 2 October 1990.

Turn right down Thielallee and take the next right into Van-t'-Hoff-Strasse, which emerges next to the Harnackhaus, which was used as the American Officers' Club during the Occupation. Cross the bridge over the U-Bahn cutting and turn left down Saargemünder Strasse. The buildings on your right were built as the headquarters of Luftgau III, the Berlin District Luftwaffe administration, and were taken over by the Americans for the headquarters of their sector of the city.

You pass the main entrance as you turn right along Clayallee, named after General Lucius D. Clay, the first American Military Governor of Germany after the war, and President Kennedy's envoy to Berlin to restore morale after the erection of the Wall in 1961. The far end of the complex is used by the American Consulate General, but the remainder has been vacant since the Americans left. The other side of Clayallee was Trumanplatz, the American shopping complex, which is now under redevelopment.

At the junction with Huttenweg, cross over to the other side of Clayallee, passing a fine statue of General Steuben, who took an active part in the American War of

The display outside the Allied Museum showing the last version of Checkpoint Charlie, a British aircraft from the Air Lift and a carriage from the French train.

The former American Sector Headquarters on Clayallee.

Independence, and you will come to the **Allied Museum**, which contains some very interesting exhibits on the Air Lift, the Cold War and the Allied Occupation in general, including a section of the Anglo-American secret tunnel used to tap Soviet communications that was betrayed by the British spy George Blake.

Allierten Museum

Free admission, open Thursdays–Tuesdays 1000–1800 hours.

Cross Clayallee and take bus **115 Güntzelstrasse** from opposite the museum fourteen stops to **Fehrbelliner Platz**. As you set off, you can see the distinctive block of former US Army married quarters on your left. Further on you leave behind the trees of the Grunewald and the road swings half right to become the Hohenzollerndamm. At the far end of this straight avenue you come to the bridge over the autobahn and S-Bahn rings. Immediately before you come to this bridge you pass a series of buildings on your right bearing the AEG label. These were formerly the German Army's Berlin District headquarters.

As you cross the bridge, you can get some idea of the value of the cutting beneath as a defensive obstacle, although admittedly the autobahn did not exist in 1945.

The building facing you straight ahead was originally known as the Margarinehaus and served as a strongpoint in the battle, as Gerhard Tillery, who was at this time serving as a panzergrenadier escort to a *Hetzer* crew, related:

> We were sent to Wilmersdorf, where we had to secure Barstrasse, where it led off Mecklenburgische Strasse. Our tanks stood at a crossroads and covered toward Mecklenburgische Strasse. Behind us were some shops, a small lake with a bridge going over it, and beyond it a cemetery and a crematorium. The Russians were already occupying the other end of the street at Mecklenburgische Strasse.
>
> Suddenly a T-34 came on to the street. Our gunner had spotted it and it

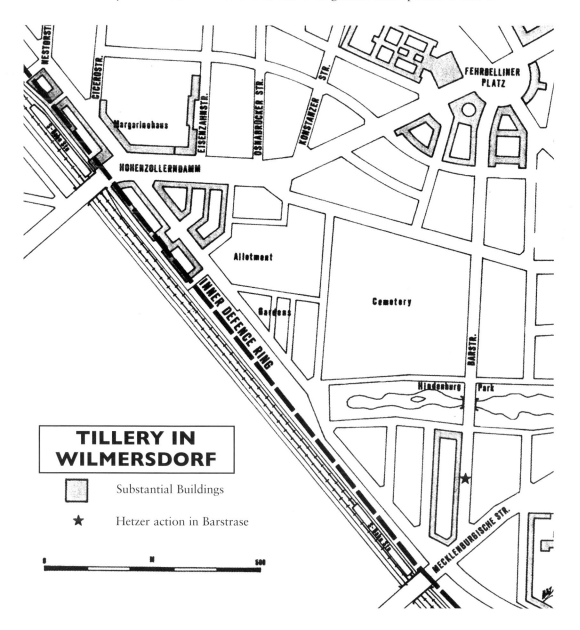

TILLERY IN WILMERSDORF

☐ Substantial Buildings

★ Hetzer action in Barstrase

Gerhard Tillery.

burst into flames with the first shot. Meanwhile the Russian infantry could be seen in the buildings, so we had to withdraw over the bridge to the cemetery.

On the 30th April we changed position again to the Margarinehaus on the Hohenzollerndamm, where there was also a Mark IV tank from our regiment. In the Margarinehaus were thousands of civilians who had lost everything in the last few days, mainly women and children. There were no supplies and the children were crying for bread. Unholy chaos reigned. There were also many soldiers here, and the Russians were only 100 metres away.

On the afternoon of the 30th we moved back to Fehrbelliner Platz, where there were some large administrative buildings. Most of the city was now in Russian hands and we were being pushed in closer together. The Russian artillery fire was steadily increasing and the city lay under constant bombardment. For days we had not had any sleep and there was no longer any warm food to be had. We would have to see how we could survive. Nevertheless, we did not go hungry, for the civilians, with whom we were

A Hetzer such as Gerhard Tillery escorted.

always in contact, kept giving us snacks. However, these were the worst days in my experience, for in the front line one knew where Ivan was, but here we had always to be ready for surprises. Often we would be in a building and a little later the Russians would come and bring the windows and cellar exits under fire.

That evening I was in a building opposite the Margarinehaus. The Russian fire had diminished and the inhabitants had come up out of their cellars. A woman brewed me a cup of tea and gave me a few biscuits. As if in normal peacetime, I was sitting in an armchair in her sitting room, although the Russians were only thirty to forty metres away. Suddenly I heard our tank and a machine gun firing. The Russians were attacking again. Fortunately it was very dark and I was able to cross over to the Margarinehaus. We withdrew back to Fehrbelliner Platz again.

During the night the Russians were able to close in on the Margarinehaus from three sides. Our Mark IV was also there and could not withdraw, because it was not known which streets were occupied by the Russians. On the morning of the 1st May, Second Lieutenant Lorenz sent me to look for a way out for them. 'Don't miss anything, though!' he said. At first I tried to reach the Margarinehaus via Eisenzahnstrasse. I ran across and was shot at by a Russian anti-tank gun, but was saved by diving into a cellar entrance as the splinters smashed into the wall above my head.

Then I tried again via Cicerostrasse and Nestorstrasse, but I was spotted in both of them and shot at. The only route remaining was via Osnabrücker Strasse [now Bielefelder Strasse]. I ran from cellar entrance to cellar entrance

The dreaded *Stalin-Organs* being loaded in a Berlin street.

and when I had to cross an open space, I opened fire on the Russians. There was not a single German soldier to be seen anywhere around. The last stretch was open ground, but I was not shot at as I had expected, and I covered it at the run. I reported to the commandant of the Margarinehaus, a lieutenant colonel who had already given up hope of further contact with the outside world. There were now some 800 men in the building and when I explained to him that there was still a chance of getting away, he immediately ordered the building to be cleared.

The Mark IV tank had left during the evening and driven back. I had now to return to my tank, which was about 300 metres away. Explosions, bangs and whistles were going on everywhere and I was only about 100 metres from my tank when suddenly a shell howled close by. I instinctively dived for cover, but was too late. I was intending to take cover behind a windowsill, but the blast caught me and blew me on top of it instead. At the same moment I felt a burning pain in my upper left arm and in my rear. I felt around with my right hand and found blood. I had splinters in my right arm and rear. I hobbled into the building, feeling quite numb. After I had shouted several times, someone answered from the cellar and two young girls of about 18 came up and took me down into the cellar, where they applied first aid dressings. After about half an hour, I hobbled back to the tank. Second Lieutenant Lorenz let me sit aboard and took me to the battalion command post, where the medical centre was located, and there I was bandaged properly.[4]

The bus takes you to **Fehrbelliner Platz** where you switch to the U-Bahn, taking the **U-1 Warschauer Strasse** two stops to **Spichernstrasse**, where you change again to the **U-9 Osloer Strasse** two stops back to the Zoo.

CHAPTER FIFTEEN

BERLIN TOUR E: WANNSEE AND POTSDAM

Wannsee – Glienicke Bridge – Potsdam Conference – KGB Prison

LIMITATIONS: The KGB Prison is only open at weekends.

AREA: This short tour covers places of interest at Wannsee in south-west Berlin and in Potsdam.

DIRECTIONS: From the Zoo take the **S-7 Potsdam** six stops to **Wannsee,** where you turn left out of the station and walk down Kronprinzenweg to Königstrasse, following the Prussian kings' route from Schloss Berlin to their palaces in Potsdam. On your right is the bight of the Grosser Wannsee lake, and below you the landing stages for the pleasure-boats operating on the Havel.

The Havel at Wannsee with Schwaneninsel in the distance to the left.

WANNSEE

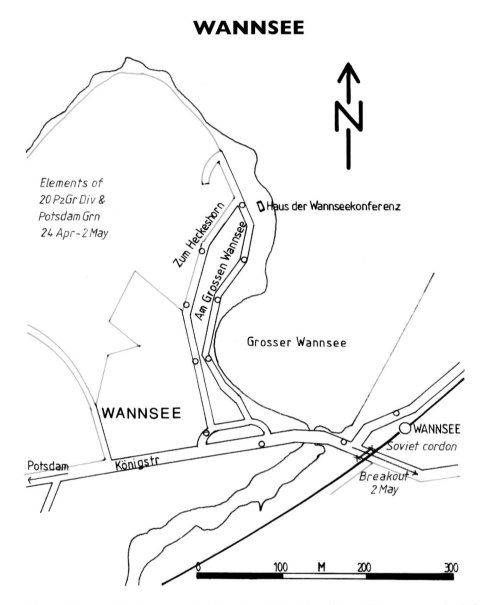

Elements of
20 PzGr Div &
Potsdam Grn
24 Apr - 2 May

Zum Heckeshorn

Am Grossen Wannsee

☐ Haus der Wannseekonferenz

Grosser Wannsee

WANNSEE

Potsdam Königstr

○ WANNSEE

Soviet cordon

Breakout
2 May

0   100   M   200   300

Turn right on a bridge over the channel linking the Kleiner Wannsee on the left with the Grosser Wannsee and you will come to Wannsee Island, surrounded by lakes and canals, and extending to the Glienicke Bridge leading into Potsdam, an important site in the battle of Berlin.

Major General Georg Scholze's 20th Panzergrenadier Division was assigned to the defence of the Teltow Canal in the Teltow–Stahnsdorf sector by General Weidling when Hitler appointed him commander of the Berlin Defence Area, but the division had been so depleted after the battle of the Seelow Heights as a result of false orders issued by so-called *Seydlitz*-troops (turn-coat German soldiers working and fighting for the Soviets) that only 92 men, including the general, actually reached this new location. So many had gone on to the Döberitz Training Area west of Berlin that they were able to reorganise as a panzergrenadier brigade, but they played no further part in the battle of Berlin.

When Marshal Koniev attacked across the canal on the morning of 24 April 1945, what was left of the division was forced back on to Wannsee Island, where it became isolated from the rest of the Berlin defence. The Wannsee Island defence was then reinforced from Potsdam by elements of Lieutenant General Hellmuth Reymann's Army Detachment *Spree*, to whose command the remnants of the division were transferred on 27 April following the suicide of Major General Scholze when he received the news of the deaths of his family in an air raid.

During the night of 28 April the 10th Guards Tank Corps of 4th Guards Tank Army, supported by the 350th Rifle Division, attacked the south-western tip of Wannsee Island and established a bridgehead across the Teltow Canal. From Marshal Koniev's memoirs, it is clear that he disapproved of this action, which he saw as an unnecessary distraction from the main objectives. As it was, the presence of these German troops effectively preoccupied the 10th Tank Corps until the very end of the battle.

The railway bridge underpass was barricaded by the Soviets, and it was through there that the Wannsee Island garrison attempted a break-out on the night of 1 May, the Soviets exacting a heavy toll. But some 2–3,000 crossed the Teltow Canal further east and subsequently fought their way through the village of Schenkenhorst, giving the headquarters personnel of the 4th Guards Tank Army a most unwelcome surprise. The survivors then went on to cross the autobahn ring, heading south-west to link up with General Walter Wenck's 12th Army, which was believed to be heading towards them. Friedrich Schöneck, one of the survivors, reported:

> Our advance is suddenly interrupted as we unexpectedly emerge from a little wood on to a Russian airfield. We can see the aircraft all lined up on it. We have no time to think. We can neither go back nor turn away. We charge on to the airfield like a crowd of demons and, before the Russian guards can grasp what is happening, grenades and *Panzerfausts* are going off and the machine guns making sieves out of the silver birds with their 'Red Star'. The chaos is complete, with screams, curses and explosions mingling. The dazed pilots try to get into their machines, and only on the far left do they succeed. With a thundering roar they race over the runway and gain height, but they don't fly away; they turn in a big loop and are then above us. Their cannon rake the airfield, shooting up the machines and the mob of German and Russian soldiers running around firing indiscriminately.
>
> The screams of the wounded mix with the sounds of cannon fire. We seek cover in the furrows of a ploughed field beyond the airfield. Lying on our backs, we aim with our weapons at the low flying IL-2s attacking us. They fly so low we can pick out the pilot's faces in their cockpits. The wounded scream and call out for medical orderlies. Some try to run for it but are shot down immediately. . . . It seems an eternity before the planes pull away, leaving the

field full of stunned and screaming people, full of collapsed, torn bodies.

But this infernal finale is not over yet. Something growls in the shadow of the trees of the little wood and tank tracks screech. Shells burst in the field with a hellish din among our lost band. Machine guns rattle, completing the deadly work. Russian infantry storm in from left and right. We no longer have a chance. Our fate is sealed.

From the two or three thousand that broke out from *Festung Wannsee* only 187 are still alive, some lightly wounded. . . . Among us are *Wehrmacht* administrators, RAD men, *Hitlerjugend*, female auxiliaries, civilians and RAD girls. The sorting out begins. The women disappear from our view, pushed into a barn. Their cries and screams, the joking and laughing of the Russian guards, drive home to us with loathing and disgust the fact that we have been conquered.[1]

Now walk across the Wannsee Bridge to the next turning off to the right, Am Grossen Wannsee, at the far end of which is the *Haus der Wannseekonferenz*, where on 20 January 1942 Reinhard Heydrich, head of the *Reichs Security Main Office* (RSHA) under Heinrich Himmler, held a conference with representatives of the various ministries involved for the implementation of the 'Final Solution' for the deportation and elimination of Europe's Jews. To visit the exhibition there, turn back to the last bus stop on Königstrasse and take bus **114 Bf. Wannsee**, which makes a circuit of the one-way system, five stops to the villa.

Haus der Wannseekonferenz

Entry free: open daily 1000–1800, except for public holidays.

Haus der Wannseekonferenz.

Continue along Königstrasse, taking bus **116 Glienicke Brücke** to the famous bridge, which is where the bus turns around. As you leave the built-up area to traverse woodland, you pass beneath a television tower on your right at the road's highest point; this is usually just visible from the Glockenturm at the Olympic Stadium. Then, as the road begins to bend, you pass alongside the park of Schloss Klein Glienicke, a small princely palace with gilded lions guarding the entrance. Alight at the Glienicke Bridge.

The original bridge connecting Wannsee Island to Potsdam was blown on 28 April 1945 to protect the defence's flank. Extending to your right along the shore of the Jungfernsee lake is a path that was connected by a pontoon bridge at the far end to the opposite bank of the Havel, enabling access to Gatow Airfield during the Potsdam Conference.

Cross the bridge, the centre of which constitutes the inter-city boundary. Here

The pontoon bridge.

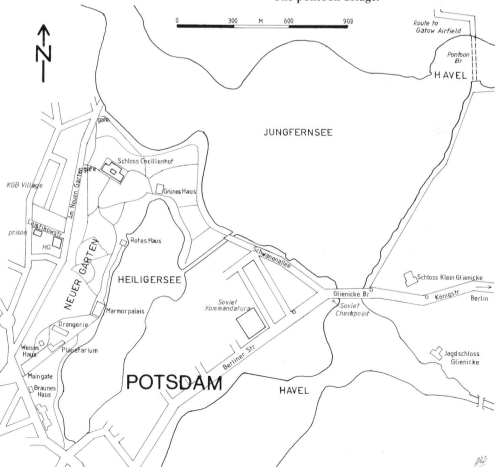

The blown Glienicke Bridge with a wrecked German tank and a Soviet temporary replacement bridge behind.

The Glienicke Bridge today and as it was at the time of the spy exchanges.

various spy exchanges took place during the Cold War, including those of Gary Powers, the American U-2 pilot shot down over the Soviet Union, and of the Jewish dissident Anatoly Scharansky in 1986.

Access to Potsdam over the bridge during the Cold War was limited to accredited diplomats to the East German government and members of the Allied military liaison missions to the commander-in-chief of the Soviet Group of Forces in

The inner courtyard with its red star.

Schloss Cecilienhof.

Stalin, Truman and Churchill with Atlee, who was to replace him halfway through the conference, behind.

Germany. These missions each had a villa as an official base in Potsdam but actually operated out of West Berlin. At the far end of the bridge in the bay on the left was located the Soviet control point, with an East German one further back on the right.

Turn off to the right down Schwanenallee and make your way into the grounds of **Schloss Cecilienhof**, the building in which the Potsdam Conference took place between 17 July and 2 August 1945.

Schloss Cecilienhof

Open 0900–1700 hours in summer, 0900–1600 hours in winter.

Guided tours at €5 are available in English.

Go past the entrance to the Cecilienhof and follow the drive out through a gate in the perimeter wall to come to the road Am Neuen Garten, where you turn left as far as Leistikowstrasse. The large building on the street corner opposite housed the headquarters of the KGB during the Cold War and was enclosed with houses beyond it into what was known as the 'KGB Village'.

As you go up Leistikowstrasse, the last building on the left was converted into the KGB prison for the Potsdam area and was where spies were lodged immediately

The KGB prison in Potsdam.

The former KGB Headquarters in Potsdam.

prior to their exchange on the Glienicke Bridge. The prison boundary walls have since been removed, and it is now run as a museum by volunteers at weekends. Entrance is up a metal staircase around the far corner. Sadly the building is in such a poor state of repair that access to the cells on the lower floor is no longer possible, but the toilet space and upper cells give some idea of the primitive and brutal conditions that prevailed. The text to the displays is in German, but an explanatory leaflet in English is available from the office.

KGB Gefängnis Potsdam

Open weekends only 1100–1700 hours.

Entry free, donations welcome.

Return via the Cecilienhof grounds and Schwanenallee to the Glienicke Bridge to take bus **116 Bf. Wannsee** back to the station, from where the **S-7 Ahrensfelder** will take you back to the Zoo.

You should bear in mind that Potsdam contains many visitor attractions, such as the royal palaces of Sans Souci and the Neues Palais, and even the old city itself, but these lie outside the scope of this guide.

The prisoners' primitive toilet facilities.

A KGB prison cell.

CHAPTER SIXTEEN

BERLIN TOUR F: COLD WAR OPTIONS

The Wall Museum – *Stasi* HQ – Hohenschönhausen Prison

AREA: As separate places of interest devoted to the Cold War, the following locations are suggested:

Erich Mielke, Minister of State Security, who controlled 85,000 full-time and 170,000 part-time spies.

A – The Wall Museum (Bernauer Strasse)

Starting from **Friedrich-strasse**, take either the **S-1 Oranienburg** or the **S-25 Hennigsdorf** two stops to **Nordbahnhof**, where you continue along the platform to the far exit, where you turn right and cross Gartenstrasse into **Bernauer Strasse**. As you cross the road, note the line in the roadway denoting the original position of the Wall. The museum is located at no. 111 on the left-hand side of the street with a display of the Wall layout opposite.

The *Stasi* HQ Museum off Ruschestrasse.

Dokumentationszentrum Berliner Mauer

Entry free: open Tuesdays–Sunday 1000–1800 hours (1700 hours in winter).

One-hour tours available at weekends at 1400 hours.

B – The Secret Police (*Stasi*) Normannenstrasse Headquarters

This has already been included as an option in Berlin Tour C, but as a separate item it can be reached from **Alexanderplatz** by taking the **U-5 Höhnow**, travelling seven stops to **Magdalenstrasse**. Emerging on Frankfurter Allee, turn up Ruschestrasse and the museum is a few yards along on your right.

C – Hohenschönhausen Prison

Again starting from **Alexanderplatz**, take tram 6 U-Bf **Schwarzkopfstr.** fourteen stops to **Gensler Strasse**, opposite the Berlin Water Works, where you alight and cross Landsberger Allee into Gensler Strasse until you come to the junction with Freienwalder Strasse, where the prison is located at Gensler Strasse 66. The obscure location of this prison, concealed in a *Stasi*-owned housing estate, was a deliberate security precaution.

Originally run by the Soviets as a special detention camp for suspected Nazis and opponents of the Communist regime, it contained up to 4,200 inmates

A water torture cell in the U-Boat – the underground part of the prison.

A line of cells in the U-Boat.

All the comforts of a cell in the modern *Stasi* prison block.

in horrendous conditions, including the underground part known as the U-Boat, where torture was commonplace, including standing-only cells and the use of water torture to extract confessions.

The *Stasi*, who took over the camp in 1951 as a remand prison, used more subtle methods to obtain the same ends. Some of the guides are former inmates.

Gedenkstätte Berlin-Hohenschönhausen

Admittance free: guided tours daily at 1100 and 1300 hours.

Advance arrangements for an English-speaking guide advisable.

Tel: 030-98-60-82-36

CHAPTER SEVENTEEN

BERLIN TOUR G

Halbe – Brand – Baruth – Kummersdorf – Wünsdorf Garrison Museum

LIMITATIONS: Private transport is required. Kummersdorf Artillery Ranges Museum is only open on Sundays from 1300 to 1700 hours. Also see the entry on the Wünsdorf Garrison Museum at the end of this section.

AREA: This tour involves visits to the battlefield and the German cemetery at Halbe, the former main Soviet airport at Brand, the Soviet cemetery at Baruth, Kummersdorf Ranges Museum, Wünsdorf Museum, the headquarters site of the Group of Soviet Forces in Germany at Zossen-Wünsdorf, and the remains of the German Army headquarters and later Soviet nuclear headquarters at Waldstadt.

DIRECTIONS: Leave Berlin on **Route 96a**, which becomes the **113 Autobahn** until the **Schönefelder Kreuz** and then becomes the **13 Autobahn** (E36/E55) for Dresden. Take exit **5a Teupitz**, turning left for **Halbe**, passing through the village to come to **Märkische Buchholz**, stopping at the junction with the **B173**.

The main square in Märkische Buchholz.

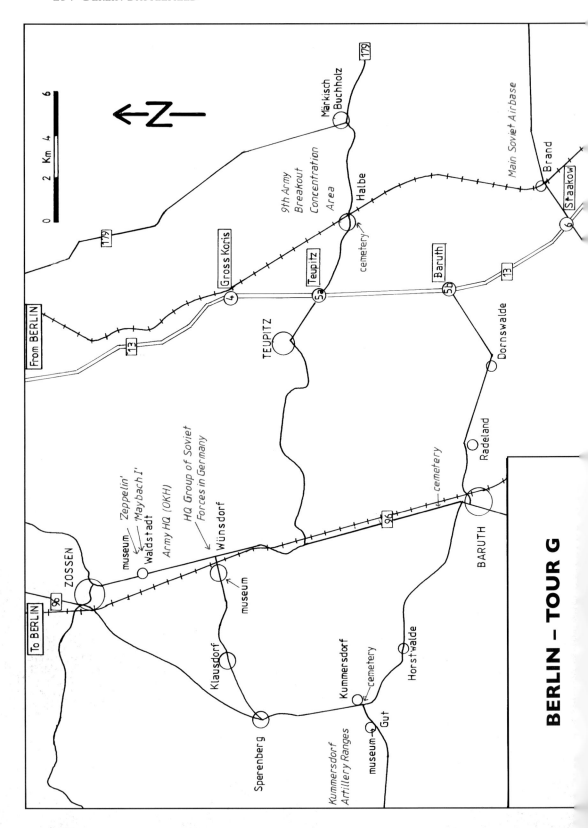

BERLIN – TOUR G

It was here that many of the columns of refugees sheltering in the Spreewald and those units and troops of the German 9th Army that had survived the main Soviet attack of 16 April 1945 converged to deploy in the woods between here and Halbe for the break-out to the west, aiming away from the Red Army to reach the American lines on the Elbe.

Wolfgang Fleisher described the desperate scene in Märkische Buchholz on 25 April 1945:

> The village was burning. The concrete bridge over the Dahme had been badly damaged in an air attack and was no longer usable by vehicles. Units of the 9th Army were making their way to the north-west, coming through the Kleine Wasserburg Forest and across the Bürgerheide Heath up to the Dahme on a broad front, leaving abandoned vehicles, discarded weapons and equipment strewn along the forest aisles.
>
> During the night sappers threw two emergency bridges across the Dahme. Because of the mainly swampy ground, heavy vehicles could only get to the river south-west of the Hermsdorf [Grossemühle] Mill and Herrlichenrath. The sappers' work was interrupted from time to time by Soviet night bombers and occasional artillery fire in between. The first vehicles crossed over once it was fully dark, the tanks grinding their way over the banks of the river with engines thundering and tracks spinning, while refugees continued to hurry across the bridges between them.
>
> Gradually the congested mass of men and vehicles made its way westwards, the Berlin road [Reichsstrasse 179] was crossed, and the Hammer Forest

Halbe railway station from the level crossing.

absorbed the refugees. An unholy chaos reigned. Soviet artillery fire kept forcing people to take cover. Hissing and howling rockets came in between and left flat, smoking craters. Sharp-edged splinters swept across the woodland and exacted numerous victims among those pressed close to the ground. Almost continuous sounds of combat could be heard to the east, south and north, heavy firing coming also from the direction of the autobahn.

Having crossed the Dahme, the units of the 9th Army moved along the Berlin road and through the Hammer Forest to Halbe. With daylight the Soviet ground-attack aircraft would be engaging the encircled troops again, making movement even more difficult. The columns became stuck at the crossroads east of Klein Köris. Several IL-2s flew along the road, firing with their machine guns and rockets, the ammunition belts and cartridges clattering down on the road surface, the tracer bullets biting into vehicles, horses and human bodies.[1]

Return to **Halbe** and stop at the level crossing. Rudi Lindner wrote of the evening of 28 April 1945:

THE BATTLE OF HALBE,
WITH BREAKOUT ROUTES

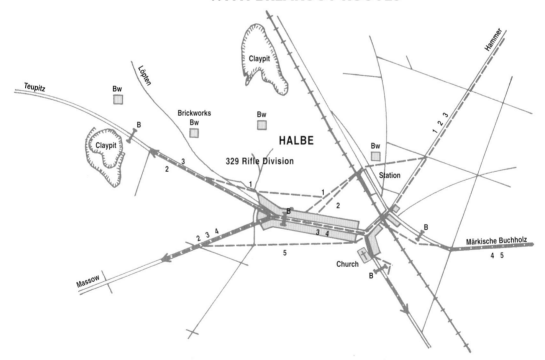

B	Anti-tank barricade
1	Hammer – Brickworks/Station – Teupitz
2	Hammer – Station – Village Centre – Massow
3	Hammer – Station – part to Teurow, part to Massow
4	Märkische Buchholz – part to Teurow, part to Massow
5	Märkische Buchholz – Level Crossing – Massow

At about 1800 hours on the 28th April, the heavy weapons fired a barrage on Halbe, after which the guns were blown up. Then at about 1830 hours our armoured column moved out of the assembly area toward Märkische Buchholz and Halbe. We thrust through Märkische Buchholz without encountering any significant resistance, then along a woodland track towards Halbe. The northern armoured spearhead of the Panzergrenadier Division *Kurmark* was also rolling along another woodland track toward Halbe. Short halts for observation and reconnaissance delayed our advance.

A Russian anti-tank barrier in front of Halbe caused the first big delay. A mortar battery went into action and fired a salvo on the nests of resistance on the eastern edge of Halbe, while our leading tank platoon engaged the barrier. The Russian security forces then pulled back into Halbe village. Our armoured vanguard was then ordered to push on into Halbe, and our *Tiger* tanks set off again. We drove into the village south of the railway station, reaching a straight street lined with trees, where the back gardens of the first houses lay.

We thought that here too we would encounter only minor resistance, but with a blast, all hell broke loose. We had driven into an ambush!

At this point I should mention that following us in the woods to the right and left of our armoured column, if a little further back, was a stream of soldiers and refugees, who kept closing up to us whenever we stopped. In their fear of losing contact and becoming prisoners of the Russians, but also because of nonexistent or insufficient combat experience, most of the soldiers were conducting themselves in a totally unmilitary fashion, so that unfortunately very many of them had to pay with their lives for it. For instance, behind each tank in Halbe there was a cluster of some 40 to 60 people seeking shelter, and every time we stopped the numbers increased. In addition, many soldiers were unarmed and most of the soldiers that were armed did not or were unable to use their weapons. In practice, only the leading tank could fire forward, while we grenadiers sitting on top fired obliquely into the roofs and windows.

It was now about 2000 hours as we drove into Halbe and another anti-tank barrier appeared before us, but this time open. The leading tank had got to within about 70 metres when it fired a shot to clear the way, drove on and stopped about 30 metres from the barrier.

Suddenly the inferno broke out with concentrated anti-tank gun fire coming from ahead, artillery and mortar fire from above, and rifle fire from the roofs and windows of the houses right and left of the street. The artillery fire with explosive shrapnel and phosphorus shells, and the mortar bombs, caused especially frightful casualties among the numerous, exposed and crammed together groups of people. The street was immediately filled with dead and wounded. Panic, confusion and deadly fear could be seen in the faces of the living, as cries for help came from the wounded and dying.

Our leading tank received a direct hit and started burning. Our second tank tried to turn, got stuck and was hit by a phosphorus shell, and also caught fire. The phosphorus shells burst with glowing white splashes on the tank, and there was phosphor everywhere on our steel helmets and tent-halves. Stinking smoke erupted as the tank began to burn. The crew baled out and we also jumped off and ran to the third tank.[2]

Drive on into the village until you come to the sign for the *Waldfriedhof* on your left and follow it through to the woodland cemetery. This vast war cemetery, the largest on German soil, came about as a result of the efforts of Pastor Ernst Teichmann and his wife. Upon his return from the war, during which he had been a padre with the *Wehrmacht*, Pastor Teichmann took over a parish in the Harz Mountains, where he started concerning himself with the graves of the war dead to be found there. He first heard about Halbe in 1947 and went to see for himself. He then applied for and was accepted for the post at Halbe four years later. Despite the indifference and even hostility encountered from the East German authorities, Teichmann and his wife, with the help of some members of the community, applied themselves assiduously to the task of identifying and reinterring the war dead from the area with reverence and care, until his death in 1983. By the end of 1958 the official record showed 19,178 reinterred, and by the end of 1989 this figure had risen to 20,222 bodies, of which some 8,000 had been identified.

Row upon row of graves fill the Halbe cemetery.

The woodland cemetery memorial at Halbe.

A dead horse gun team.

Not all the war dead came from the immediate vicinity, for the East German expansion of opencast coal mining in the Lausitz area resulted in most of the war dead from that area being transferred to Halbe. Remains are still being discovered at a rate of about 200 per year to add to the cemetery's total. It also contains the remains of some 4,500 prisoners who died in the Soviet 'Special Camp No. 5' in Ketschendorf, near Fürstenwalde, during the period 1945–7.

Return to the autobahn and turn left to the second exit **6 Staakow**. After driving along this stretch of the autobahn shortly after the breakthrough by the 9th Army, the Soviet writer Konstantin Simonov described the scene:

Shortly before reaching the great Berlin Ring, I came across a sight that I will certainly never forget. In this area the autobahn is enclosed on both sides by thick woods that had been split by a cutting whose ends were out of sight.

The German troops that had still been standing on the Oder when the fighting in Berlin had already started, had used this route to try to thrust their way across the autobahn. The intersection of the cutting and autobahn that we had reached had apparently before dawn, only a few hours previously, become the site of their final defeat. In front of us lay Berlin, on our right the cutting completely blocked with quite improbable scenes – a pile

Some of the dead scattered around in the forests.

of tanks, cars, armoured cars, trucks, specialised vehicles, ambulances, all literally piled up on top of each other, tipped over, sticking up in the air. Apparently while trying to turn round and escape, these vehicles had knocked down hundreds of trees. And in this chaos of iron, wood, weapons, baggage, papers, lie burnt and blackened objects that I couldn't identify, a mass of mutilated bodies. And this extended all along the cutting as far as one could see. And all around in the woods dead, dead and yet more dead, the corpses of those that fell while running around under fire. Dead and, as I then saw, some alive among them. There were wounded lying under blankets and greatcoats, sitting leaning against trees, some bandaged, others bleeding and not yet bandaged. Some of the wounded, as I only later noticed, were lying alongside the edge of the autobahn. Then I saw some figures moving among the wounded, apparently doctors or medical orderlies. That was all on the right-hand side.

The autobahn ran down the centre, a broad asphalted road that had already been cleared for traffic. Along a stretch of two hundred metres it is pocked with small and large craters that the military vehicles driving to Berlin have to zigzag round.

The cutting continues on the left-hand side, and part of the German column that had already crossed the autobahn was destroyed here. Again, as far as the eye could see, a mess of burnt-out, smashed, overturned vehicles. Again dead and wounded. As an officer hastily informed me, the whole of this vast column had come under fire from several regiments of heavy artillery and a few regiments of *Katyushas* that had previously been concentrated in the vicinity and had fired on the cutting on the assumption that the Germans would try to break through here.

We left this scene of horror and after a few kilometres saw a convoy of five or six ambulances coming towards us. Apparently someone had summoned reinforcements from our medical battalions but, considering the scale of the slaughter, these five or six vehicles would be no more than a drop in the ocean.[3]

At the **Staaken** exit turn left for **Brand**, about 2 kilometres away, to cross the railway line and enter the former main Soviet air base in Germany. The base was stripped by the Soviets before they left, but there is still quite a lot to be seen. In the centre of the airfield is a vast new hangar that was built after Unification in order to construct a large cargo-carrying airship. The project failed when the company concerned went into liquidation for lack of funding, but the hangar has since been taken over by a company calling itself 'Tropical Islands'.

Return by the same route and turn right on the autobahn to the next exit **5b Baruth/Massow** and then turn left for the town of **Baruth**, passing through the villages of Dornswalde and Radeland on the way.

A major action took place in the woods immediately north-west of Baruth on the night of 25 April 1945 as a result of a premature break-out plan by General Theodor Busse of the German 9th Army, who had hoped to achieve a purely military breakthrough unencumbered by refugees, but then failed to support the

A model of the vast airship hangar at Brand.

attacking troops when they ran into difficulties. The battle groups of Colonel Hans von Luck's Panzergrenadier Regiment 125 with the remaining *Panthers* of Panzer Regiment 22 and SS-Colonel Rüdiger Pipkorn with his SS Police Grenadier Regiment 35 and the remaining tanks of the SS Panzer Division *Frundsberg* converged on Baruth, but they were expected by the Soviets, who had set up a blocking position that included dug-in *Stalin* tanks. By dawn it was clear that the Germans were making no headway, and they were rapidly running out of ammunition, as was reported back to General Busse, but the latter ordered them to wait for the arrival of the remainder of the 9th Army. However, Colonel von Luck ordered his force to disband and try to break through in small groups. SS-Colonel Pipkorn was killed and von Luck captured on his way back to report his decision to Busse. Some of their men actually reached the Elbe, but most were either killed or captured.

Elisabeth Schulz described the arrival of the Soviets in Baruth:

I was then 19 years old and working as an auxiliary nurse in Schloss Baruth. At about 0900 hours on 20 April 1945 we were told that it was everyone for themselves. The wounded could not be taken along with us. We were three nurses, two medical orderlies and two *Hiwis* [Russian volunteers]. We decided to stay until all the wounded were gone. Some left on wagons with the nurses and doctors.

With part of the Schloss already on fire, we put the last 18 severely wounded on a haycart. They were only wearing shirts, as the quartermasters had shut up shop and made off. What the poor boys had to suffer was indescribable. But there were no complaints, they were grateful for being saved, as they thought. The Hiwis had found two horses and we set off across the Schloss park. By the time we reached the meadows, the Russian tanks had

The Soviet cemetery outside Baruth.

already passed us, and there was firing from all sides. We quickly laid the wounded down on the grass and took cover. Everything then happened very quickly. We watched the Russians charge across the meadows and shoot the medical orderlies, nurses and wounded. I have to thank my fellow nurse, Hedwig Steicke, for saving my life. She ran back with me across the park.

We lay there all night long and then joined the refugees from Baruth next morning, running for our lives across the meadows and being shot at by low-flying aircraft.[4]

At the junction with the **B96** in **Baruth** turn right until you come to the Soviet cemetery on your right. This was established in 1947 and contains 1,300 Red Army soldiers in 22 mass graves.

Then return to Baruth, taking the road leading to **Horstwalde** on the right at the entrance to the town. Pass through Horstwalde and you will come to a crossroads at the entrance to **Kummersdorf Gut**, where you turn left. Just beyond the first bend in the road there is an inhabited area on your right and Kosumstrasse 5, where the museum is located.

Museum Kummersdorf Schiessplatz

Open Sundays only 1300–1700.
Tel: 033703-77048

SS-Lieutenant Bärmann wrote of his experience here:

At dawn we came to the station for the Kummersdorf Training Area. Again anti-tank guns everywhere. The station, workshops and fuel depot were on fire. We broke through to the station, the dead remaining where they fell. A couple of lads rolled up a barrel of fuel. We still had five tanks left and each needed its share. One tank commander who had lost his vehicle appropriated a T-34, marked it with a swastika flag and SS pennant and took over the lead.

We went round the ranges in a big curve and hid ourselves in the woods. A bit of peace at last, but nothing to eat.[5]

And SS-Captain Lobmeyer wrote:

We fought our way across the Kummersdorf ranges, having to deal with some *Seydlitz* units, who kept pressing us to surrender, but we fought on to the west. More and more tanks and other vehicles had to be blown up and abandoned due to fuel or ammunition running out.[6]

As day broke on 30 April 1945 the last *Tigers* of SS Heavy Panzer Battalion 502 moved across the eastern firing range and then crossed over to the western firing range and stopped in the woods to the north-west. There was an industrial railway track on the second firing range, so the wounded were loaded on to wagons and towed along to the end of the ranges by a *Tiger*.

The exhausted troops had to rest and the various combat teams needed a chance to reorganise. A security screen was established and reconnaissance patrols sent out, which reported back that there was a strong Russian cordon with tanks and anti-tank guns deployed along the line of the Trebbin–Luckenwalde road (B101).

Königstiger no. 231 of the SS Heavy Panzer Battalion 502 abandoned in a swamp near Beelitz, after running out of fuel.

The German cemetery at Kummersdorf Gut.

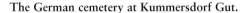

German command vehicles abandoned in Dobbrikow.

Go back to the crossroads in **Kummersdorf Gut**. Across the road, just off to the right, is the cemetery containing the German victims of the fighting in this area. Continue along the main road to the left, passing through Sperenberg and Klausdorf to reach **Wünsdorf**. Entering the village, take the second street to the right, Schulstrasse, go round a bend to the right and you come to the old schoolhouse, which is now a museum mainly devoted to the local area in general, but containing some highly interesting military material and well worth a visit.

Museum des Teltow

Open March–October weekdays 1000–1700 hours, weekends 1400–1700 hours, November–February weekdays 1000–1600 hours; weekends 1300–1600 hours. Entry €1.

Return to the main road and turn right and continue to the central crossroads, where you take Chausseestrasse straight on, cross the railway and turn left on the **B96**, here called Berliner Strasse. You are now passing through the centre of the old Wünsdorf Garrison area, later developed during the Third Reich to accommodate a tank training school and then to accommodate the wartime establishments of the *Oberkommando der Wehrmacht* (Armed Forces GHQ) and the *Oberkommando des Heeres* (Army GHQ).

During Marshal Koniev's advance on Berlin from the south, he exhorted the commander of the 3rd Guards Tank Army: 'Comrade Rybalko, you are moving like a snail. One brigade is fighting, the rest of the army standing still. I order you to cross the Baruth/Luckenwalde line through the swamps along several routes and deployed in battle order. Report fulfilment. Koniev.'

The 3rd Guards Tank Army duly advanced 37 miles on 27 April, taking Baruth and almost reaching Zossen before disaster struck. The leading brigade of the 6th Guards Tank Corps ran out of fuel and was destroyed piecemeal with *Panzerfausts* close to the *Maybach* bunker complex by either *Hitler Youth* or *Volkssturm* units.[7]

HQ GSFG with its statue of Lenin.

The Wünsdorf camp guard company together with six to eight tanks from the training establishment had set off to block the Soviet approach route at Luckau, but by 0600 hours that morning they reported being bypassed by Soviet armour. Only 20 survivors of this 250-strong group returned.

The complex was then taken over as the headquarters of the Soviet Group of Forces in Germany (GSFG). Some of the buildings, which the Russians stripped before leaving, have been restored and some allowed to rot.

Continue along this road until you come to Waldstadt at the far end of what was a closed-off area while occupied by Soviet troops. Here you turn off right and follow the main road through this newly resettled village to reach the parking lot outside the Wünsdorf Garrison Museum at 9 Gutenbergstrasse. The museum has a restaurant and an interesting display on the everyday life of a Soviet soldier, but it also offers various tours of the adjacent former German and Soviet installations as follows:

A – *Maybach I* and *Zeppelin*

100-minute tour of the *Maybach I*, the secret wartime headquarters of the *Oberkommando des Heeres*, and of the still-intact *Zeppelin* bunker that had

The series of armoured doors protecting the entrance to the GSFG nuclear command bunker.

Bunks lining the wall of a passageway in the GSFG bunker.

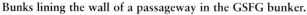

housed the communications centre for the German armed forces and was later converted into the nuclear warfare headquarters for the GSFG. Mondays–Fridays 1400 hours; weekends November–March 1300 and 1500 hours, April–October 1200, 1400 and 1600 hours. Price €9.

B – Special Tour of *Maybach I* and *Zeppelin*

This 4^1/2-hour tour is available only with prior booking. Price €25.

C – In the Russians' Footsteps

A 2-hour tour of the Soviet 16th Air Army's installations, including *UK 20* and *Panzir*, only by prior arrangement on Saturdays at 1000 hours. Price €10.

D – Four Bunkers

A 2^1/2-hour tour of *Maybach I*, *Zeppelin*, *Panzir* and *UK 20*, for groups only. Price €12.

E – 'The Forbidden City'

A 1-hour tour of the former Soviet enclosed area, for groups only by prior arrangement. Price €3.

Garrison Museum Wünsdorf

Schulstrasse 15, D-15838 Wünsdorf.
Tel: 033702-9600.

From the museum return to the **B96**, turn right and follow this road back to Berlin.

PART THREE

REICHSTAG BATTLEFIELD

THE BATTLE FOR THE REICHSTAG

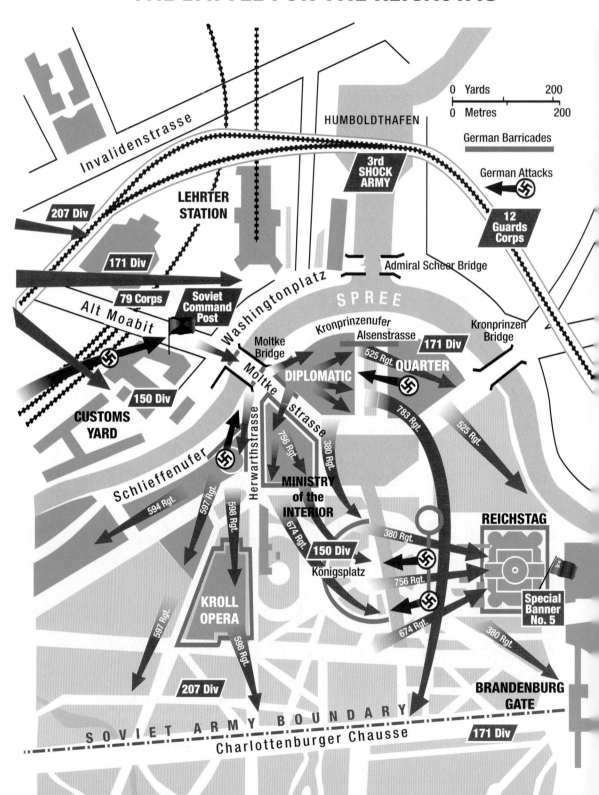

CHAPTER EIGHTEEN

REICHSTAG BATTLE SYNOPSIS

The Soviet objective in Berlin was the Reichstag, a building the Russians saw as the German equivalent of their Kremlin, the centre of governmental power, even though it had been a burnt-out ruin since soon after Hitler came to power in 1933. As the various Soviet armies converged on the city centre, including Marshal Koniev's 3rd Guards Tank Army from the south, it became a race to get there first. Fortunately, amid the burning ruins of the city, this building stood apart and had an easily identifiable outline.

It so happened that the 79th Rifle Corps of the 3rd Shock Army won the prize and fought a battle for the building that was like a play within a play, for it took place as a separate action in an area only 700 metres square as the reduction of the city took place all around it.

Major General S.N. Perevertkin's 79th Rifle Corps had already conducted two

The Reichstag battlefield with the smoke of artillery bombardment seen from a Soviet biplane. The Spree curves through the picture, in the middle of which light is reflected off the flooded pit for the diversion of the river.

assault canal crossings in the city by the time the lead scouts spotted the Reichstag through the murk that hung over the burning city, and had suffered many casualties. However, it had been able to refill its ranks with released prisoners of war on the way, so was virtually up to strength when it reached the banks of the Spree on the afternoon of 28 April 1945. Orders from above were that the Red Flag was to be hoisted on the Reichstag in time for the 1 May celebrations, so General Perevertkin was under considerable pressure to achieve his aim.

The vertical banks of the river provided no option but to cross by the Moltke Bridge, which was barricaded at either end and mined for demolition. Extending from the far end of the bridge, Moltkestrasse pointed directly at the Reichstag, but was lined on the left by the ruined remains of the near wedge of the Diplomatic Quarter, and on the right by the massive Prussian Ministry of the Interior, which would clearly have to be taken as a preliminary to the attack on the Reichstag itself.

The Moltke Bridge in earlier times with the Customs Yard, Lehrter station and Washingtonplatz on the left, and the near corners of the Diplomatic Quarter and the Prussian Ministry of the Interior on the right.

Then came a formidable obstacle in the form of the great pit that had been dug for the diversion of the Spree under Königsplatz as part of the abandoned plans for *Germania*, with the cutting for a U-Bahn curving into it from the far side; it was all now flooded, so that the attack would have to go around the pit. (Curiously enough, the Soviet maps depicting this battle omit the pit and show the 'anti-tank ditch', as they called the cutting, as a straight line across Königsplatz.) The Soviet plan for the attack involved a two-battalion attack across the bridge after the near barricade had been cleared, seizure of the near wedge of the Diplomatic Quarter, then the taking of the Ministry of the Interior building as a start point for the attack on the Reichstag.

For this task the 79th Rifle Corps had three rifle divisions, each consisting of two three-battalion regiments and one two-battalion regiment with establishments of

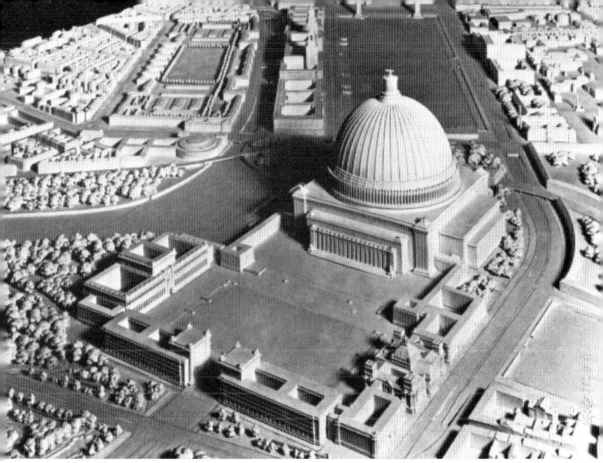

This photograph of the planning model shows how the vast dome of the Great Hall would dominate the Reichstag. On the left-hand side of the square is Hitler's palace, with the Chancellery and War Office bounding the southern side of the square.

about 500 men per battalion. Also under command were the 23rd Tank Brigade and the 10th Independent Flame-Thrower Battalion. Close air support had had to be withdrawn as the battlefield was now dangerously narrow, only 1,500 metres separating the 79th Corps from their comrades on the Landwehr Canal to the south and Friedrichstrasse to the east. However, the massed heavy artillery of four Soviet armies, plus that of the Front Reserve, were all concentrating their efforts on the centre of the city in which the Reichstag stood, and there was no shortage of ammunition.

The Soviets estimated the German opposition as 5,000 troops of various kinds, but this was a wild exaggeration. Apart from an unknown number of police officials guarding the Ministry of the Interior building, the area between the Moltke Bridge and the Brandenburg Gate was defended by a 100-strong company of Waffen-SS potential NCOs under Lieutenant Babick, later reinforced by about 100 *Volkssturm* and some 250 sailors who had just arrived in Berlin equipped as an honour guard and were totally untrained for infantry combat. Another company of the same improvised Waffen-SS Regiment *Anhalt* was deployed between the bridge and Schloss Bellevue.

General Perevertkin decided to mount a surprise attack by one battalion from each of his two leading divisions. They would push straight across the Moltke

The Diplomatic Quarter side of Moltkestrasse with the Reichstag beyond.

The Prussian Ministry of the Interior with a glimpse of the Schlieffenufer buildings behind.

Bridge with a view to establishing a primary foothold in the near corner building of the Diplomatic Quarter. Once this was achieved, the remainder of these two divisions would be pushed through to expand their hold over the whole of the Diplomatic Quarter block and the Ministry of the Interior, thus providing a firm base for their eventual attack on the Reichstag.

As night fell, the corps artillery was brought forward and deployed either side of the Moltke Bridge on Washingtonplatz and the Customs Yard, and was engaged by the odd rocket and mortar shell, the latter firing at extreme range from Potsdamer Platz S-Bahn station.

The attack across the bridge was launched at midnight and by daybreak most of the two assault divisions had squeezed through the corner cellar window on the Diplomatic Quarter and were consolidating their position inside. At daybreak the 128mm guns of the Zoo Flak-tower came into action against the guns and armour

Later in the battle, self-propelled guns and a tank line up at the entrance to Moltkestrasse.

on the northern bank of the Spree with devastating effect, and the German defence mounted a counterattack. A company about 100-strong from the 9th Parachute Division that had been cut off by the Soviet advance in the goods station yard then took advantage of the situation to charge through the Soviet lines and across the bridge. The bridge was then blown but only half of the southern span collapsed into the water, leaving sufficient room for tanks to cross.

The 150th Rifle Division attacked across the centre of Moltkestrasse into one of the main entrances of the Ministry of the Interior at 0700 hours, but the building was so large and so well defended that it took until 0400 hours next day, 30 April, to secure it.

Time was running out and General Perevertkin ordered the exhausted troops to launch an attack on the Reichstag half an hour later. This was rapidly squashed, for as the troops wheeled round to face the Reichstag they came under fire from the front, side and rear, where the Germans had fortified the Kroll Opera House.

General Perevertkin had no option but to call in his reserve 207th Rifle Division

Looking back at the Moltke Bridge from the corner of the Diplomatic Quarter on the morning of 29 April 1945. The missing parapet shows where the bridge has been blown.

The Kroll Opera House after the battle.

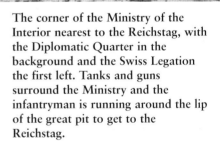

The corner of the Ministry of the Interior nearest to the Reichstag, with the Diplomatic Quarter in the background and the Swiss Legation the first left. Tanks and guns surround the Ministry and the infantryman is running around the lip of the great pit to get to the Reichstag.

A close-up of the same corner.

Wrecked Soviet tanks at the end of Moltkestrasse.

The approach to the Reichstag.

to sweep down Hewerthstrasse at the rear of the Ministry of the Interior and secure the Schlieffenufer and Kroll Opera House complexes. As soon as this attack made some progress, he was able to bring forward tanks, self-propelled guns, rocket-launchers and artillery pieces to reinforce the 150th Rifle Division in preparation for the next assault on the Reichstag.

The next attack by the 150th Rifle Division took place at 1130 hours and reached as far as the railway cutting before it was checked. Another attempt was made at 1300 hours but was again foiled when the Zoo Flak-tower's guns intervened.

It was then appreciated that no further advance was possible without the cover of nightfall that was expected as early as 1800 hours because of the heavy pall of smoke hanging over the city. Meanwhile the 171st Rifle Division succeeded in securing both wedges of the Diplomatic Quarter and reaching a position where it could provide flanking fire for the assault on the Reichstag.

The final assault took place at 1800 hours closely supported by Soviet armour and a horizontally held mortar was used to smash a way through the bricked-up

The staged hoisting of the Red Banner on the Reichstag.

entrance, after which fighting took place in the dark and unfamiliar surroundings.

A special banner assigned to the 150th Rifle Division was brought forward by a picked team that eventually found its way to the roof at the rear of the building and mounted it on an equestrian statue there in accordance with the demand to have the Red Banner hoisted on the Reichstag by 1 May.

Fighting continued within the now burning Reichstag building until about noon on 2 May, when news of the surrender reached the defenders.[1]

The Red Banner flying from the top of the Reichstag later on 2 May.

The Reichstag became the centre of attraction for the victorious Soviet soldiers.

CHAPTER NINETEEN

REICHSTAG BATTLEFIELD TOUR

OBJECTIVE: This tour walks the battle for the Reichstag and goes on to the Soviet War Memorial, the Charlottenburger Chaussee air strip, the Brandenburger Gate, Pariser Platz and briefly along the Unter den Linden to end near Alexanderplatz.

DIRECTIONS: From the Zoo station take any of the following S-Bahn trains:
S-3 Erkner
S-5 Strausberg
S-7 Ahrensfelder
S-9 Flughafen Berlin-Schönefeld
S-75 Wartenberg
three stops to the **Hauptbahnhof (Lehrter Bahnhof)**.
Alternatively, from Alexanderplatz take any of the following S-Bahn trains:
S-3 Westkreuz
S-5 Spandau
S-7 Potsdam Hbf
S-9 Westkreuz
S-75 Spandau
three stops to the **Hauptbahnhof (Lehrter Bahnhof)**.
Alighting from the train go along the platform in the direction of the Zoo and take the walkway extension to descend the stairs to street level and turn left to the junction with Alt Moabit. Here you go right up Alt Moabit a short distance to the bridge and cross the road to look down on the site of the former Lehrter goods station.

THE SITE: This was where a company of German parachutists was cut off when the first Soviet scouts of the 79th Rifle Corps approached along Alt Moabit. There is now a police station in what had been the Customs Offices where General Perevertkin rushed forward to establish his command post. He then called forward the 150th Rifle Division to this area, with the 171st Rifle Division across the road on the left and the 207th Rifle Division in reserve further back up Alt Moabit.

As you go back down Alt Moabit you get your first glimpse of the Reichstag from this direction, as the Soviet scouts did, and approach the near end of the Moltke Bridge, which, at the time the Soviets arrived, was still intact, although prepared for demolition and with barricades across either end. Here General

Perevertkin deployed his artillery to fire at virtually point-blank range from the Customs Quay on the right and Washingtonplatz on the left.

Turn right and go down the steps leading to the quayside below the bridge. Across the river is the vast structure of the new Federal Chancellery (Germany's 10 Downing Street), while the pleasure-craft probably passing by on the river are 'going on the Spree' – indeed, they gave rise to the expression!

The bridge has three spans across the river. The far one was blown by the Germans, but only the near side of the roadway fell into the river, leaving enough room for tanks to pass on the far side. The bridge has since been completely restored. Note the griffin on the far end of the bridge, then turn round and see the original one behind you. The upper part of the figure has been completely shot away, showing the intensity of fire at that point. Under the bridge you can see a copperplate engraving of a photograph taken from the corner house of the Diplomatic Quarter diagonally opposite during the fighting and reproduced here.

Go back up to the near end of the bridge, where the German barricade was bulldozed clear by Soviet tanks, and cross over to the far side, keeping to the Federal Chancellery side. Today the road leading off the bridge is Willy-Brandt-Strasse, but it was then Moltkestrasse. On the far side were four embassies, the middle two having their coach entry side in the centre, from where the 150th Rifle Division's attack on the Ministry of the Interior was launched at 0700 hours on the morning of 29 April 1945. On the near side the massive Prussian Ministry of the Interior building came to a point with Hewerthstrasse leading off behind it to the Kroll Opera House facing directly across Königsplatz to the Reichstag, and the Schlieffenufer street of houses leading off to the right. This was the area attacked by the 207th Rifle Division on 30 April. Today the southern edge of the Federal Chancellery equates to that of the former Ministry of the Interior building, so we can still get a good idea of the 1945 layout.

The remains of the Griffin from the south-west end of the bridge demonstrates the intensity of the crossfire.

The Moltke Bridge today

The Federal Chancellery.

The only remaining building on the old Diplomatic Quarter site is that of the Swiss Embassy, then a Legation, which refused to move when the others did and now has a rather ugly extension to its eastern end.

Walk forward to the front of the Federal Chancellery, whose size reflects that of its first occupant, Helmut Kohl. It has been dubbed by the Berliners the 'washing machine'. Opposite lies the new block of parliamentary offices that conveniently now defines the width of the vast pit that reached to within a street's width of the Ministry of the Interior. This pit had been dug to re-route the Spree underground beneath the square that Albert Speer had designed to cater for the Great Hall of the People, which was to be flanked by palaces for Hitler and Göring and also, surprisingly, the Reichstag.

Cross over to the pavement bordering the lawn in front of the Reichstag. It took the 150th Rifle Division 21 hours to clear the Ministry of the Interior building behind you of its German defenders, so that it was 0400 hours on 30 April before the first assault on the Reichstag could be made. Coming out of the Ministry of the Interior to wheel left towards the Reichstag, the Soviets were caught in fire coming from the Kroll Opera House behind them and the Tiergarten on their flank. This was the stage when General Perevertkin called in the 207th Rifle Division to clear the Schlieffenufer and Kroll Opera House. Behind them he sent forward tanks and self-propelled guns to reinforce the infantry, while rocket-launchers were dismantled and reassembled on the roof of the Ministry of the Interior.

The scene Hitler wanted to create with his palace facing the Reichstag, his Chancellery on the left and the OKW on the right, all to Speer's design.

The approach to the Reichstag today. The parliamentary offices on the left cover the site of the great pit intended to divert the Spree.

Try to imagine the nature of the ground as it then was: an abandoned building site strewn with rubble, with some new bunkers near the main building and other subsidiary constructions. The Reichstag, following the fire of 1933, had its doors and windows bricked up, leaving ventilation holes like gun-ports on a man-of-war. However, there were people sheltering in the cellars, including the defenders and the *Hitler Youth* gun-crews of two 88mm anti-aircraft guns from Zehlendorf that had been deployed outside, and there was also a maternity hospital, for which some emergency generators outside the back of the building provided power for light and water supplies. Unfortunately, the generators soon fell victim to artillery bombardment. The guns had been used somewhat ineffectively in a field artillery role until knocked out.

However, the second attack at 1130 hours, which was supported by the 350th Rifle Regiment wheeling around the great pit from the Swiss Embassy building, stalled at the flooded tunnel cutting that curved around the base where the Victory Column had stood. The third attempt two hours later was effectively squashed by the heavy guns firing from the Zoo Flak-tower, so the Soviets decided to wait for the cover of darkness, which came early because of all the smoke in the air, and made their fourth and final attempt at 1800 hours, backed by flanking fire from the rest of the 171st Rifle Division, which had meantime taken the remainder of the Diplomatic Quarter.

Approach the left-hand side of the Reichstag. As you advance, note the shape of the building. It was opened in 1894 to the design of Paul Wallot, with the central dome representing the imperial crown and the four corner towers the kingdoms of Bavaria, Saxony, Baden-Würtemburg and Hanover. At the time of the battle all its doors and windows were bricked up, while the dome was a different shape and slightly smaller than it is now. It was crowned by a sort of crow's nest that housed machine guns. Centrally in front of the dome over the front entrance is a platform, which then carried a Goddess of Victory, on which a group of gunners under Captain V.N. Makov secured the first Soviet flag on the roof of the Reichstag. They were later awarded the Order of the Red Banner.

The new dome is open to the public free of charge, but access is usually easier in the evenings when the queues for admittance are much shorter than during the daytime. A security check is involved and the public are excluded at 10 p.m.

Before Sir Norman Foster took over the renovation of the Reichstag, it had a brief moment of glory while still dome-less as a large 'parcel' that attracted the attention of tens of thousands in 1994 when Christo wrapped the entire edifice in a reflective sheeting that responded well to the different coloured lights played on it.

Look at the large windows to the left of the main entrance. The one on the bottom row, second from the right, is where Friedrich Ebert announced the birth of the new German Republic on 9 November 1918 following the abdication of the Kaiser.

Walk past the left-hand side of the building to the riverbank. Before Unification a hedge ran from the corner of the building towards the river's edge. Along it were displayed white crosses commemorating those who lost their lives attempting to cross into West Berlin; this is where Prime Minister Margaret Thatcher laid a wreath during her visit to the city on 29 October 1982. Today some of the crosses are displayed against the riverbank railing here, but most are now on the corner of the Tiergarten opposite the far end of the building. A line of bricks set in the pavement denotes the line of the former Wall, behind which stood a small watchtower at the river end.

In fact the sector boundary ran in a straight line through the lampposts and pillars at the rear entrance to the Reichstag, which meant that the British Military Government had to tell the Soviet Embassy to inform the

The banks of the Spree spanned by the new parliamentary offices.

The rear of the Reichstag.

East German authorities in turn whenever inspection or renovation work was required on the rear of the building. The Reichstag building within its square of pavements was recognised as Federal property throughout the Allied Occupation.

Go across to the reddish building opposite. This was the residence of the President of the Reichstag, the equivalent of the Speaker of the House of Commons, who at the time of the fire was Hermann Göring. Looking back from here, you can see a line of opaque glass blocks set in the pavement leading towards the rear of the Reichstag building. Another similar line comes in from the new building next door. These mark the tunnels by means of which the Nazis were suspected of having set fire to the building on 28 February 1933, only four weeks after coming to power. They then accused the Communists of being responsible and used this as an excuse to bring in drastic legislation to curb and suppress their political opponents. Eventually a young Dutchman of limited intelligence was accused of the deed and given a show trial by Göring that ended in his execution.

Move along a little further and look up at the parapet opposite. On the roof at either side of the rear entrance are two platforms, on which equestrian statues used to stand. Below the left-hand platform you can make out the windows of a staircase. This was the route taken by the 150th Rifle Division's specially appointed standard bearers to reach the roof, where they eventually found a suitable spot to wedge the staff of the banner on the equestrian figure there. This was reported to have happened at 2250 hours on 30 April 1945, only seventy minutes before May Day, but was in fact accomplished well after midnight. Although the Soviet aim of hoisting the banner on the Reichstag had officially been achieved and the building was surrounded, the German defenders held out until 1300 hours on 2 May 1945.

The Story of the Banners

A unique feature of Operation Berlin was the reintroduction of the carrying of unit standards into battle as a morale booster. Upon reaching Berlin the military council of the 3rd Shock Army had issued special banners with extra large hammer and sickle emblems to its rifle divisions for hoisting on prominent objectives.

At 1425 hours on 30 April the commander of the 150th Rifle Division reported that he thought he had seen a red flag over the steps of the Reichstag near the right-hand column. This news sped up the channel of command and led to Marshal Zhukov reporting to Moscow that the Reichstag had been taken, which became worldwide news. It now became even more urgent to turn wishful thinking into fact.

However, it was only some considerable time after the final assault at 1800 hours that one of the attacking battalions was able to report by telephone that it had reached the first floor. The 150th Rifle Division's 'Special Banner No. 5' escort party under Politruk Lieutenant Alexei Berest was then sent forward with orders to get the banner flying from the rooftop by midnight at all costs. Eventually they found a staircase at the rear of the building that took them up

Captain Makov and one of his gunners re-enact their triumph.

to the roof, where they wedged the shaft of the standard on an equestrian statue, but this was not until well past midnight.

Meanwhile at 2250 hours Artillery Captain V.N. Makov and some of his NCOs, who had lost their guns on the far side of the Spree and fought on as infantry, fixed their banner on the Goddess of Victory statue above the front entrance, to be followed shortly after by Lieutenant Sergei E. Sorkin's reconnaissance platoon and its banner, again ahead of the official party.

The following afternoon, after the surrender of the German garrison, these events were re-enacted for the benefit of the cameras in daylight. Realising that a picture of 'Special Banner No. 5' against the sky was of no significance, the photographer had the banner party change places so that he could take them apparently fixing the banner to the third 'pepper-pot' from the corner tower with the Brandenburg Gate in the background. However, when the picture was printed the exposed wrist of the man holding the banner was seen to be ringed with looted watches that had to be painted out before publication.

Honours for participants were distributed on the first anniversary of this battle. Sergeants M.A. Yegorov and M.V. Kantaria of the special banner party became 'Heroes of the Soviet Union', but Lieutenant Berest, who had meanwhile fallen foul of Marshal Zhukov, had his name struck off the honours list. Captain Makov's and Lieutenant Sorkin's parties received the lesser Order of the Red Banner, but later on one of the artillery NCO's names was struck off the history books when he was arrested for 'hooliganism'.

Cross over to the Tiergarten and walk past the Wall victim memorial plaques and turn right down the Strasse der 17. Juni to reach the **Soviet War Memorial**, which was deliberately built on the site of the Siegesallee (Victory Avenue) and was

The Soviet War Memorial against the battlefield. Guardrooms were later built behind the memorial.

formally opened on Armistice Day, 11 November 1945, in a ceremony in which guards of honour from the Western Allies participated.

This was also the point where the east–west and north–south axes were meant to meet, so tunnels had been prepared to enable the traffic to flow from one to the other. These tunnels were used by the German defence as shelters and stores during the fighting but have since been sealed off.

The two tanks flanking the entrance are of the old T-34/76 type, then already obsolete. The statue of a Red Army rifleman dominating the edifice is known to the Berliners as 'the unknown rapist', with good reason. It is estimated that there were some 95–130,000 cases of rape in the city during and after the battle, leading to about 10,000 suicides. Slabs in the foreground bear the names of senior officers killed in the fighting for the Reichstag, while other names are recorded on the columns behind, each of which bears the insignia of one of the services involved. Behind are the two guardrooms that accommodated the 24-hour guard. These now display pictures of historic interest.

The bodies of the 2,200 Soviet soldiers killed in this battle are interred behind the hedges on either flank of the memorial. The 79th Corps claimed to have taken some 2,600 prisoners and counted 2,500 enemy dead.

The memorial was the scene of parades commemorating Red Army Day, May Day and VE Day, the participants being escorted by the Royal Military Police from the Invalidenstrasse crossing point; parking was organised for them on the south side of the Strasse der 17. Juni opposite. A broad procession of generals and Eastern Bloc diplomats, headed by the Soviet Ambassador and the Commander-in-Chief of the Group of Soviet Forces in Germany, would form up on the north side of the street and walk up to the memorial for a wreath-laying ceremony attended by a large military band and a battalion from a Guards regiment, which would conduct a march-past before dispersing. These ceremonies were regularly observed by members of BRIXMIS (the British liaison mission to the GSFG) and the Public Safety branch of the British Military Government to ensure that all went smoothly.

The security of the Soviet War Memorial posed a problem for the British sector authorities over the years as anti-Soviet feeling among the civilian population waxed and waned. At one time the British Army had to maintain a camp close by to accommodate a guard detachment. Later on a German student fired at one of the Soviet sentries from the Tiergarten opposite, as a result of which that section of the Strasse der 17. Juni between the Entlastungsstrasse crossroads and the Brandenburg Gate was sealed off by gates and only official and privately owned vehicles of the Western Allies were allowed in by Berlin Police guards. Tourist coaches were also allowed into the sealed area, but their passengers were not allowed to alight, unlike Allied visitors, who could climb the so-called Kennedy observation stand to take their photographs of the Brandenburg Gate and the bare expanses behind the Wall.

The road between the Brandenburg Gate and the Victory Column (*Siegesäule*) was used as an airstrip during the last days of the siege, involving the cutting down of Albert Speer's lampposts and trees on either side of the road. At 1030 hours on 26 April 1945 two Junkers 52 transport aircraft landed with their cargoes of tank ammunition. They took off again half an hour later laden with wounded, but one

The airstrip on the Charlottenburger Chaussee looking towards the Brandenburg Gate from the top of the Siegesäule, showing how the trees had been cleared back from the road and Speer's lampposts removed.

The wreckage of a Fieseler *Storch* near the Siegesäule.

crashed into an obstacle on take-off killing all on board, so this method of supply had to be abandoned. In addition, six Fieseler *Storch* aircraft flying in from Rechlin were shot down, as were twelve Junkers 52 transports carrying Waffen-SS reinforcements.

However, the airstrip continued to be used by light aircraft, including an extraordinary and unnecessary visit by Albert Speer on the 23rd, apologising to Hitler for his opposition to the latter's 'scorched earth' policy, and then on the 26th Hanna Reitsch landed a Fieseler *Storch* carrying Colonel General Robert Ritter von Greim. Hitler had summoned von Greim from Munich to appoint him head of the Luftwaffe in succession to the disgraced Hermann Göring. Von Greim brought with him his girlfriend Hanna, who was famous throughout Germany for her exploits as an aviatrix. (Among other things, she had flown the prototype of a helicopter inside the audience-filled Deutschlandhalle in Berlin and had even volunteered to fly the manned prototype of the V-2 to discover what had caused previous fatal accidents in getting it to fly correctly. She was also the first woman to obtain an airline pilot's licence, to become a test pilot, to fly a helicopter and to fly a jet, her exploits earning her the Iron Cross 1st and 2nd Class.)

Flying first to Rechlin Air Base, where they had intended taking one of the last remaining helicopters in service to fly into the besieged city, only to find it damaged, they were then flown to Gatow airfield in a Focke-Wulf 190, which only had one passenger seat, so the diminutive and determined Hanna was stuffed into the luggage compartment near the tail. Most of the aircraft escorting them were shot down on the way.

At Gatow, which was already under siege, they transferred to the two-seater *Storch* with von Greim flying and Hanna seated behind. While passing over the

Grunewald residential area, von Greim was severely wounded in the legs and Hanna had to take over the controls from over his shoulders. After being treated for his wounds in the *Führerbunker*, von Greim and Hanna Reitsch were flown out again on 28 April in an Arado 96 by the same fighter pilot who had previously flown them in from Rechlin, their *Storch* having been wrecked by artillery fire meanwhile. (Hanna was to continue flying until her death in 1979 at the age of 67, having established a new women's world long-distance gliding record of 805 kilometres only four months previously.) All in all, this proved an expensive way of promoting von Greim, which could just as easily have been done by teleprinter.

The famous aviatrix Hanna Reitsch.

This stretch of road was also used by the Soviets and Western Allies for a series of victory parades in the summer of 1945, including reviews by Marshal Zhukov, Field Marshal Sir Bernard Montgomery and others; a review by Sir Winston Churchill during the Potsdam Conference ended with a combined Allied victory parade in September.

We now turn back to the **Brandenburg Gate**. Yet another snag that evolved from post-Unification development in this area was the reconstruction of the buildings on either side of the Brandenburg Gate, which proved unsuited for modern traffic and so had to be sealed off and a diversion introduced, breaking the old east–west axis, whereas Albert Speer's plans had left the Gate isolated with traffic flowing on

The Allied Victory Parade on the Charlottenburger Chaussee in September 1945. Marshal Zhukov shares the tribune with Lieutenant-General Sir Brian Robertson, General Louis Koeltz and General George S. Patton.

either side. The traffic flow problem has been further exacerbated by the construction of the new American Embassy on the corner between the diversion and Pariser Platz.

The Brandenburg Gate was constructed to a design by Paul Langhans over the period 1789–93 to adorn the western entrance of the then walled city and to serve as a customs post. It was of no especial consequence until Napoleon arrived in 1805 and ordered the Quadriga's removal to Paris. Its subsequent return to Berlin following Napoleon's downfall was conducted like a triumphal progress, symbolising Prussian national pride.

The badly damaged Brandenburg Gate after the battle.

The Quadriga and Gate were seriously damaged during the Second World War, but the original moulds for the Quadriga were found in the western part of the city and an agreement was reached between the East and West city governments in 1958 for the restoration of the Gate and Quadriga, the latter without its original imperialistic emblems.

When the Wall was built in 1962, the half circle in front of the Brandenburg Gate was the only section of the Wall constructed with horizontally laid concrete slabs as an anti-tank barrier. As the vertical sections of the Wall had been constructed from vertical slabs capped by a rounded section of a diameter too wide to provide a grip, this horizontal section was the only part of the Wall on which people could stand when it

The new Quadriga awaiting installation.

The wreckage in Pariser Platz after the battle.

The reinforced Hotel Adlon entrance in 1945.

German wounded on Unter den Linden after having being removed from the Hotel Adlon.

was eventually breached. As elsewhere, the line of the Wall is marked in the roadway and pavements by a line of bricks.

Walk through the Brandenburg Gate into Pariser Platz, which was a scene of desolation after the fighting. The whole area has had to be rebuilt since Unification. The ground floor of the Hotel Adlon had been fortified against bombing and was used as a meeting point for diplomats. During the battle it was used as a field dressing station, and afterwards its copious bar stocks attracted the victors, who set the place on fire during their celebrations so that only the servants' quarters remained in use as a hotel during early DDR times. The Hotel Adlon has since been rebuilt to its previous size but with an extra storey squeezed into the design.

Continue down the Unter den Linden, passing the Russian Embassy complex on your right. This was the first post-war construction in East Berlin and was built with the security of a fortress. The stained-glass windows of the main building depict the Kremlin.

Cross the junction with Friedrichstrasse and look at the magnificent statue of Frederick the Great, which survived the war intact, boxed in at this location, despite all the bombing and shelling. He is depicted surrounded by his leading generals and ministers of state. The East German government had him moved to Potsdam after the war, but he was brought back again in 1981.

Next on the right is Bebelplatz, in the centre of which is an unusual subterranean memorial commemorating the Nazis' burning of the books they had proscribed on 10 May 1933. Pass the Staatsoper, Berlin's principal opera house, and you come to a garden containing the statues of famous Prussian generals, such as Blücher, the saviour of Waterloo. Across the road from here is the Neue Wache (the equivalent

The East German honour guard at the Neue Wache.

of the Tomb of the Unknown Warrior). The East German Army's *Felix Dzerzhinsky* Regiment, named after the founder of the *Cheka* (later the NKVD) and a recruiting ground for the *Stasi* (State Secret Police), provided the honour guard here during the Cold War. Next to the Neue Wache is the Zeughaus (Arsenal), which now houses the German Historical Museum.

Deutsches Historisches Museum

Open daily, except Wednesdays, 1000–1800 hours.

You now come to the Schlossbrücke over the Kupfergraben Canal, which used to provide a defensive moat for the Schloss or royal palace beyond, forming an island with the Spree. The Schloss was destroyed by the East German government after the war and replaced by their parliament building (Volkskammer), which is now being dismantled with much controversy over the future role of the site.

The tour ends just short of Alexanderplatz at the Red Town Hall (*Rotes Rathaus*), seat of the city government. This was attacked by the 266th Rifle Division of the 26th Guards Corps, 5th Shock Army, late on 29 April 1945, and was defended by elements of the 11 SS *Nordland* Panzergrenadier Division. The attack was supported by tanks and self-propelled artillery but made no progress until holes had been blown through the walls from an adjacent building to enable access. The Soviets were then obliged to fight for every room in turn through the dense clouds of smoke that filled the burning building, and it was not until early the next morning that it was secured.[1]

Regretfully, the area around Alexanderplatz has been so considerably altered since the time of the battle that it is no longer possible to trace events here in detail.

Looking back across the barricaded Schloss Bridge with the boxed statue of Frederick the Great in the distance.

The severely damaged Rotes Rathaus (Red Town Hall) after the battle.

NOTES

Introduction
   1. Tony Le Tissier, *Zhukov at the Oder*, p. 158.

Chapter 1: Seelow Battle Synopsis
   1. Tony Le Tissier, *Zhukov at the Oder*.

Chapter 2: Seelow Tour A
   1. Tony Le Tissier, *Death Was Our Companion*, pp. 64–70.
   2. Tony Le Tissier, *Death Was Our Companion*, pp. 53–6.
   3. Tony Le Tissier, *Zhukov at the Oder*, p. 159.
   4. Vassili I. Chuikov, *The End of the Third Reich*, pp. 179–80.
   5. Tony Le Tissier, *With Our Backs to Berlin*, pp. 107–25.

Chapter 3: Seelow Tour B
   1. Tony Le Tissier, *With Our Backs to Berlin*, pp. 112–14.
   2. Tony Le Tissier, *Zhukov at the Oder*, p. 172.
   3. Tony Le Tissier, *Zhukov at the Oder*, p. 172.
   4. Tony Le Tissier, *Zhukov at the Oder*, p. 173.
   5. Tony Le Tissier, *With Our Backs to Berlin*, pp. 89–90.
   6. Tony Le Tissier, *Death Was Our Companion*, pp. 57–63.
   7. Tony Le Tissier, *With Our Backs to Berlin*, pp. 58–83.
   8. Tony Le Tissier, *Death Was Our Companion*, pp. 87–9.

Chapter 4: Seelow Tour C
   1. Tony Le Tissier, *With Our Backs to Berlin*, pp. 46–7.
   2. Marshal Georgi K. Zhukov, *Reminiscences and Reflections*, p. 322.
   3. Tony Le Tissier, *Zhukov at the Oder*, pp. 172–3.
   4. Tony Le Tissier, *Zhukov at the Oder*, p. 195.
   5. Tony Le Tissier, *With Our Backs to Berlin*, pp. 49–50.

Chapter 5: Seelow Tour D
   1. Helmut Altner, *Berlin Dance of Death*.

Chapter 8: Seelow Tour G
   1. Colonel A.H. Babadshanian, *Hauptstosskraft*, pp. 246–7.
   2. Tony Le Tissier, *With Our Backs to Berlin*, p. 106.
   3. Joachim Engelmann, *Geschichte der 18. Panzergrenadier-Division*, pp. 634–7.
   4. Vassili I. Chuikov, *The End of the Third Reich*, pp. 150–1.

Chapter 10: The Berlin Battle Synopsis
1. Tony Le Tissier, *Race for the Reichstag*.

Chapter 11: Berlin Tour A
1. Tony Le Tissier, *Race for the Reichstag*, p. 129.
2. Henrik Bering, *Outpost Berlin*, pp. 167–9.
3. Vassili I. Chuikov, *The End of the Third Reich*, pp. 188–94.
4. Tony Le Tissier, *Race for the Reichstag*, p. 135.
5. Tony Le Tissier, *With Our Backs to Berlin*, p. 170
6. Vassili I. Chuikov, *The End of the Third Reich*, pp. 197–9.
7. Vassili I. Chuikov, *The End of the Third Reich*, p. 202.
8. Tony Le Tissier, *Death Was Our Companion*, pp. 199–200.
9. Tony Le Tissier, *With Our Backs to Berlin*, pp. 124–6.
10. Tony Le Tissier, *With Our Backs to Berlin*, pp. 128–9.

Chapter 12: Berlin Tour B
1. Tony Le Tissier, *Race for the Reichstag*, p. 184.
2. Helmut Altner, *Berlin Dance of Death*, pp. 143–9.
3. Tony Le Tissier, *Death Was Our Companion*, p. 171.
4. Helmut Altner, *Berlin Dance of Death*, pp. 130, 139–41.
5. Tony Le Tissier, *Race for the Reichstag*, p. 184.
6. Helmut Altner, *Berlin Dance of Death*, pp. 128–30, 134, 136–9, and Tony Le Tissier, *Death Was Our Companion*, pp. 166–7.
7. Helmut Altner, *Berlin Dance of Death*, pp. 204–5.
8. Tony Le Tissier, *Death Was Our Companion*, pp. 187–8.
9. Tony Le Tissier, *Farewell to Spandau*, pp. 63–6.
10. Tony Le Tissier, *Race for the Reichstag*, p. 163.
11. Tony Geraghty, *BRIXMIS*, pp. 133–42.
12. Helmut Altner, *Berlin Dance of Death*, pp. 151–8.

Chapter 13: Berlin Tour C
1. Tony Le Tissier, *Race for the Reichstag*, pp. 90–1.
2. Tony Le Tissier, *With Our Backs to Berlin*, pp. 160–1.
3. Tony Le Tissier, *Death Was Our Companion*, pp. 135–8.
4. Tony Le Tissier, *Death Was Our Companion*, p. 140.
5. Tony Le Tissier, *Death Was Our Companion*, pp. 143–4.
6. Tony Le Tissier, *Death Was Our Companion*, p. 147.
7. Tony Le Tissier, *Race for the Reichstag*, pp. 185–6.
8. Tony Le Tissier, *With Our Backs to Berlin*, pp. 187–92.

Chapter 14: Berlin Tour D
1. Tony Le Tissier, *Death Was Our Companion*, pp. 156–8.
2. Tony Le Tissier, *Death Was Our Companion*, pp. 202–3.
3. Tony Le Tissier, *Race for the Reichstag*, p. 149.
4. Tony Le Tissier, *With Our Backs to Berlin*, pp. 51–4.

Chapter 15: Berlin Tour E
1. Tony Le Tissier, *With Our Backs to Berlin*, pp. 193–4.

Chapter 17: Berlin Tour G

1. Tony Le Tissier, *Slaughter at Halbe*, p. 73.
2. Tony Le Tissier, *Slaughter at Halbe*, pp. 125–7.
3. Konstantin Simonov, *Kriegstagebücher*, pp. 105f.
4. Tony Le Tissier, *Slaughter at Halbe*, pp. 214–15.
5. Tony Le Tissier, *Slaughter at Halbe*, p. 179.
6. Tony Le Tissier, *Slaughter at Halbe*, p. 179.
7. Tony Le Tissier, *Race for the Reichstag*, p. 34.

Chapter 18: Reichstag Battlefield Synopsis

1. Tony Le Tissier, *Race for the Reichstag*.

Chapter 19: Reichstag Battlefield Tour

1. Tony Le Tissier, *Race for the Reichstag*.

BIBLIOGRAPHY

Altner, Helmut, *Berlin Dance of Death* (Spellmount, 2002)

Babadshanian, Colonel A.H., *Hauptstosskraft* (Militärverlag der DDR, 1981)

Chuikov, Vassili I., *The End of the Third Reich* (Moscow, Progress Publishers; London, Panther edition, London, 1969)

Geraghty, Tony, *BRIXMIS – the untold exploits of Britain's most daring Cold War spy story* (London, HarperCollins, 1997)

Le Tissier, Tony, *Death Was Our Companion* (Stroud, Sutton, 2003)

Le Tissier, Tony, *Farewell to Spandau* (Ashford, Buchan & Enright, 1994)

Le Tissier, Tony, *Race for the Reichstag* (London, Frank Cass & Co., 1999)

Le Tissier, Tony, *Slaughter at Halbe* (Stroud, Sutton, 2005)

Le Tissier, Tony, *With Our Backs to Berlin* (Stroud, Sutton, 2001)

Le Tissier, Tony, *Zhukov at the Oder* (Praeger Publishers, 1995)

Simonov, Konstantin, *Kriegstagebücher* (Militärverlag der DDR, 1982)

Zhukov, Marshal Georgi K., *Reminiscences and Reflections* (Moscow, Progress Publishers, 1974; English translation, 1985)

INDEX

MILITARY INDEX

POLISH ARMED FORCES

SOVIET ARMED FORCES